CHRISTIANS, MUSLIMS, AND MARY

Como os mouros sacarõ a omagẽ do mar. e aposerõ no muro.

E pescarõ sas redes. e sacarõ tãto pescado q̃ as nõ podiã tirar.

CHRISTIANS, MUSLIMS, AND MARY

A History

RITA GEORGE-TVRTKOVIĆ

Paulist Press
New York / Mahwah, NJ

Cover image: A Falnama (Book of Divination) painting of the Virgin Mary and Jesus (c. 1600)
Cover design by Sharyn Banks
Book design by Lynn Else

Library of Congress Cataloging-in-Publication Data is available upon request.

ISBN 978-0-8091-5328-2 (paperback)
ISBN 978-1-58768-676-4 (e-book)

Published by Paulist Press
997 Macarthur Boulevard
Mahwah, New Jersey 07430

www.paulistpress.com

Printed and bound in the
United States of America

To my teachers

CONTENTS

PREFACE

Mary, Bridge or Barrier?

The Church regards with esteem also the Moslims....
They also honor Mary, His virgin Mother; at times they
even call on her with devotion.

—*Nostra Aetate* 3, Second Vatican Council, 1965

Until recently, I took it for granted that Muslims and Christians "share" Mary. My uncritical acceptance was due mainly to the fact that since 1965, the document quoted above has shaped how Catholics like me have viewed Islam and engaged in dialogue with Muslims. In the last twenty years, I have attended countless interfaith meetings at which Mary's importance to Islam and Christianity has been repeated. I have read speeches by high-level church officials affirming the shared Mary, from Cardinal William Keeler to Pope John Paul II.[1] Likewise, Muslims eager to build relationships with Christians also point to Mary, highlighting the similarity between her veil and the Muslim hijab. Furthermore, my own scholarship has focused on two medieval Dominicans, William of Tripoli and Riccoldo da Montecroce, both of whom wrote positively about the Muslim Mary. Of these two friars, William is especially complimentary. Noting parallels between the biblical and qur'anic Marys, he reaches a surprising conclusion: "One can infer that God gave this book [the Qur'an], if the book is from God and not from man, only to praise and glorify Christ

Jesus and his mother Mary."[2] The similarities between the medieval view of Mary expressed by William and the modern view expressed by *Nostra Aetate* seemed obvious to me, and I assumed that the ideas found in the latter were simply a continuation of the former. After all, if texts from both the thirteenth *and* twentieth centuries affirmed Mary as a bridge between the two religions, didn't this show continuity in the Christian tradition?

Continuity in the tradition is crucial because it legitimizes current Christian doctrines and practices by linking them to Jesus, the apostles, and the early church. If there were continuity in the tradition such that one could say "the church has always" seen Mary as a bridge between Christianity and Islam, this would be an exceptional and noteworthy claim indeed, given that most historical writings on Christian-Muslim relations stress disagreement, not concord, between the two religions.

But it seems I was wrong about continuity. What jolted me out of the false assumption that "the church has always seen Mary as a bridge" was reading from a historical period outside my area of expertise. A colleague introduced me to a sixteenth-century book by the Catholic Arabist Guillaume Postel, in which twenty-eight doctrinal points shared by Muslims and Protestants are enumerated.[3] I did a double take when I read number 6 on the list, which declares that Muslims and Protestants are equally deficient in honoring Mary.[4] In Postel's eyes, Mary was not an interfaith bridge at all. Rather, she was an interfaith barrier, and she divided not only Christians and Muslims, but Catholics and Protestants, too.

Postel's book forced me to rethink my assumptions. True, in 1965 the Catholic Church declared that Christians and Muslims share a devotion to Mary. But had I been too quick to assume that Christians had *always* viewed Mary as a bridge between the two religions? *Nostra Aetate*'s sentence on Mary does not include a footnote, so I started to wonder: how deeply rooted is this idea in Christian tradition after all? I began to suspect that the thirteenth-century Dominicans who had been the subject of my research might be the exception rather than the rule. Yes, William and Riccoldo (along with a few others) knew that Islam respects the Virgin Mary, that the nineteenth chapter of the Qur'an is named after her, and that some Muslims frequent Marian shrines. But the fact is, for the bulk of history, most Christians either criticized qur'anic

Mariology as deficient, or raised standards of Mary in wars against Muslims. The idea that the Blessed Virgin actively fights Muslims has not gone away; in the years since 9/11, blog posts such as this one, from February 2015, have increased: "Mary the mother of Jesus is one of the greatest warriors against jihad." Therefore, the belief that Mary is an interfaith bridge has *not* been held continuously by Christians through time. Rather, Christian knowledge of the Muslim Mary has produced a wide range of responses: from viewing her as a bridge on the one hand, to viewing her as a barrier on the other.

This book examines the complicated history behind *Nostra Aetate*'s affirmation of Mary. My goal is not to be exhaustive, but rather to sketch out the basic contours of a broad historical trajectory that has vacillated between two opposite ideas: Mary as interfaith bridge, and Mary as interfaith barrier. As the book moves through the years, we will examine in detail a select number of key historical moments. Each of the eight chapters will highlight pivotal texts, artworks, theologians, events, or shrines that have brought Christians, Muslims, and Mary together in significant ways. The fundamental questions driving my inquiry are as follows:

- First, given the variant details about Mary found in Islamic and Christian texts, in what sense can Muslims and Christians say they "share" Mary at all? (And should they?)
- Second, when and by whom has she been seen as a bridge, when and by whom has she been seen as a barrier, and why? I would like to suggest that Christian views of Mary vis-à-vis Islam are in constant flux, depending on her polemical or irenic usefulness at a particular time and place.
- Third, how has the shared figure of Mary, as seen by believers at different times and places, influenced the development of a Christian theology of Islam (and to a lesser extent, a Muslim theology of Christianity), as well as popular practice?[5]
- Fourth, how does knowledge of this history of Mary (full or fragmented, nuanced or revisionist), along

with new ideas about her, affect Christian-Muslim relations today?

The book begins with scriptural accounts of Mary from the Bible, Qur'an, and Christian Apocrypha; the stories are placed side by side for easy comparison. Chapter 1 also introduces some caveats when considering the possibility of a "shared" Mary. Chapter 2 covers the rise of Marian doctrine and devotion in early Eastern Christianity. Chapter 3 presents traditional Muslim views of Marian doctrine and devotion: while all respect her as the virgin mother of Jesus, they disagree about her spiritual status and the proper way Muslims should approach her. Chapter 4 spotlights the unusually positive views two medieval Latins, William of Tripoli and Nicholas of Cusa, had about qur'anic Mariology. Chapter 5 describes Mary's emerging identity as "Our Lady of Victory" in the sixteenth-century Catholic fight against Turks and Protestants, while chapter 6 discusses the long history of Christians who imagined Mary as a tool for mission among Muslims—a history that stretches from medieval Spain to early modern India to modern North Africa. The last two chapters move into the contemporary period. Chapter 7 centers on mid-twentieth-century changes in the Catholic theology of Islam that culminated in the 1965 Vatican II Council document *Nostra Aetate*. Chapter 8 concludes the book by returning to the four questions above, and then considering the problems and opportunities that arise when considering Mary as a model for dialogue—especially as she relates to feminism, ecumenism, and violence. What is Mary's role (or lack thereof) in Christian-Muslim relations today? What should it be going forward?

ACKNOWLEDGMENTS

I happily begin with gratitude. First, I wish to thank my colleague Christine Isom-Verhaaren, an Ottoman historian, whose invitation to collaborate across the medieval–early modern divide resulted in the "a-ha" moment that sparked the idea for this book. Second, I am grateful to Christopher Bellitto—fellow Cusanus scholar, church historian, and Paulist Press editor—who championed this project from its inception and offered valuable feedback the whole way through. Third, I would have been unable to devote a full academic year to completing this book without the generous support of the Louisville Institute's Sabbatical Grant for Researchers, plus the sabbatical leave granted by my home institution, Benedictine University in Illinois.

The following libraries were essential to my research: Edinburgh University Main Library, El Escorial Madrid/Patrimonio Nacional, JKM Library of the Lutheran School of Theology in Chicago, Köln Historisches Museum, Loyola University Chicago's Special Collections, Newberry Library Chicago, OMI General Archives in Rome, Victoria and Albert Museum London, and Wheaton College Special Collections. I am also much obliged to Fr. Maciej Michalski, OMI, archivist at the Oblate General Archives in Rome for sending me copies of the unpublished Yves Plumey-Louis Massignon correspondence. Two photos of overseas Marian sites were kindly provided by David Collins, SJ (Pius V Lepanto mosaic in Rome), and Flo Merkl-Deutsch (Meryem Ana Evi shrine in Turkey). Thanks also go to colleagues who read portions of this book or its entirety, and offered helpful comments or other key information: Scott Alexander, Audrey Berns, John Borelli, Andreatte Brachman, Mara Brecht, John Castañeda, Emanuele Colombo, Jordan

Denari Duffner, Sidney Griffith, Kathryn Heidelberger, Sharon Klein, Christian Krokus, Matthew Levering, Rana Lahham, José Martínez Gázquez, Matthew Milliner, Lucinda Mosher, Azam Nizamuddin, Trent Pomplun, Gabriel Said Reynolds, Devorah Schoenfeld, Iris Shagrir, William Toma, Kim Wagner, Melanie Webb, and Zaki Zaheer. This book has been greatly enriched by the inter- and intrareligious dialogues I have shared with these colleagues. Naturally, any errors are my own. I would be remiss if I did not also give a nod to my neighborhood coffeehouse for creating an ambience conducive to writing and thinking, and for intentionally fostering community among local scholars: Metropolis Café on Granville Avenue in Chicago. Of course, the deepest gratitude and most love always go to my family—Zoran, Luka, and Anya Lucia—for their fidelity and encouragement during this and every scholarly project. I could not do it without you, *moje ljubavi*.

And finally, in thanksgiving for a lifetime of learning, I dedicate this book to my most influential teachers, those whose pedagogical example I seek to emulate: Kim Rohde, John Bowlin, Peter Stromberg, Ali Asani, John O'Malley, SJ, Janice Farnham, RJM, Rabbi Michael Signer, David Burrell, Thomas Prügl, Joseph Wawrykow, and most especially my very first teachers, my parents, Anthony and Arlene George. *"Train children in the right way, and when old, they will not stray"* (Prov 22:6).

Rita George-Tvrtković
Feast of the Annunciation of Mary
March 25, 2017
Chicago, Illinois

LIST OF
ILLUSTRATIONS

Frontispiece. The Muslims and Christians of Faro retrieve Mary from the sea. Detail from Cantiga 183, *Cantigas de Santa Maria*, 13th century, El Escorial Madrid MS T.I.1, folio 242r. Copyright © Patrimonio Nacional. Used with permission.

Figure 1. The Annunciation to Mary, *Kitab al-Athar al-Baqiya* (Chronology of Ancient Nations), Al-Biruni, 14th century illustration, Or. Ms 161, Edinburgh University Main Library, Folio 141 v. Reproduced under a "CC-BY" license. (chapter 3)

Figure 2. *Triumphus SS.mi Rosarii*, 17th century, Köln, Kölnisches Stadtmuseum (RM 1936/1031). Photo: © Rheinisches Bildarchiv Köln, rba_224251. Used with permission. (chapter 5)

Figure 3. A Muslim venerating an image of Mary. Cantiga 46, *Cantigas de Santa Maria*, 13th century, El Escorial Madrid MS T.I.1., folio 68v. Copyright © Patrimonio Nacional. Used with permission. (chapter 6)

Figure 4. The Muslims of Faro throw a statue of Mary into the sea. Cantiga 183, panel 2, *Cantigas de Santa Maria*, 13th century, El Escorial Madrid MS T.I.1, folio 242r. Copyright © Patrimonio Nacional. Used with permission. (chapter 6)

NOTE ON TEXTS AND TRANSLATIONS

1. Quotations from the Bible are taken from the New Revised Standard Version Bible: Catholic Edition, copyright 1989, 1995, Division of Christian Education of the National Council of the Churches of Christ in the United States of America. Used by permission. All rights reserved.

2. Quotations from the Qur'an are taken from The Qur'an, Revised English Translation, by M. A. S. Abdel Haleem (Oxford University Press, 2016). Used with permission.

3. Quotations from the *Protevangelium of James* are from the translation by J. K. Elliott in *The Apocryphal New Testament* (Oxford: Clarendon Press, 1993), 57–67. Used with permission.

4. All translations of Latin and French primary source materials are my own, unless otherwise noted. For Arabic transliterations, I have generally followed the IJMES system; however, to simplify reading, most diacriticals have been omitted, except the *ayn* (ʿ) such as in *ʿIsa* (Jesus), and the medial *hamza* (ʾ) such as in *Qur'an*. Those who are scholars of Arabic know where the diacriticals should be; those who are not will hopefully appreciate a more simplified read.

5. The following parts of the book are adapted versions of conference presentations and published articles,

the latter of which are used with permission. An earlier version of chapter 4 was published as "Bridge or Barrier? Mary and Islam in William of Tripoli and Nicholas of Cusa," *Medieval Encounters* 22, no. 4 (2016): 307–25. An earlier version of chapter 7 was published as "Meryem Ana Evi, Marian Devotion, and the Making of *Nostra aetate* 3," *Catholic Historical Review* 103, no. 4 (Autumn 2017): 755–81. Sections of chapters 6 and 7 were taken from my presentation, "Mary and Popular Devotion," given at the Catholic Theological Society of America conference in 2015. Portions of chapter 5 appeared in papers given at the 2013 Boston College Historical Theology Colloquy; the 2014 Islam and Religious Orders conference at DePaul and Benedictine in 2014; and the 2017 Renaissance Society of America conference.

Chapter 1

SCRIPTURAL PRELUDE

The angel said to her, "Do not be afraid, Mary, for you
have found favor with God. And now, you will conceive
in your womb and bear a son."...Mary said to the
angel, "How can this be, since I am a virgin?"

—Luke 1:30–31, 34

He said, "I am but a messenger from your Lord,
[come] to announce to you the gift of a pure son."
She said, "How can I have a son when no man has
touched me? I have not been unchaste."

—Qur'an 19:19–20

The above verses from the Bible and Qur'an describe the
annunciation to Mary. Points of similarity are clear: the angel
claims to speak for God, he tells Mary she will have a child, the child
will be a boy, and Mary is a virgin who is therefore understandably
surprised. In the larger story of Mary's gestation and motherhood,
there are many other parallels between the Muslim and Christian
accounts. But there are also significant differences. For example,
the Qur'an describes Mary as moving to a remote location to be
alone during her pregnancy (Sura 19:22). The childbirth takes

place under a palm tree, and is so difficult that Mary exclaims, "I wish I had been dead and forgotten long before all this!" (Sura 19:23). Just days after the baby is born, Jesus miraculously speaks to defend his mother against relatives who suspect fornication (Sura 19:27–32). In contrast, the Gospel of Luke says that the pregnant Mary does not seek solitude but rather the company of her relative Elizabeth, with whom she stays for three months (Luke 1:36, 39–41, 56). Unlike the qur'anic Mary, the biblical Mary does not complain; instead, she sings a song of praise, the Magnificat: "My soul magnifies the Lord…" (Luke 1:46–55). The Bible does not give us any details about the actual delivery, only that it took place while Mary and Joseph were out of town, couldn't find a place to stay, and thus had to give birth in a barn (Luke 2:6–7). Nor does the biblical baby Jesus speak. Given these differences, in what sense can Christians and Muslims say this is the same story, or that they share Mary?

In his recent book *Inheriting Abraham*, Jon Levenson argues that while Jews, Christians, and Muslims all claim Abraham as a spiritual ancestor, in reality, each religion has divergent ideas about who Abraham is and what he means.[1] Muslim scholar Timothy Winter takes Levenson's caveat one step further, suggesting that Mary "is an emblem of what Islam and Catholicism find superficially recognizable in each other but which investigation discloses as alienating."[2] Likewise, my book begins with the premise that while the Virgin Mary is "shared" in some sense by Muslims and Christians, the Marys of the Bible and Qur'an remain distinct, not only due to variant biographical details, but also because of discrete theological meanings constructed over time. For example, the first difference one might detect when comparing Muslim and Christian views of Mary is a certain degree of unevenness: Mary is theologically more important for Christians than she is for Muslims, simply because her son Jesus is more central to Christianity than he is to Islam. Christian understandings of Mary's identity have a direct bearing on their understanding of Christ's identity as "true God, true man."[3] In other words, Christian Mariology is always intimately connected to Christology, in particular to the central doctrine of the incarnation ("God made flesh"). Islamic Mariology is likewise connected to its own distinctive Christology. For example, since Muslims believe that Jesus was a completely human prophet and not the Son of God, their Mariology emphasizes his humanity. Indeed, one of the most common Muslim epithets for Jesus, *'Isa ibn Maryam* (Jesus son of Mary), underscores Jesus' human origins, and in so doing implicitly contradicts the Christian view. For Muslims, the fact that Jesus has an identifiable human mother proves that he is *not* divine, which is important if they are to preserve one of the most—if not *the* most—significant of Islamic doctrines: *tawhid*, the oneness of God.[4] Furthermore, despite the fact that Mary is the only woman named in the Qur'an, and that a smattering of Muslim scholars have even accorded her quasi-prophetic status, she still remains a relatively minor personage within Islam when compared to other revered figures such as Ibrahim (Abraham), Musa (Moses), Muhammad, Fatima, 'Aisha, and others.[5] Mary's overall theological importance in Islam is therefore lower than in Christianity.[6] This unevenness should be kept in mind whenever it is suggested that Christians and Muslims "share" Mary. (And this doesn't even address another more fundamental question: whether Christians and Muslims *should* share her at all. We will return to that question in chapter 8.)

This chapter treats scriptural accounts of Mary found in two key Christian sources (the Bible and the apocryphal *Protevangelium of James*) and one Muslim source (the Qur'an). The texts are presented side by side for easy comparison, and are organized around three topics: (1) Young Mary, (2) Annunciation and Birth of Jesus, (3) Postpartum Mary. The chapter will end with some theological commentary on these verses.

One final introductory note: brief mention must be made of the differing levels of authority these scriptural texts carry within each religion. The descriptions of Mary found in the Bible (mainly from the Gospel of Luke) are considered by Christians to be of the highest authority, since they believe it to be divine revelation. The story of Mary found in the apocryphal (extrabiblical) text known as the *Protevangelium* of James has much less authority than the Bible, for it was never accepted into the official canon of Scripture by the Church, nor are most Christians today even aware of its existence.[7] Yet the mid-second-century *Protevangelium*, the earliest extant Christian "biography" (more properly, hagiography) of Mary, is important for its widespread and long-standing influence; in fact, some scholars argue that no other Christian apocryphal text was more influential in late antique and medieval theology, liturgy, and popular imagination.[8] Originally written in Greek, it was soon translated into Coptic, Syriac, Ethiopian, Georgian, Arabic, and Armenian. Its stories reached Europe long before its 1552 translation into Latin by Guillaume Postel (see chapter 5), yet Postel's edition remains important partly for giving us the name *Protevangelium*, so called because the events it discusses, like Mary's birth, predate the Gospel narratives. Ancient manuscripts are entitled *The Birth of Mary, the Apocalypse of James*.[9]

While the *Protevangelium* is not biblical and thus not as authoritative as the Gospel of Luke, it still carries weight, especially among Catholic and Orthodox Christians.[10] Furthermore, the *Protevangelium* influenced the development of Marian liturgy and devotion in early Christianity—inspiring popular hymns among Oriental Orthodox Christians, and serving as the impetus for liturgical feasts such as Mary's Presentation (November 21), Mary's Conception (December 9), and Mary's Nativity (September 8).[11] (See chapter 2 for more about the development of Marian liturgy and piety in the early Church.) Also, the information found in the *Protevangelium* has always been part of the Church's received tradition, even if the source itself has been unacknowledged.[12] This means that while the vast majority of ordinary Catholics and Orthodox have never read (or even heard of) the *Protevangelium*, they nevertheless still know much of the information contained therein. For example, if asked to identify the parents of Mary, many would say Joachim and Anna, even though these names are not in the Bible, but come from the *Protevangelium*.

A similar hierarchy of authoritative texts is present in Islam. Like the Bible for Christians, the Qur'an for Muslims possesses the highest level of authority because it is considered divine revelation. Second in importance is the Hadith literature (traditions describing the words and deeds of Muhammad). Other early genres of Islamic literature such as Tafsir (qur'anic exegesis) and Sira (biographies of Muhammad) have less authority than the Qur'an and Hadith but are still quite influential. Some scholars have noted the complex relationships between scriptural and extrascriptural literature within and between Islam and Christianity during the earliest centuries of their development.[13] This context should be kept in mind when comparing the following Christian and Muslim accounts of Mary.

SIDE-BY-SIDE SCRIPTURAL ACCOUNTS OF MARY

YOUNG MARY

Bible[14]	Protevangelium of James[15]	Qur'an[16]
No details about Mary's birth or child-hood are given.	**Annunciation of Mary's Birth** "And behold an angel of the Lord appeared to her and said, 'Anna, Anna, the Lord has heard your prayer. You shall conceive and bear, and your offspring shall be spoken of in the whole world.' And Anna said, 'As the Lord my God lives, if I bear a child, whether male or female, I will bring it as a gift to the Lord my God and it shall serve him all the days of its life.'" (4:1–2)	**Annunciation of Mary's Birth** " 'Imran's wife said, 'Lord, I have dedicated what is growing in my womb entirely to You; so accept this from me. You are the One who hears and knows all.'" (Sura 3:35)
	Birth and Naming of Mary "In the ninth month, Anna gave birth. And she said to the midwife, 'What have I brought forth?' And she said, 'A female.' And Anna said, 'My soul is magnified this day.' And she lay down. And when the days were completed, Anna purified herself and gave suck to the child, and called her Mary." (5:2)	**Birth and Naming of Mary** "But when she gave birth, she said 'My Lord! I have given birth to a girl'—God knew best what she had given birth to: the male is not like the female—'I name her Mary and I commend her and her offspring to Your protection from the rejected Satan.'" (Sura 3:36)
	Young Mary "[Anna] made a sanctuary in [Mary's] bedroom and did not permit anything common or unclean to pass through it. And she summoned the undefiled daughters of the Hebrews, and they served her. On the child's first birthday Joachim made a great feast, and invited the chief priests and the priests and the scribes and elders and all the people of Israel. And Joachim brought the child to the priests, and they blessed her saying, 'O God of our fathers, bless this child and give her a name eternally renowned among all generations.'" (6:1–2) "And Mary was in the temple of the Lord nurtured like a dove and received food from the hand of an angel." (8:1)	**Young Mary** "Her Lord graciously accepted her and made her grow in goodness, and entrusted her to the charge of Zachariah. Whenever Zachariah went in to see her in her sanctuary, he found her supplied with provisions. He said, 'Mary, how is it you have these provisions?' and she said, 'They are from God: God provides limitlessly for whoever He will.'" (Sura 3:37)

ANNUNCIATION AND BIRTH OF JESUS

Bible	Protevangelium of James	Qur'an
Annunciation of Jesus	**Annunciation of Jesus**	**Annunciation Account A**
"In the sixth month the angel Gabriel was sent by God to a town in Galilee called Nazareth, to a virgin engaged to a man whose name was Joseph, of the house of David. The virgin's name was Mary. And he came to her and said, 'Greetings, favored one! The Lord is with you.' But she was much perplexed by his words and pondered what sort of greeting this might be. The angel said to her, 'Do not be afraid, Mary, for you have found favor with God. And now, you will conceive in your womb and bear a son, and you will name him Jesus. He will be great, and will be called the Son of the Most High, and the Lord God will give to him the throne of his ancestor David. He will reign over the house of Jacob forever, and of his kingdom there will be no end.' Mary said to the angel, 'How can this be, since I am a virgin?' The angel said to her, 'The Holy Spirit will come upon you, and the power of the Most High will overshadow you; therefore the child to be born will be holy; he will be called Son of God. And now, your relative Elizabeth in her old age has also conceived a son; and this is the sixth month for her who was said to be barren. For nothing will be impossible with God.' Then Mary said, 'Here am I, the servant of the Lord; let it be with me according to your word.' Then the angel departed from her." (Luke 1:26–38)	"Behold, a voice said, 'Hail, highly favored one, the Lord is with you, you are blessed among women.' And she looked around to the right and to the left to see where this voice came from. And, trembling, she went into her house and put down the pitcher and took the purple and sat down on her seat and drew out the thread. And behold, an angel of the Lord stood before her and said, 'Do not fear, Mary; for you have found grace before the Lord of all things and shall conceive by his Word.' When she heard this she considered it and said, 'Shall I conceive by the Lord, the living God, and bear as every woman bears?' And the angel of the Lord said, 'Not so, Mary; for the power of the Lord shall overshadow you; wherefore that holy one who is born of you shall be called the Son of the Most High. And you shall call his name Jesus; for he shall save his people from their sins.' And Mary said, 'Behold, (I am) the handmaid of the Lord before him: be it to me according to your word.'" (11:1–3)	"The angels said to Mary: 'Mary, God has chosen you and made you pure: He has truly chosen you above all women. Mary, be devout to your Lord, prostrate yourself in worship, bow down with those who pray.' This is an account of things beyond your knowledge that We reveal to you [Muhammad]: you were not present among them when they cast lots to see which of them should take charge of Mary, you were not present with them when they argued [about her]. The angels said, 'Mary, God gives you news of a Word from Him, whose name will be the Messiah, Jesus, son of Mary, who will be held in honour in this world and the next, who will be one of those brought near to God. He will speak to people in his infancy and in his adulthood. He will be one of the righteous.' She said, 'My Lord, how can I have a son when no man has touched me?' [The angel] said, 'This is how God creates what He will: when He has ordained something, He only says, "Be," and it is. He will teach him the Scripture and wisdom, the Torah and the Gospel, He will send him as a messenger to the Children of Israel…'" (Sura 3:42–49)
		Annunciation Account B
		"Mention in the Scripture the story of Mary. She withdrew from her family to a place east and secluded herself away; We sent Our Spirit to appear before her in the form of a normal human. She said, 'I seek the Lord of Mercy's protection against you: if you have any fear of Him [do not approach]!' but he said, 'I am but a Messenger from your Lord, [come] to announce to you the gift of a pure son.' She said, 'How can I have a son when no man has touched me? I have not been unchaste,' and he said, 'This is what your Lord said: "It is easy for Me—We shall make him a sign to all people, a blessing from Us."' And so it was ordained: she conceived him." (Sura 19:16–22)

Continued

Birth of Jesus

"[Joseph] went to be registered with Mary, to whom he was engaged and who was expecting a child. While they were there, the time came for her to deliver her child. And she gave birth to her firstborn son and wrapped him in bands of cloth, and laid him in a manger, because there was no place for them in the inn....When the angels had left them and gone into heaven, the shepherds said to one another, 'Let us go now to Bethlehem and see this thing that has taken place, which the Lord has made known to us.' So they went with haste and found Mary and Joseph, and the child lying in the manger. When they saw this, they made known what had been told them about this child; and all who heard it were amazed at what the shepherds told them. But Mary treasured all these words and pondered them in her heart." (Luke 2:5–7, 15–19)

Birth of Jesus

"And having come half-way [in their journey], Mary said to him, 'Joseph, take me down from the she-ass, for the child within me presses me to come forth.' And he took her down from the she-ass and said to her, 'Where shall I take you and hide your shame? For the place is desert.' And he found a cave there and brought her into it, and left her in the care of his sons and went out to seek for a Hebrew midwife in the region of Bethlehem. Now I, Joseph, was walking...and behold, a woman came down from the hill-country and said to me, 'Man, where are you going?' And I said, 'I seek a Hebrew midwife.' And she answered me, 'Are you from Israel?' And I said to her, 'Yes.' And she said, 'And who is she who brings forth in a cave?' And I said, 'My betrothed.' And she said to me, 'Is she not your wife?' And I said to her, 'She is Mary, who was brought up in the temple of the Lord, and I received her by lot as my wife, and she is not yet my wife, but she has conceived by the Holy Spirit.' And the midwife said to him, 'Is this true?' And Joseph said to her, 'Come and see.' And she went with him. And they stopped at the entrance to the cave, and behold, a bright cloud overshadowed the cave. And the midwife said, 'My soul is magnified today, for my eyes have seen wonderful things; for salvation is born to Israel.' And immediately the cloud disappeared from the cave and a great light appeared, so that our eyes could not bear it. A short time afterwards that light withdrew until the baby appeared, and it came and took the breast of its mother Mary. And the midwife cried, 'This day is great for me, because I have seen this new sight.' And the midwife came out of the cave, and Salome met her. And she said to her, 'Salome, Salome, I have a new sight to tell you about; a virgin has brought forth, a thing which her condition does not allow.' And Salome said, 'As the Lord my God lives, unless I insert my finger and test her condition, I will not believe that a virgin has given birth.'" (17:3; 18:1–2; 19:1–3)

Birth of Jesus

"She withdrew to a distant place and, when the pains of childbirth drove her to [cling to] the trunk of a palm tree, she exclaimed, 'I wish I had been dead and forgotten long before all this!' but a voice cried to her from below, 'Do not worry: your Lord has provided a stream at your feet and, if you shake the trunk of the palm tree towards you, it will deliver fresh ripe dates for you, so eat, drink, be glad, and say to anyone you may see: "I have vowed to the Lord of Mercy to abstain from conversation, and I will not talk to anyone today."'" (Sura 19:22–26)

POSTPARTUM MARY

Bible	Protevangelium of James	Qur'an
Boy Jesus "After three days they found him in the temple, sitting among the teachers, listening to them and asking them questions. And all who heard him were amazed at his understanding and his answers. When his parents saw him they were astonished; and his mother said to him, 'Child, why have you treated us like this? Look, your father and I have been searching for you in great anxiety.' He said to them, 'Why were you searching for me? Did you not know that I must be in my Father's house?' But they did not understand what he said to them. Then he went down with them and came to Nazareth, and was obedient to them. His mother treasured all these things in her heart." (Luke 2:46–51)	*No details about Mary postpartum are given.*	**Baby Jesus Speaks** "She went back to her people carrying the child, and they said, 'Mary! You have done something terrible! Sister of Aaron! Your father was not a bad man; your mother was not unchaste!' She pointed at him. They said, 'How can we converse with an infant?' [But] he said: 'I am a servant of God. He has granted me the Scripture; made me a prophet; made me blessed wherever I may be. He commanded me to pray, to give alms as long as I live, to cherish my mother. He did not make me domineering or graceless. Peace was on me the day I was born, and will be on me the day I die and the day I am raised to life again.' Such was Jesus, son of Mary." (Sura 19:27–34)
Wedding at Cana "On the third day there was a wedding in Cana of Galilee, and the mother of Jesus was there. Jesus and his disciples had also been invited to the wedding. When the wine gave out, the mother of Jesus said to him, 'They have no wine.' And Jesus said to her, 'Woman, what concern is that to you and to me? My hour has not yet come.' His mother said to the servants, 'Do whatever he tells you.' Now standing there were six stone water jars for the Jewish rites of purification, each holding twenty or thirty gallons. Jesus said to them, 'Fill the jars with water.' And they filled them up to the brim. He said to them, 'Now draw some out, and take it to the chief steward.' So they took it. When the steward tasted the water that had become wine, and did not know where it came from (though the servants who had drawn the water knew), the steward called the bridegroom and said to him, 'Everyone serves the good wine first, and then the inferior wine after the guests have become drunk. But you have kept the good wine until now.' Jesus did this, the first of his signs, in Cana of Galilee, and revealed his glory; and his disciples believed in him. After this he went down to Capernaum with his mother, his brothers, and his disciples; and they remained there a few days." (John 2:1–12)		
True family "Then his mother and his brothers came; and standing outside, they sent to him and called him. A crowd was sitting around him; and they said to him, 'Your mother and your brothers and sisters are outside, asking for you.' And he replied, 'Who are my mother and my brothers?' And looking at those who sat around him, he said, 'Here are my mother and my brothers! Whoever does the will of God is my brother and sister and mother.'" (Mark 3:31–35)		
At the Cross "Meanwhile, standing near the cross of Jesus were his mother, and his mother's sister, Mary the wife of Clopas, and Mary Magdalene. When Jesus saw his mother and the disciple whom he loved standing beside her, he said to his mother, 'Woman, here is your son.' Then he said to the disciple, 'Here is your mother.' And from that hour the disciple took her into his own home." (John 19:25–27)		

SOME OBSERVATIONS

The Bible mentions just one detail about the pre-annunciation Mary: she was betrothed to Joseph before becoming pregnant (Matt 1:18). Much more information about the young Mary can be found in the *Protevangelium* and the Qur'an. Both texts include an annuciation story where an angel proclaims Mary's birth to her mother—named Anna in the *Protevangelium* and "the wife of 'Imran" in the Qur'an.[17] Also in both accounts, the future baby is promised to God, and once Mary is born, her mother expresses amazement that the child is a girl, since the angel had not previously revealed the baby's gender. This declaration of surprise is followed by an unequivocal affirmation of the equal worth of females and males. Finally, both stories emphasize the purity and blessedness of the young Mary. Her chastity is preserved throughout her childhood; she is described as living in a specially protected place. Both accounts offer many examples of Mary's favor in God's eyes; for example, both stories say that the girl was miraculously provided with food.

One significant difference between the stories of young Mary is that the Qur'an says God entrusted her "to the charge of Zachariah" (Sura 3:37). This shift in male guardianship is puzzling. Since her mother has already been identified as the "wife of 'Imran" (Sura 3:35), and Mary herself is identified in Sura 66:12 as "Mary, daughter of 'Imran," one would assume that she would have been raised by her father 'Imran.[18] The Qur'an does not offer an explanation for why the child is given to Zachariah, but most Muslim exegetes suggest that 'Imran's death is implied.[19] To further complicate matters, the connections between Mary, Zachariah, and Elizabeth are slightly different in the two accounts. In the Bible, Zachariah is the husband of Mary's cousin, Elizabeth (Luke 1:36), and Zachariah and Elizabeth are the parents of John the Baptist (Luke 1:60). In the Qur'an, Elizabeth is not mentioned by name (she is referred to as the wife of Zachariah in Sura 19:2–7; 3:40; and 21:90), nor is she identified as Mary's relative, and Zachariah is both the guardian of Mary and the father of John the Baptist, who is known as Yahya ibn Zakariya (Sura 19:7; 3:39).

All three texts have an annunciation story; in fact, the Qur'an has two. As noted earlier, these stories share many similarities. But there are important differences; some of the most striking can be found between the two Christian texts. The *Protevangelium*'s annunciation story contains many details about the young Mary that are not found in the Bible. The angel is described as coming to Mary while she is weaving purple threads. The context behind this can be found in the preceding chapter, which describes the girl being chosen by the Jewish high priest to weave the purple cloth that would become the temple curtain; this task could only be accomplished by a virgin dedicated to God. The *Protevangelium* spends many chapters painting an image of Mary as a chaste young girl whose purity and holiness are recognized by everyone, including the Jewish authorities. Another interesting difference between the *Protevangelium* and Bible on Mary is that the former describes her family as "very rich" in the first line, while the latter suggests her poverty.

All three annunciation accounts underscore a significant aspect of Mary: her paradoxical identity as virgin-mother. Therefore all must deal with the same "problem"—how to explain her pregnancy. Readers of the Bible and Qur'an are explicitly told that she conceived by the power of God, therefore preserving her virginity (Luke 1:35; Sura 3:47). This explanation is presented during the annunciation, in response to Mary's confusion and subsequent questioning of the angel (Luke 1:29, 34). Mary is satisfied with the answer, and assents to God's plan (Luke 1:38). But the people around Mary are not privy to her dialogue with the angel. So how could they be convinced of the virgin's chaste conception and birth? The Qur'an solves the problem by having baby Jesus speak to defend his mother when relatives question her virtue (Sura 19:26–34). The Bible solves the problem by describing how Joseph—who wants to break off their engagement after discovering Mary's pregnancy—has a dream in which an angel assures him of Mary's chastity and the divine origins of her child (Matt 1:18–25). The *Protevangelium* expands on the Joseph dream story: others discover Mary's pregnancy and subject her (and him!) to a test, and they are both forced to drink water "of the conviction of the Lord," which confirms her chastity. Later, after Jesus' birth,

Mary is questioned once again, this time by a midwife who physically examines Mary to verify her virginity (chapter 20).

Another interesting difference between the birth stories is in the Qur'an, where Mary is described as delivering Jesus under a palm tree and is miraculously provided with dates to eat (Sura 19:22–25). Neither the Bible nor the *Protevangelium* mention a palm tree or dates, but these details can be found in other Christian apocryphal texts like the *Infancy Gospel of Thomas*, the *Gospel of Pseudo-Matthew*, the *Apocryphal Gospel of Matthew*, and the *Book of Mary's Repose*.[20] In fact, the fourth-century *Book of Mary's Repose*, which describes the dormition (assumption) of Mary, is part of a group of texts known as the "palm traditions" for depicting her with a palm from the tree of life.[21] Another difference between the qur'anic and biblical accounts of Mary is that the Muslim Mary has no husband—neither Joseph nor anyone else. Some have suggested that details highlighting Mary's complete solitude in the Qur'an (having no husband, distancing herself from her family when pregnant, giving birth alone under a palm tree) are meant to demonstrate her total dependence on God, a key tenet in Islam.[22]

Finally, it is noteworthy that the Qur'an says little about the postpartum Mary (nor does the *Protevangelium*). The only story takes place soon after Jesus' birth, when the baby speaks to defend his mother's honor, as noted earlier. The Bible has more detail about the postpartum Mary, but not much more: she is mentioned in accounts of the circumcision and presentation of Jesus (Luke 2:21–40), in a conversation with twelve-year-old Jesus teaching in the temple (Luke 2:41–52), at the wedding at Cana (John 2:1–12), with her other children looking for Jesus (Mark 3:30–35; Luke 8:19–21), when Jesus speaks to her from the cross (John 19:25–27), and praying with the apostles in the upper room, after Christ's ascension (Acts 1:14).

The fact that Scripture has given us scant information about Mary has not stopped the development of a robust Mariology in both religions. When comparing Christian and Muslim scriptural accounts of Mary, what theological issues emerge? Here are a few possibilities for further dialogue:

CHOSENNESS

For both Muslims and Christians, Mary is exceptional, for she is handpicked by God. Indeed, in all three annunciation accounts, the angel explicitly calls Mary chosen, blessed, or favored over other women: Luke 1:30, "Do not be afraid, Mary, for you have found favor with God"; *Protevangelium* chapter 11, "Hail, highly favored one, the Lord is with you, you are blessed among women… you have found grace before the Lord of all things"; Sura 3:42, "Mary, God has chosen you and made you pure: He has truly chosen you above all women." Mary is unique because God selected her to conceive and give birth in a unique way, to a special person, Jesus—considered a prophet by Islam and the Son of God by Christianity. Even Mary herself seems to understand her chosenness; in the Magnificat, she says "all generations will call me blessed" (Luke 1:48). And indeed they have (hence this book!). But Mary's chosenness also presents some problems: yes, Mary was a mother and an ordinary woman, a teenage mom, and a refugee. But she was also visited by God's angel, got pregnant through divine power, and gave birth to one of the most important persons in history. How can ordinary women relate to this extraordinary woman? (See chapter 8 for more on this question.) Furthermore, Muslims might argue that the notion of "chosenness" is more apt when comparing the Christian Mary and the Muslim Fatima (daughter of Muhammad), rather than the Christian Mary and the Muslim Maryam.[23]

RESPONSE TO GOD'S CALL

Despite Mary's uniqueness, her exchange with the angel can be seen by both Christians and Muslims as one of the best examples of a *human* (not just female) response to God's call. Her response is exemplary for both female and male believers. And what was the nature of her response? According to the Gospel of Luke, Mary freely and courageously says yes: "Here am I, the servant of the Lord; let it be with me according to your word" (Luke 1:38), using language that might seem surprisingly "Muslim," given Mary's clear submission to God's will (submission to God is the meaning of the word *islam*). Her assent came only after some initial hesitation and questions: "But she was much perplexed by his words and pondered what sort of greeting this might be" (Luke 1:29) and "How can this be, since I am a virgin?" (Luke 1:34). Likewise, in the Qur'an, Mary also challenges the angel. In Sura 19:18, she actually tells him to go away (!), and then after he announces God's plan, she wonders how the pregnancy could even have happened, given her virginity (Sura 19:21), using language that is reminiscent of Luke 1:34. An interesting conversation between Christians and Muslims today would be to discuss the nature of Mary's dialogue with the angel: her questions and internal concerns, and her assent (whether explicit or not) to God's plan in both the qur'anic and biblical accounts of the annunciation.

PURITY

For both Christians and Muslims, Mary's purity and chastity are paramount. Christians often refer to her simply as "the Virgin" without using her name; everyone knows this is Mary the mother of Jesus, not one of the many other virgin-saints of the Church. Muslims call her *al Batul* (pure or "detached").[24] The question is, what is meant by purity: is it physical, spiritual, or both? Orthodox and Catholic Christians consider her both spiritually and sexually pure, calling her "ever-virgin" because they believe she conceived by the power of the Holy Spirit, had a virgin birth, and abstained from marital relations postpartum. Furthermore, the more recent Catholic doctrine of the immaculate conception highlights Mary's sinlessness from the moment she was conceived.[25] In Islam, scholars view Mary's purity in various ways; interpretations include purity from unbelief, from sin, from bad habits, from sexual intercourse, or from physical impurities such as menstruation.[26] There are Hadiths (e.g., from Bukhari and Muslim, whose collections are considered the most authoritative) that say that Mary and Jesus are unique for being the only two humans in history who escaped the "pricking of the devil" at birth, an idea that is connected to the Islamic doctrine of *isma*, "the innate quality of impeccability or immunity from sin and error."[27] It is important to note that while both religions stress Mary's sinlessness from birth, there is no doctrine of original sin in Islam.

Both religions say Mary is pure, but they ascribe different meanings to Mary's physical purity. While some Christians view

13

Mary's virginity as a model for monastic celibacy, Muslims see the ascetic life as exceptional. In Islam, a proper sexual relationship within marriage is considered normative. Thus, for Muslims it is better to imitate Fatima, the daughter of Muhammad, and not Mary, since Fatima was a normal, married mother, while Mary was an unmarried mother who conceived through exceptional means.[28] Furthermore, as noted earlier, Muslims prefer to call Mary *al Batul* (detached) rather than *al Adhra* (virginal), the title used for Mary by Christian Arabs, because *al Batul* is understood in the sense of living as a pious worshiper in isolation from everyone (not just sexual partners), "and hence, a virgin only by implication."[29] For Muslims, therefore, it is not so much Mary's *sexual* purity that makes her special, but her *overall physical demeanor* as one who is modest (Sura 19:16–17), obedient, who prostrates herself humbly before God (Sura 3:43), and is chaste (Sura 21:91; 66:12). These other aspects of her physical purity, and not her sexual purity per se, make her a model Muslim (*muslim* means "one who submits to God").[30] Mary's physical purity and spiritual devotion are likewise linked in Sura 66:11–12, where she is described as both "chaste" and a "believer": "God has also given examples of believers...Mary, daughter of 'Imran. She guarded her chastity, so We breathed into her from Our spirit. She accepted the truth of her Lord's words and Scriptures: she was truly devout." Mary has traditionally been considered by Muslim scholars as "chief lady of the women of Paradise," and first of the four holiest women in Islam (followed by Fatima, Khadija, and Asiya, wife of Pharaoh).[31] A question for a broader dialogue could be this: How is Mary a model of purity for both men and women, not just women?

MARY'S RELATIONSHIP TO JESUS

In both religions, Mary's main function is to point to Jesus' true identity. Mariology and Christology are therefore always intimately linked.[32] In Christianity, she is called *Theotokos* (God-bearer), while in Islam, her name is frequently mentioned in reference to Jesus; in fact, the most common title for Jesus in the Qur'an is *'Isa ibn Maryam* (Jesus, son of Mary). In Christianity, Mary's purity, both physical (virginity) and spiritual (sinlessness), is required for her to be God-bearer. But her importance as mother of Jesus goes beyond conception, pregnancy, and delivery. Aside from the biblical verses describing Mary at the very beginning of Jesus' life, there are several others showing later interactions between mother and child, for example, the boy Jesus in the temple, the wedding at Cana, and the crucifixion. Christians therefore recognize Mary as exceptional in her role as the Virgin Mother of God, but also consider her to be an exemplar of virtues anyone can emulate: courage, mercy, fidelity, obedience to God.[33] In Islam, Mary's purity and sinlessness highlight ʿIsa (Jesus) as an important prophet. Islam considers Jesus to be one of Islam's four main messengers, along with Abraham, Moses, and Muhammad. He is also the only Islamic prophet to be called a "word" (*kalima*) and "spirit" (*ruah*) of God in the Qur'an (Sura 4:171). But the Qur'an also stresses repeatedly—and sometimes quite explicitly contra Christians—the Islamic belief that Jesus is a human prophet, and not at all divine (e.g., Sura 5:75; 19:30–36; 21:26–29). Aside from baby Jesus speaking in her defense, the Qur'an has no stories about Mary postpartum, nor any stories describing interactions between her and Jesus, although mother and son are sometimes listed as a unit; for example, in Sura 21:91, they are both singled out as "signs for all people." Furthermore, there are few qur'anic references to the adult Jesus at all—only a few brief allusions to his future character (Sura 3:45–46; 19:30–33), his miracles (Sura 2:87; 3:49), a conversation with his disciples (Sura 5:112–14), and a denial of his crucifixion (Sura 4:157). In the Qur'an, there is no chapter named after Jesus, nor is there even a major section devoted to him; there is only the chapter named for Mary (19), which contains more information about her than Jesus. Some Hadith and other later sources, including Sufi poetry, do expand on Jesus and Mary, because they are important figures in Islam. But Muslim scholars through history have always debated the precise theological meaning of Mary and Jesus in Islam, especially given competing Christian views.[34] (See chapter 3 for more on Muslim Mariology.)

Now that our survey of Marian scripture passages is complete, the next two chapters will explore the development of Mariology in early Christianity and early Islam, along with Mary's role in nascent Christian-Muslim relations. As we shall see, Greek-speaking Christians saw Mary as a protective barrier between themselves and Muslim outsiders, while Arabic speakers—be they Christian or Muslim—had a more complicated view, since they lived in proximity to one another and shared the same language and culture.

Chapter 2

EARLY EASTERN CHRISTIAN VIEWS

Hail, deliverance from pagan worship....
Hail, immovable tower of the Church.
Hail, impregnable wall of the Kingdom....
To you, our leader in battle and defender,
O Theotokos, I, your city, delivered from sufferings,
ascribe hymns of victory and thanksgiving.
Since you are invincible in power,
free me from all kinds of dangers.[1]

        —Akathistos hymn, ca. 5th–6th century

"Muslims are pagans" but "much more right-minded"
because "they confess that [Jesus] was born of a
virgin and she was chaste."[2]

        —Nonnus of Nisibis, late 800s

The story of Christians, Muslims, and Mary begins with the rise of Christian Mariology in late antiquity, years before Islam was born. Scholars have traditionally identified the fifth century as a key moment in mariological development, due mainly to the Council of Ephesus (431), which declared Mary to be *Theotokos* (God-bearer).[3] After Ephesus, "Mary emerged like a comet in

Christian devotion and liturgical celebration throughout the world."[4] And indeed, one can readily see the "stuff" of a Marian cult bursting forth in the fifth and sixth centuries: new churches were built in her honor, official feast days were proclaimed, hymns were written, relics were venerated, and a rich iconography developed.

Two hundred years after Ephesus, Islam as both a religion and political entity arose in Arabia, and quickly spread to nearby Mesopotamia, Greater Syria, Palestine, and Egypt—places where Christians already lived and would remain in the majority for centuries to come. Since Christians and Muslims were living together in these areas, what were they saying to each other? Scholars argue that early Islamic theology, which developed in these very locations, was shaped by its encounter with Christianity.[5] Likewise, Eastern Christians living "in the shadow of the mosque" could not afford to ignore Islam when doing their own theologizing, even though Christianity, like Judaism before it, was a complete system with no internal need to mention religions that came later.[6]

When, how, and why does Islam enter early Christian theological writings, and how does Mary fit in? From the seventh through tenth centuries, Eastern Christians writing about Islam brought up Mary only briefly, usually to highlight her as a point of commonality, before launching into differences.[7] Mary was almost never the focus of these writings. Rather, she was mentioned only insofar as she related to the main topics of debate at this time, which were usually defensive, meaning that Christians were not driving the discussion, but rather, they were responding to Muslim questions. The main topics of debate were Trinity, incarnation, baptism, Eucharist, veneration of the cross, and direction of prayer.[8] Mary was most often mentioned in connection to the incarnation. Some, like John of Damascus (d. 749), whose catalogue of heresies includes one of the earliest descriptions of Islam in Greek, do not mention her at all.[9] Those who do mention Mary, usually Arabic- or Syriac-speaking Christians living in Muslim-controlled lands, acknowledge belief in the virgin birth as a key commonality. This affirmation can be seen in the quote from Nonnus of Nisibis (d. 886) at the beginning of this chapter: he derides Muslims as pagans in one breath, but in the next he adds that they are "more right-minded" than pagans because at least they believe Mary is the virgin mother of Christ. Nonnus's paradoxical statement shows the fine line Eastern Christians had to walk: they stressed commonalities between the two religions because they needed to maintain good relations with their Muslim overlords, but they could not ignore differences because they wanted to prevent Christians from converting to Islam.

Byzantine Christians had a different approach. They rarely if ever saw Mary as a figure shared by Christians and Muslims. As early as the fifth century, Byzantines began to describe Mary as a powerful barrier against all non-Christian enemies, eventually including Muslims.[10] This idea was expressed in myriad ways, from the famous *Akathistos* hymn quoted at the beginning of this chapter (where Mary is described as a bulwark against "pagan" foes), to stories of her standing on Constantinople's walls to shield the city with her robe during sieges by Avars (626), Arabs (717–18), and Russians (830). As we will see in later chapters, the Greek idea of Mary as a protectress was eventually transferred to the Latin West, where she continued to fight all manner of "pagans" for centuries to come: as *La Conquistadora* against the Moors in medieval Spain, Our Lady of Victory against the Ottomans in early modern Croatia, and Our Lady of the Rosary against modernists and communists in the twentieth century.[11]

This chapter will consider the following topics. First, we will review the development of Marian devotion in early Christianity, asking this question: Which came first, doctrine or devotion? The answer has implications for our understanding of Mariology not only in Christianity, but also in Islam. Second, we will examine how Mary was used in the earliest Christian writings against Islam (seventh to tenth centuries). What topics were discussed, and how was she used in dialogue, debate, and even war with Muslims? Third and finally, we will compare the differing emphases of Arabophone and Byzantine Christians when they talked about Muslims and Mary. It seems that in late antiquity, Mary played multiple and even contradictory roles, depending on the Christians. For Arabic-speaking Christians, Mary was simultaneously a bridge to harmonious relations with their Muslim rulers, and a barrier preventing apostasy to Islam among their confreres. The necessarily dual stance of Eastern Christians (who shared a common culture, language, and homeland with Muslims and lived under Islamic rule) has been called "a discourse of accommodation and a discourse of resistance."[12] But for Byzantine Christians, most of whom did not know any Muslims nor live under Islamic rule, there was no dual stance. It seems they saw Mary only as a barrier, one that protected them from external attack by non-Christian foes like Muslims.[13] There is scant evidence that Greek-speaking Byzantines of this time ever saw Mary as a bridge. Is this because they did not understand Islamic theology well enough to recognize the affinities between the two religions, or because they felt they didn't need a bridge, since they were not under Islamic rule and therefore could afford to ignore the religion?

MARY BEFORE ISLAM: WHICH CAME FIRST, DEVOTION OR DOCTRINE?

Christian doctrines about Mary did not develop in isolation. Rather, they evolved in tandem with doctrines about Christ, such that both Mariology and Christology were articulated at the Council of Ephesus and its sequel, Chalcedon (451).[14] As noted earlier, there is ample material evidence for a Marian cult immediately following these two councils, but not so much before. However, some scholars have recently begun to question the assumption that Marian devotion came after these fifth-century councils. Instead, it has been suggested that widespread popular devotion to Mary was a contributing *cause*, not effect, of the councils.[15]

Evidence is needed to make such a claim, but Marian devotion prior to the fifth century has not been well studied.[16] Several reasons have been suggested as to why not. The first is that many pre-fifth-century Marian writings (aside from the second-century *Protevangelium of James*) have been ignored, perhaps because they were written or preserved in less-studied early Christian languages such as Georgian, Ethiopian, Armenian, Coptic, and Syriac. Examples of such writings dating from the third to fourth centuries include the *Gospel of Mary*; *Georgian Chantbook*; *Book of Mary's Repose*; *Six Books Dormition Apocryphon*; and *Under Your Protection* (*Sub Tuum Praesidium*).[17]

Another possible reason pre-fifth-century Marian devotion

has been ignored is that some of these early texts, and thus Marian devotion itself, were often connected to heterodox Christian movements. Even though orthodox fathers like Athanasius, Gregory Nazianzus, Gregory of Nyssa, and Ephrem the Syrian all wrote of Mary's importance by the late fourth century, using titles like *Theotokos* and describing popular devotional practices, they may have been reluctant to say too much because Marian devotion seems to have developed in heterodox (i.e., theologically marginal) communities.[18] For example, the *Six Books Apochryphon* just mentioned is associated with the Kollyridians, also known as the Marianites, a fourth-century Christian group condemned as heretical. The Kollyridians were accused of worshiping Mary, giving women priestly powers, and offering Mary a kind of bread Eucharist. Due to the possible connections between Marian piety, the Kollyridians, and other heterodox groups, early theologians may have been hesitant to elaborate on Mary until the fifth-century councils gave her legitimacy.[19] The connection between heterodoxy and Christian Mariology is important to keep in mind when considering Islamic Mariology, because even today, the Marian piety of ordinary Muslims is considered suspect if not heretical by many clerics.

Likewise, Christian theologians have always been concerned about the orthodoxy of Marian doctrine and devotion. To counter accusations of idolatry, one traditional explanation for Mariology's rise in the fifth century is that it was needed to support orthodox Christology, which was under fire at the time. Thus, the three most popular Byzantine epithets for Mary—*Theotokos* (God-bearer), *Aeiparthenos* (Ever-Virgin), and *Panagia* (All-Holy)—were intended to say something about Christ, not Mary; the original goal of these titles was to "safeguard orthodox Christological dogma, not provide the foundations for a mariology which supplants an adequate theology."[20] Yet there have been times in history when Marian doctrine *does* seem to have supplanted an adequate (meaning Christ-centered) theology. When Mary is disassociated from Christ and presented as a stand-alone theological topic, some Christians worry about idolatry; indeed, this was one of the main concerns the sixteenth-century Reformers had with the Catholic Church.

The final reason pre-fifth-century Marian piety has been neglected is that theologians have sometimes privileged doctrine over devotion. In so doing, they have ignored an important principle, *lex orandi, lex credendi* ("the law of prayer is the law of belief"), which means that liturgy and popular piety often drive doctrine, rather than the other way around. For example, a third-century Coptic liturgical text, *Sub Tuum Praesidium* (*Under your protection*), includes one of the earliest extant intercessory prayers to Mary: "We take refuge beneath the protection of your compassion, *Theotokos.* Do not disregard our prayers in troubling times, but deliver us from danger, O only pure and blessed one."[21] Here, the faithful already deem Mary worthy of *hyperdulia*, a form of devotion unique to her and greater than that accorded to other saints (*dulia*), but less than the worship given to God alone (*latria*).

Sub Tuum and other early liturgical texts suggest that Marian devotion existed at the grassroots level decades and perhaps even centuries before the formal Marian doctrines of the fifth century. However, as already noted, after the Councils of Ephesus and Chalcedon, the cult of Mary grew exponentially, giving rise to new feast days, churches, shrines, hymns, relics, and icons. Liturgy, in particular, helped to spread Marian piety throughout the empire, and indeed, four feast days dedicated to Mary emerge at this time. Two of them, the Annunciation (March 25) and Presentation (February 2), have biblical roots and a dual Mary-Jesus focus; their dates were officially set by Justinian in 561. The other two feasts, the Dormition/Assumption (August 15) and the Nativity of Mary (September 8), were established later. The latter two are distinctive for their focus on Mary alone (no Jesus), and roots not in the Bible but in apocryphal texts such as the *Protevangelium.*[22] To celebrate these feasts, elaborate processions developed in both Rome and Constantinople by the end of the seventh century. Pope Sergius (r. 687–701) declared that on all four Marian feasts, Rome's faithful would process from Sant'Adriano to Santa Maria Maggiore.[23] Constantinople followed suit, with processions at Blachernai for the Feasts of Dormition and Presentation, and Chalkopraeia for the Annunciation and Mary's Nativity.

Also in the fifth century, we see the rise of churches and shrines dedicated to the *Theotokos.* One of the earliest Marian shrines is the Kathisma Church, located midway between Jerusalem and Bethlehem.[24] In Greek, *kathisma* means "seat," and legend has it that a pregnant Mary stopped to rest here on her way to giving birth in Bethlehem. The Kathisma is important not only for being one of the first churches devoted to the Virgin, but also because it hosted the Feast of the Theotokos, unique for commemorating a theological concept rather than an event like the Nativity.[25] Also in the fifth century, three major Marian churches were built in Constantinople—Blachernai, Chalkopraeia, and Hodegoi—all founded with the help of Empress Pulcheria, a major promoter of Marian devotion in the empire.[26]

In addition to the building of new shrines and churches, the fifth century saw the writing of new Marian hymns. The *Akathistos* is perhaps the most famous, and is still sung in Orthodox churches today.[27] Its twenty-four stanzas tell the story of Jesus' birth, praise Mary's powers, and implore her aid. Each verse includes numerous titles for Mary, such as "Bright Dawn," "Bride Unwedded," and "Womb of Divine Incarnation."[28] Other titles depict Mary as a defender and warrior, such as "Protection and Defense," and "Impregnable Wall of the Kingdom."[29] The latter titles may be surprising to Western Christians, who are more familiar with gentler names for Mary such as "Mother of Mercy," "Mystical Rose," and "Morning Star." But in the *Akathistos*, Mary is not meek and mild. Rather, she is the invincible one who protects Constantinople and brings victory to her people; in so doing she looks a bit like classical goddesses Tyche and Victoria.[30] In this famous Byzantine hymn, Mary seems a long way from the "clement, loving, sweet virgin" of the medieval Latin *Salve Regina*.[31]

Mary's ability to protect and fight, which is so praised in the *Akathistos*, was connected to various relics housed at Constantinople's churches. For example, the monastery of Blachernai, situated just outside the city walls and thus in constant danger of foreign attack, contained a powerful relic: Mary's mantle (robe), which the faithful "activated" in a weekly Friday service and procession.[32] Also at Blachernai was an annual feast thanking *Theotokos* for helping the Christian city to secure victory over its enemies; the feast itself was called the Akathistos, after the hymn sung during the celebration. Thus, at Constantinople's Blachernai, we can see how shrine, relic, and liturgy came together in the fifth century to encourage popular Marian devotion.

MARY, PROTECTRESS AND GENERAL

Two images from the *Akathistos* hymn are particularly relevant to our discussion of Christians, Muslims, and Mary: protectress and general. Mary's power in these two roles was derived from her paradoxical status as Virgin (*parthenos*) and Mother of God (*Meter Theou*).[33] As both protectress and general, Mary acted on behalf of Christians at war with non-Christians. As protectress, she was on the defensive. But as general, she was on the offensive, and sometimes shockingly so. For example, one poem says she "incinerates the barbaric insolence," while an account of the Avar siege (626) describes General Mary waging war thus:

> Upon slaughtering the enemies in the hands of the Christian soldiers, she brought down to earth the aggression of the barbarians and enfeebled their whole army.... The intervention of the Virgin Mary gave courage to our soldiers, who knew her power through experience and believed that it was truly the *Theometor* [mother of God] who would protect her city and fight. And the Virgin appeared everywhere, winning uncontested victory and inflicting horror and fear on the enemies....In the sea battle, the Virgin sank men and boats together before our Blachernai monastery....It was proved most clearly that the Virgin alone fought this battle and won the victory."[34]

Particularly notable about these two quotes (apart from the graphic verbs used to describe Mary's actions: *slaughter*, *incinerate* and *inflict horror*!) is that they describe her as personally fighting the enemy, and that enemy is explicitly called "infidel" or "barbarian." Mary's use of force to defeat a non-Christian enemy is justified in an early homily by Severian of Gabala, who compares the violent actions of *Theotokos* to those of biblical women Deborah and Jael (Judg 4):

> And we also have Saint Mary the Virgin and Theotokos who intercedes for us. For if an ordinary woman [Deborah or Jael] can be victorious, how much more will the mother of Christ humiliate the enemies of truth? The

enemy, armed to the teeth, thought that the woman was worthy of derision, but he found her to be a valiant general…he was put to death by her.[35]

It has been suggested that Severian's homily (ca. 400) is the oldest extant reference to a militarized Mary.[36] His homily predates even the *Akathistos* hymn, which also describes Mary fighting pagan error. For example, the hymn's eleventh strophe says, "Shining upon Egypt the Light of Truth, you dispelled the darkness of falsehood, for her idols, O Saviour [Mary], fell down unable to endure your power," and calls Mary the one who "trampled upon the delusion of error" and "refuted the deceit of the idols."[37] This terminology is significant, for one can see how easily the image of Mary fighting Egyptian idolaters could turn into an image of her fighting Muslim "infidels."

The way Mary was seen as protecting Constantinople from non-Christian invaders evolved over time: early Byzantine texts depict her as being directly involved in battles, while later writings ascribe her power to relics and icons rather than to her person.[38] For example, eyewitness accounts of the Avar siege of 626 describe Mary walking on the city walls and fighting the enemy herself.[39] Her help is due to her physical presence. But eventually, Mary's power was transferred from her person to her robe, such that later accounts (of Avar, Arab, and Russian sieges) describe Christians processing with Mary's robe along the city walls.[40] Still later accounts transfer Mary's power from her robe to her icon, and describe elaborate processions centered on specific Marian icons known for their power.[41] An account of a war with the Muslims of Aleppo in 1030 claims that by this time it was tradition for Byzantine emperors to carry a Marian icon with them into battle. This icon was nicknamed "Blachernitissa" because it was from Constantinople's Blachernai church. A second Marian icon, called "Hodegetria," from the Hodegoi church, never left Constantinople, so that she could protect the city. Thus, by the eleventh century, Byzantine Christians were relying on two different Marian icons to help them fight infidels: one stayed home to protect them from invasion, and one traveled abroad to secure victory.[42]

How did the Greek image of Mary as protectress get transferred to the Latin West? An anonymous text from eleventh-century

Iberia preserved Byzantine accounts of the Virgin's robe protecting Constantinople from Arab attack.[43] It is not surprising that this story would appeal to medieval Iberians, given their own wars against Muslims at the time. In fact, the famous thirteenth-century illustrated book *Cantigas de Santa Maria* refers often to the Muslim sieges of Constantinople. For example, *cantiga* 28 depicts Mary above the city, staring down its Muslim attackers and "gently spreading her mantle so it deflected the blows dealt by the thick-lipped sultan."[44] It is not clear whether *cantiga* 28 is referring to the Arab siege of 717–18, or a Byzantine victory over Arabs on August 15, 963.[45] But no matter which, the same key details apply: Constantinople is besieged by Muslims, and the city is successfully defended by Mary's robe. Interestingly, *cantiga* 28 adds a new detail to the old story: it says that during the battle, the sultan had a vision of Mary: "When he raised his eyes up to heaven, he saw the Mother of God, wrapped in her veil, hovering over the city with her mantle outstretched, fending off the blows."[46] Immediately after this vision, the sultan converts to Christianity (but secretly). Aside from the *Cantigas*, there are other cases of the Mary-as-protectress idea transferring from East to West. For example, images of Madonna di Costantinopoli and Madonna d'Itria (the latter is a corruption of Hodegetria), who is depicted standing on city walls, became popular in late medieval Naples, Sicily, and Sardinia.[47] As chapter 5 will show, "Our Lady of Victory" was the preferred image of Western Christians, who succeeded in turning back Muslim advances into their territory. But after the seventh century, some scholars have argued that the Orthodox communities of Southeastern Europe began embracing not "Our Lady of Victory" but "Our Lady of Defeat," since their lands eventually came under the orbit of the Ottomans.[48]

The case was different for another group of early Eastern Christians—those living in the Muslim-ruled lands of Mesopotamia, Syria, Palestine, and Egypt. Did they ever see Mary as a protector? Given their distinct cultural milieu, how did early Christians living in the Middle East describe Mary vis-à-vis Islam? Certainly, the differences between Greek and Middle Eastern Christians have something to do with the fact that for the former, Muslims were external to their own culture, while for the latter, Muslims were integral to it.

MARY AND EASTERN CHRISTIAN RESPONSES TO ISLAM

Unlike Greek and Latin Christians in Europe, Christians living in the eastern Mediterranean could not ignore Islam.[49] This was true even when they wrote about their own religion; most Arabophone Christian theology composed in the eighth century and later had Islam in mind.[50] Aside from genres that were explicitly polemical or apologetic, even Christian-centric texts implicitly engaged in dialogue with Islam.[51] This can be seen in an early Arabic "summa" of Christian theology called the *Summa Theologiae Arabica* in Latin (copied ca. 877). The book's long title in Arabic, *Summary of the Ways of Faith in the Trinity of the Unity of God, and in the Incarnation of God the Word from the Pure Virgin Mary*, doubles as a list of the most important interfaith topics.[52] It is notable that Mary is mentioned here along with the Trinity, God's unity (*tawhid*—an important Islamic concept), and the incarnation.

Eastern Christians incorporated Mary into their thinking about Islam, but they used her differently than the Byzantines. For the Byzantines, she was a protectress or general against all infidels including Muslims; in short, she was a barrier. But for Eastern Christians, Mary was more complicated. Unlike the Byzantines, they had to balance acknowledging similarities (to preserve good relations with their Muslim neighbors and overlords) with highlighting differences (to prevent Christians from converting to Islam).[53] Their main topics of interfaith discussion were the Trinity, incarnation, Scripture, veneration of the cross, and direction of prayer, with Mary brought up only tangentially. Only a few theologians devoted substantive space to Mary in their arguments against Islam, for example, Jacob of Edessa's *Letter on the Genealogy of the Virgin*, the *Apology of Timothy*, and the *Apology of Al-Kindi*. In these writings, Mary and Islam connect to the following topics: shared belief in her virgin birth and Davidic ancestry; differing opinions on her perpetual virginity; and the supposed qur'anic confusion between Mary the mother of Jesus and Miriam the sister of Moses (see Sura 19:27–28).[54]

Before exploring these writings, some mention must be made of the distinctive cultural and religious milieu of Middle Eastern

Christians. While Islam as a political entity spread swiftly from the Arabian Peninsula throughout the eastern Mediterranean in the seventh century, it took several decades for the region to become fully Arabicized and Islamicized, with the language being accepted first, followed by the religion, which took some centuries to move beyond the minority ruling class. Non-Muslim communities such as Christians and Jews were tolerated as "people of the book" and thus protected (and restricted) under Islamic law. But beginning in the 690s, the government began to push key Islamic tenets like the *shahada* through official means such as coins and building inscriptions.[55] Some of these proclamations were explicitly anti-Christian. For example, Jerusalem's Dome of the Rock, built circa 690, has numerous qur'anic inscriptions that expressly condemn Christian doctrines such as the Trinity and incarnation.[56] In response to this new religious offensive, Christian leaders began to compose more extended anti-Islamic tracts. They also began to write more apologetical works, due to increasing fears of mass conversion to Islam by the turn of the eighth century.[57]

Middle Eastern Christianity at the time included three main groups: Melkites, Jacobites, and Nestorians. These were the product of the first major splits in Christianity in the fifth century, due to disagreements about the Christology (and Mariology) proclaimed at the Councils of Ephesus and Chalcedon. Melkites were called Chalcedonians for their acceptance of Chalcedon's "two natures, one person" christological formula, while Jacobites and Nestorians were called non-Chalcedonians. Melkites, who had ties to Byzantium, lived mainly in the Levant (Palestine, Lebanon, Syria, and Jordan). Jacobites (called *monophysites* for their "one nature" Christology), who also lived throughout the Levant and Mesopotamia, are theologically related to other monophysites such as the Copts and Ethiopians of Africa, and the Armenians and Georgians of Central Asia. Nestorians (called *dyophysites* for their alleged "two natures" Christology) lived mainly in Iraq and Iran. All three Eastern Christian groups—Jacobites, Nestorians, and Melkites—were to have a profound influence on early Islam's understanding of Christianity.[58] Furthermore, the Jacobites and Nestorians were considered heretical by Latin and Greek Christians, a label that influenced subsequent European views on *all* religiosity in the Middle East—be it Christian or Muslim. Recall the Kollyridians (Marianites) mentioned earlier; they were thought to have originated in southern Arabia, a place Latin and Greek Christians considered an especially fertile breeding ground of heresy. In fact, Western Christians accused Islam itself of being a heresy created by Muhammad, Nestorian Christians, and Jews.

Today, thanks to improved ecumenical relations, some of the theological differences that once divided Eastern and Western churches have now been resolved. For example, in 1994 the Roman Catholic Church and the Assyrian Church of the East (formerly called "Nestorian," which is now considered pejorative), signed a common christological declaration stating that *Theotokos* (God-bearer) and *Christotokos* (Christ-bearer)—terms for Mary that were fought over in the fifth century—are now both theologically acceptable.[59] Beyond theology, Eastern and Western Christians differ liturgically and linguistically.[60] Geography has also created another relevant difference: the majority of Eastern Christians have lived among Muslims for centuries, sharing a language and culture; thus their experience of Islam has been very different from that of Western Christians.[61]

How did this context affect Eastern Christian writings about Islam? At first, not so much; early polemics against Muslims were modeled on older arguments against Jews and heretics.[62] But as Eastern Christians learned more about Islamic theology, they began to tailor their arguments accordingly. One of the earliest Christian texts to discuss Mary and Islam at length is the *Letter on the Genealogy of the Virgin* by Jacob of Edessa (d. 708).[63] Jacob, bishop of Edessa (now in Turkey, near the Syrian border), was one of the first church leaders to legislate Christian-Muslim relations.[64] He wrote about Christians and Muslims eating together (mostly forbidden), Christians attending Muslim funerals (mostly allowed), and rebaptism after apostasy (not required). In his *Letter on the Genealogy of the Virgin*, which is addressed to a fellow Christian, Jacob touches on all the major Christian-Muslim issues of the time, such as Trinity and incarnation. But his main goal is to prove that Mary is descended from King David, despite the conflicting genealogies found in the Gospels. Evidently, Mary's Davidic ancestry was a common topic of discussion at the time, not only between Christians and Muslims but also among Christians. For example, several homilies of Andrew of Crete (d. 740) center on this topic.[65]

While Jacob's letter is addressed to a fellow Christian, it is not meant for Christians alone. In fact, Jacob explicitly and repeatedly states that he is targeting both Christians and Muslims, to show them that "Mary the Holy Virgin and Mother of God is of the race of David."[66] To do this, Jacob notes which aspects of Christology and Mariology are shared by the two religions, and which are not: "Even though the Muslims do not recognize Jesus Christ as God or the son of God, they still confess without hesitation that he is the messiah and will come again as the prophets say."[67] Jacob also thinks that Muslims revere the Old Testament (they do not), and thus quotes frequently from prophetic books like Isaiah to prove his claims. He says that the prophets "will be sufficient to show clearly to a Christian or Muslim who discuss this subject that Mary is of the race of David."[68] Not only does this quote affirm Jacob's belief in a shared Scripture, but also a shared Mary. Jacob knew that both religions believe in the Virgin. Christians and Muslims of his time were not arguing about whether to honor her; it was simply taken for granted that they did. Rather, they were discussing the finer points of Mariology: for example, whether she was of the race of David, or whether she remained a virgin after the birth of Christ.

Jacob does something else in his letter. At one point, he broadens the list of religions that believe in the Messiah to include Christians, Muslims, and Jews: "That the messiah is in his flesh of the race of David…is confessed by all, and is like a fundamental dogma for Jews and Muslims and Christians."[69] But he then goes on to use the Jesus shared by Christians and Muslims as leverage to attack Jews. He notes that where Jesus is concerned, Muslims

> have no controversy with us, rather they have a bigger controversy with the Jews, when they establish against them, through the force of argument, that he was announced by the prophets, born of the race of David, and that the messiah who would come would be born of Mary….This is confessed strongly by the Muslims and no one among them contests it, because they say always and to all that Jesus son of Mary is the true messiah, they also call him the word of God.[70]

30

A few pages later, Jacob intensifies his polemic by listing all the usual Christian arguments against Jews: they wait for the messiah in vain, their hearts are blind to Christ, and so on.[71] He adds that Muslims are better than Jews, because they share some (but not all) of the same beliefs about Mary and Jesus. In so doing, Jacob foreshadows a technique that would be used during the sixteenth century, when Catholics and Protestants brought a third party (Muslims) into bilateral debates, with the sole purpose of disparaging their interlocutor. For example, Protestants accused Muslims of being bad but still better than Catholics, while Catholics argued the opposite. (See chapter 5 for more on this topic.) Centuries earlier, Jacob of Edessa did the very same thing, by arguing that Muslims are bad but Jews are worse, because although Muslims believe in Mary and Jesus imperfectly, Jews do not believe in them at all.

Another early Eastern Christian text that mentions both Islam and Mary is the late eighth century *Apology of Timothy*, framed as a dialogue between Mar Timothy, a Nestorian patriarch, and Mahdi, the Abbasid caliph.[72] Mary is first brought up by the Muslim, who asks how Timothy can be such a wise leader yet believe that God "married a woman and begat a son."[73] This question leads into an extended discussion of Christ. But then the Muslim returns to Mary, asking Timothy to affirm his belief in the virgin birth: "'Do you not say that He was born of the Virgin Mary?' And I [Timothy] said to [Mahdi]: 'We say it and confess it. The very same Christ is the Word born of the Father, and a man born of Mary.'"[74] But after confirming a shared belief in Mary's virgin birth, Timothy brings up a point of disagreement, Mary's perpetual virginity: "From the Father he is therefore born eternally, and from the mother he is born in time, without a father, without any marital contact, and without any break in the seals of the virginity of his mother."[75] The Muslim is skeptical about her perpetual virginity: "That he was born of Mary without marital intercourse is found in the [Qur'an] and is well known, but is it possible that he was born without breaking the seals of the virginity of his mother?" Timothy responds by asking, If God could allow Mary to conceive without intercourse, then why couldn't God have also allowed her to remain a virgin after giving birth? Mahdi answers by saying that while Adam is proof of birth without intercourse, there is no scriptural proof for virginity after childbirth: "That a man can be born without breaking his mother's virginal seals we have no proof, neither from Book nor from nature."[76] Timothy responds by saying that there *is* scriptural proof of this, but the evidence he gives is weak: he says Eve was born from Adam's side without rupturing it, and Jesus ascended to heaven without rending the skies. The anonymous Christian author of the *Apology of Timothy* does not allow the Muslim to respond. Instead, the two interlocutors return to christological questions.

The *Apology of Timothy* discusses all the other polemical topics common to Christian-Muslim debates at this time. But despite obvious theological disagreement, the overall tone is quite positive; Timothy addresses the Muslim caliph as "*Our* King," repeatedly calling him "God-loving," "gracious," "wise," and "victorious." When asked what he thinks of Muhammad, Timothy says he is "worthy of praise by reasonable people," and while he does not go as far as to call him a prophet, he does say that Muhammad "walked in the path of the prophets, and trod in the track of the lovers of God," and praises him for getting the Arabs to reject polytheism and accept one God.[77] For a Christian polemicist to describe Muhammad in such positive terms would later become rare among Western Christians.

Another Eastern Christian text on Mary and Islam is the famous Arabic-language polemic, *Risalat al-Kindi* (ca. ninth–tenth century), which would have great influence in Western Europe beginning in the twelfth century, when Peter the Venerable commissioned its translation into Latin along with several Islamic texts, most notably the Qur'an.[78] The *Risalat* purports to be a letter exchange between a Christian and a Muslim, but both letters were probably written by a single unknown Christian author, and intended for an internal audience. One clue of its Christian authorship and audience is the fact that the Christian's letter is five times as long as the Muslim's! The *Risalat* is an example of an "epistolary exchange," a literary genre popular among early Eastern Christian apologists.[79]

Al Kindi's tone is less irenic than Timothy's. While he covers many of the same topics, he introduces some new stereotypes that would have great longevity in the West: Islam is a violent, satanic religion; the Qur'an is a mendacious, disorderly book;

Muslim rituals are superficial and ineffective; and Muhammad was an evil, violent, promiscuous polygamist. But the *Risalat* also includes a short section on the qur'anic and biblical annunciation stories, which al Kindi says should prove to Muslims that Christ is the fulfillment of the prophets and the Son of God. The section begins with quotations from Luke's annunciation account, along with some details from the *Protevangelium*, such as the name of Mary's father, Joachim. His description of Mary lists qualities that Christians and Muslims can both affirm: purity, virginity, chastity, holiness, and chosenness. Al Kindi encourages his Muslim interlocutor to listen to the Christian annunciation story with an open mind, and to "lay aside the ignorance and prejudice that blind you."[80] Directly following the biblical annunciation come extensive quotes from the qur'anic annunciation (Sura 3:42–50), which Al Kindi says "differs from ours [Christian account] and yet confirms our argument."[81]

The above quote shows that even in more polemical writings like Al Kindi's, Eastern Christians still acknowledged Mary as a bridge. In fact, Mary seems to have been more of a bridge than Jesus, for references to Jesus in these texts were often the beginning of an argument. But Mary and her good qualities remained something both sides could agree on. In fact, Mary's preferability over Jesus as an interfaith bridge can be seen when one considers their names in Arabic. Early Eastern Christians writing in Arabic wanted to distinguish between Muslim Christology and Christian Christology, and thus sometimes used two different words for Jesus: *Yasu'* for the Christian Jesus, and *'Isa* for the Muslim Jesus.[82] But they made no distinction between the Muslim Mary and the Christian Mary. In Arabic, she was and still is called only Maryam in both cases.

CONCLUSION

In the first few centuries of Muslim-Christian interaction, Mary played multiple and sometimes competing roles. Eastern Christians often highlighted commonalities between Christian and Muslim mariologies. They saw Mary as a bridge that might allow for harmonious interfaith relations between themselves and their Muslim overlords. Because they shared a language and culture, Eastern Christians knew Islamic literature and praxis well, and were thus able to stress similarities. For example, Bartholomew of Edessa, writing in the twelfth century, observed, "In the entire Qur'an there do not occur any praises of Muhammad or his mother Aminah, such as are found about our Lord Jesus Christ and about the Holy Virgin Mary, the *Theotokos*."[83] His argument is that since the Qur'an praises Mary more than anyone else—not only revered Muslim women like Aminah, but even the Prophet Muhammad himself—this proves that Islam acknowledges what Christians already believe about Mary: that she is the mother of God. Bartholomew believed that the Qur'an itself recognizes Christian claims about Mary, even if Muslims do not. Of course, he also believed that this fact should lead Muslims to convert. However, Eastern Christians could not just stress commonalities; they had to discuss differences too. Thus, after agreeing with their Muslim interlocutors about Mary's virgin birth, they argued over her perpetual virginity. Thus, Mary also became a barrier against Christian apostasy. But debates about the finer points of mariological doctrine could never have taken place without both sides having good knowledge of the other, and a foundation of commonalities from which to draw. This was not the case in Byzantium, where Christians and Muslims did not live together, nor did they share a common language and culture. For Byzantines, Mary was a barrier protecting them from external attack by non-Christians. She was not a bridge. And it was this idea of Mary as barrier, not Mary as bridge, that transferred to most places in the Latin West. Only where Christians and Muslims were neighbors—medieval Iberia and Sicily, for example—did Mary take on the more complex role as both bridge and barrier, as found among Eastern Arabophone Christians.

Aside from her use in debates, there is one other way Mary connects early Islam and Christianity: the development of Mariology itself. For Mary is central to neither religion. In fact, there have been leaders on both sides who have criticized the excesses of Marian devotion, if not the devotion itself. Yet, in both religions, Marian piety flourishes among ordinary believers who truly love her. Religious practices surrounding Mary—icon veneration, pilgrimages to shrines, intercessory prayers, and so forth—might be considered heterodox by the elite and sometimes even condemned, but such practices have remained strong at the grassroots level. As Jane Baum has observed, "The people-led nature of Marian belief holds true in East and West."[84] By East and West, Baum meant Eastern and Western Christianity, but her idea could be extended to Islam as well. Is the development of Mariology in both religions— where the liturgy and practice of ordinary believers has influenced official doctrine—an example of *lex orandi, lex credendi* at work? This chapter suggests that the answer is yes for Christianity. The next chapter, which introduces Muslim Mariology, will help us to consider the question for Islam.

Chapter 3

MUSLIMS ON MARY: PROPHET OR IDOL?

When God says, "Jesus, son of Mary, did you say to people, 'Take me and my mother as two gods alongside God'?" He will say, "May you be exalted! I would never say what I had no right to say."

—Qur'an, Sura 5:116

The truth is that Mary was a prophetess because God communicated revelation [*wahi*] to her through an angel, as he did to other prophets.

—Al-Qurtubi (d. 1273)[1]

Islam was born in the seventh century of the Common Era, but did not see itself as a new religion. Rather, Muslims believe that *islam* (submission to God's will) is the original human religion. They also consider themselves related to two older religions, Judaism and Christianity, which the Qur'an dubs *ahl al-kitab*, "people of the book." Early Muslim writings, therefore, strove to demonstrate both Islam's connectedness to its predecessors and also its superiority over them. In some ways this paralleled early Christianity's declaration of its rootedness in, and supersession of, Judaism (supersessionism was not explicitly and officially refuted by Christians until after World War II).[2] However, unlike early Christian writings, many of which contain strongly anti-Jewish sentiments, early Islamic writings often speak well of Christians. And Mary features prominently in several of these texts. For example, Ibn Ishaq's eighth-century biography of Muhammad recounts the story of Muslim refugees who fled to Ethiopia, where they recite qur'anic verses about Mary and Jesus to Ethiopia's Christian King Negus, who declares that the two religions only differ as much as a stick is long.[3] The refugees did not select verses from Sura 5, which criticizes Christians for idolizing the Virgin. Instead, they chose passages from Sura 19 (Maryam), which they knew the Christian king would recognize, thus showing an early Muslim acknowledgment of Mary as a potential bridge between the two religions.

In addition to her usefulness as an interfaith bridge, Mary is also a significant Islamic figure in her own right. But what exactly is her status in Islam? Muslims have long debated this point. One contemporary scholar lays out the possibilities: "Is she to be considered as the righteous (*siddiqa*) only, or as a saintly, holy woman (*wali-yya*), or a prophetess?"[4] There has never been a consensus answer to this question. Some Muslims have wondered whether it is possible for any female to be a prophet, while others have focused on the question of whether Mary in particular—among other prominent women such as 'Aisha, Asiya, and Fatima—should be called a prophet. A second and related issue is how Islam should evaluate Christian doctrines about Mary. While Muslims disagree about Mary's status within their own religion, they have generally agreed that some of what Christianity says about her is not only erroneous but also blasphemous; many Muslims consider the Christian Mary to have devolved into an idol who compromises the oneness of God (*tawhid*), one of Islam's most important doctrines. (Sixteenth-century Protestants were equally critical of what they saw as Catholic Mariolatry.) Most Muslims through history, therefore, have seen Mary as a barrier between Christianity and Islam, since she highlights significant theological differences between the two religions. In short, viewing Mary as an interfaith barrier is a conclusion many Muslims and Christians have long shared.

Unlike all the other chapters in this book, which discuss the historical Christian theology of Islam, this chapter is unique for offering a brief glimpse into the historical *Islamic* theology of Christianity as it relates to Mary. It is important to note that the "Islamic theology of Christianity" is not a traditional subject in Islamic theology (nor is it in patristic or medieval Christian theology, for that matter). However, there have been some Muslim scholars, both medieval (Ibn Hazm, al-Ghazali) and contemporary (Nasr, Gülen), who have written on Islamic views of other religions, and the last decade has seen an increase in Islamic treatments of this subject.[5] Furthermore, there has long been an implicit Islamic theology of Christianity, or perhaps more correctly, an Islamic theology of "people of the book" (*ahl al-kitab*), present in traditional Islamic jurisprudence, but a full discussion of that would be well beyond the scope of this book.

This chapter has three parts, covering three interrelated topics. Part one will outline Islamic Mariology, which is rooted in an interpretation of Sura 3:42: "Mary, God has chosen you and made you pure: He has truly chosen you above all women." Is she righteous, a saint, or even a prophet? Part two will consider the devotional practices and art that flow from Islamic Mariology. Part three will discuss historical Islamic arguments against Christian Mariology. It is this last section that best parallels the rest of the book, since Muslims through history have used Mary in their polemics against Christianity, just as Christians through history have used Mary in their polemics against Islam.

As far as Mary's spiritual status is concerned, the disagreements are not only interreligious (that is, between Christians and Muslims), but also intrareligious (that is, among different kinds of Muslims). In fact, some of the internal Muslim arguments about Mary could be likened to internal Christian (e.g., Protestant vs. Catholic) arguments about her. But whether the debate is interreligious or intrareligious, both Christianity and Islam have had to grapple with some of the same theological questions about the Virgin Mary: who is she, what is her status, and why does she matter to believers?

ISLAMIC MARIOLOGY

While Muslims disagree about Mary's precise spiritual status and how she is to be approached, they all nevertheless agree that she is an important figure. In Islam, the Virgin Mary is exceptional indeed: she is one of only two sinless human beings in history (the other is Jesus); she is the only woman mentioned by name in the Qur'an; and an entire sura (19) is named after her. In fact, there are more verses about Mary in the Qur'an than in the Bible.

So who do Muslims say Maryam is? She is significant first and foremost as the Virgin Mother of Jesus ('Isa), an important prophet and messenger in Islam. Her connection to Jesus is underscored by the Qur'an, Hadith, and other early Islamic literature, all of which frequently mention her and Jesus together. The most common title for the Prophet Jesus in Islamic texts is 'Isa ibn Maryam (Jesus, son of Mary). In early Islam, therefore, just as in early Christianity, Mariology is intimately linked to Christology.[6] But just as is the case with the Christian Mary, the Islamic Maryam has good qualities of her own, apart from her connection to Jesus. These include faith (66:12), obedience (66:12; 3:43), pious submission, and even *ma'rifah* (secret knowledge of the divine).[7] Like the Bible, the Qur'an highlights the fact that Maryam has been chosen by God above all other women: "The angels said to Mary, 'Mary, God has chosen you and made you pure. He has truly chosen you above all women'" (Sura 3:42; cf. Luke 1:28, "And he came to her and said, 'Greetings, favored one! The Lord is with you'").[8] Besides chosenness, Sura 3:42 mentions purity as another key Marian quality; in fact, Islamic tradition singles out Mary and Jesus as the only human persons untouched by Satan.[9] Early Islamic exegetes argued about whether her purity was spiritual or physical, or both.[10] In any case, thanks to all of the above qualities possessed—virginal motherhood, faith, obedience, submission, secret knowledge, chosenness, and purity—the Qur'an says Mary is one of two women given by God to be "examples of believers," along with Pharaoh's wife (Sura 66:11–12).

One key point stressed by Islamic Mariology is that Mary is a human being, and not at all divine. For example, the Qur'an says, "The Messiah, son of Mary was only a messenger...his mother was a virtuous woman; both ate food [like other mortals]," (Sura 5:75), and "When God says, 'Jesus, son of Mary, did you say to people, "Take me and my mother as two gods alongside God"?' He will say, 'May you be exalted! I would never say what I had no right to say'" (Sura 5:116). Christians agree with Muslims that

Mary is only a human being, but they disagree about Jesus. Christians believe Jesus is "true God and true man," while Muslims believe Jesus is a prophet and thus only a man. These verses are clearly a qur'anic polemic against two central Christian doctrines: the incarnation and the Trinity. However, the argument in Sura 5:116 seems to be based on the mistaken notion that the Christian Trinity includes Mary as one of the three divine persons. It must be noted that most Muslims do know that Christians do not believe Mary to be a member of the Trinity or to be divine at all; for example, the eleventh-century Muslim polemicist 'Abd al-Jabbar (d. 1025) records a Christian refutation of Sura 5:116: "The Christians say, 'This is a lie for although we said about Christ that he is a god we did not say about his mother than she is a God.'"[11]

In addition to Suras 3 and 19, which contain the most extended qur'anic treatment of Mary (these chapters include stories of her youth, the annunciation, and the birth of Jesus), she is also mentioned briefly elsewhere, for example, in Sura 21, where she is listed along with Abraham, Moses, Aaron, Jacob, Isaac, Lot, Noah, David, Solomon, Job, Zechariah, and John. Islam considers every single one of these men to be prophets; in fact, Sura 21 itself is entitled *Anbiya* (Prophets). In this chapter, Maryam is introduced in the same way that all the male prophets in the sura are: "Remember [name]." The only difference is that Maryam is not named explicitly, but rather, she is alluded to by events unique to her: "Remember the one who guarded her chastity. We breathed into her from Our Spirit and made her and her son a sign for all people" (Sura 21:91). The only other person in the Sura referred to by identity rather than by name is "her son," that is, 'Isa, whom Islam recognizes as a prophet. By this logic, one can see why a few Muslim scholars have concluded that Maryam is a prophet according to the Qur'an.

The case for Maryam's prophethood has been debated throughout Islamic history, although her advocates have been in the minority. Several champions for her status as a prophet come from the Zahirite school of thought in medieval Andalusia, where several qur'anic women were identified as prophets, including Mary and the mother of Moses.[12] One of the strongest supporters of Mary's prophethood was Ibn Hazm (d. 1064) of Andalusia, who points out that the Qur'an calls her a "virtuous woman"

(5:75), which he claims is the same language used to describe the Prophet Joseph (12:46). (This is Joseph, son of Jacob, not Joseph, husband of Mary; the latter is not mentioned in the Qur'an.) Ibn Hazm suggests four female prophets in Islam: Maryam; Sarah (mother of Isaac); Moses' mother; and Asiya bint Muzahim, the Pharaoh's wife.[13] He defines prophethood as "verbal inspiration (*wahy*) designed for those whom God intends to inspire....This verbal inspiration takes the form of the appearance of an angel or a recited speech."[14] Ibn Hazm argues that these four women received such inspiration. In the case of Maryam, he notes that Jibril (Angel Gabriel) gave her inspiration when he spoke to her at the annunciation, and that what happened to Mary during the annunciation should be seen as parallel to what happened to Muhammad when he received the Qur'an.[15] In the case of Sarah, the mother of Isaac, Ibn Hazm says that she received information through a delegation of angels, and they gave her the unlikely message that she would conceive Isaac despite her age. As for Moses' mother (who is nameless in the Qur'an), Ibn Hazm argues that she received inspiration when she was instructed by God to save her baby by throwing him into the river (Sura 28:7).[16]

While Ibn Hazm argues that these four women were prophets because they received special knowledge from God, he doesn't go as far as to say that they were messengers. In Islam, this is an important distinction: a messenger is a prophet who brings a book. Not all prophets are messengers, while all messengers are prophets. (Examples of messengers in Islam include Abraham, Moses, Jesus, and Muhammad.) Ibn Hazm agrees that there were never any women messengers in Islam.[17] Many scholars who object to the idea that Maryam is a prophet base their objections on the qur'anic verse that states, "All the messengers We sent before you [Muhammad] were simply men" (Sura 16:43). But Ibn Hazm is quick to point out that this verse is talking about messengers, not prophets. Thus he concludes that his assertion—that Mary is a prophet but not a messenger—still stands.

While most Muslim scholars through history have disagreed with Ibn Hazm, denying that any female could be a messenger or prophet, a few others have also affirmed Maryam's prophethood. For example, Al-Qurtubi (d. 1273), an Andalusian like Ibn Hazm, based his argument for Maryam's prophethood on two qur'anic points. First, her perfection is acknowledged: a hadith calls Mary a spiritually perfected person, and according to Al-Qurtubi, perfection is equated to prophethood.[18] Second, her divine chosenness is revealed in Sura 3:42. Other Muslim scholars who have leaned toward acknowledging Mary as a prophet include Shah Wali Allah (d. 1762),[19] who calls her a sage because she possessed both miracles and the "quality of maleness."[20] Interestingly, Shah Wali Allah's argument that Mary's exceptional qualities are rooted in her "masculinity" mimics a similar argument among early Christians, many of whom likewise attributed the virtues of extraordinary women to a deep-seated "manliness." For example, the saint and martyr Perpetua (d. ca. 202), whose *Passion* is one of the earliest extant writings by a Christian woman, even describes herself in this way: "And there came out against me a certain ill-favored Egyptian with his helpers, to fight with me....And I was stripped naked, and I became a man."[21] Finally, while the famous Muslim poet Rumi (d. 1273) never took a stand about Mary's prophethood, his frequent poetic allusions to Mary and Jesus suggest that he considered them both to be spiritual examples for Sufis. Rumi calls Jesus a "spring breeze" who transforms hearts, and describes Mary as a model ascetic whose suffering has the power to bear spiritual fruit: "It is pain that guides a person in every enterprise....It was not until the pain of labor appeared in Mary that she made for the tree....Those pangs brought her to the tree, and the tree which was withered became fruitful."[22]

One contemporary Muslim scholar agrees with these few historical affirmations of Mary's prophethood, but for a unique reason: Hosn Abboud argues that the Virgin should be considered a prophet because she is "an important link in a genealogically determined chain of prophets," which in Jesus' case can only be "traced through Mary's lineage," since he has no human father.[23] Abboud notes that Jesus' matrilineal lineage is emphasized through his Islamic name: 'Isa bin Maryam (Jesus, son of Mary), a name that both acknowledges Jesus' unique conception without a father, and also indicates Mary's singular importance for his identity as an Islamic prophet.[24]

Most Muslim scholars throughout history, however, have argued against the prophethood of any woman, including Mary. One of the most prominent is the exegete Fakhr al-Din al-Razi

(d. 1210), who attributes Mary's miraculous sustenance in Sura 3 to sainthood, not prophethood.[25] Al-Razi explicitly notes that his conclusion is shared by most Muslim scholars: "No prophethood was granted to Maryam, as is well known. This is the opinion of mainstream Sunna and the Shi'ites."[26] Nawawi (d. 1277) and Qushayri (d. 1073), both declare Mary to be a *waliya* ("friend of God" or saint), but not a prophet; Ibn Kathir (d. 1373) calls Mary righteous (*siddiqa*).[27] But even though Ibn Kathir denied Mary's prophethood, whenever he wrote her name he adds the honorific phrase, "Peace Be upon Her," which is normally reserved only for prophets. He did this for Mary alone, and not for any other holy woman in Islam.[28]

POPULAR AND ARTISTIC VIEWS OF MARY IN ISLAM

As the above examples show, there has always been a "considerable and unresolved controversy over Mary's precise spiritual status" among Islamic scholars.[29] Despite this long history of scholarly debate about who Mary is, she has nevertheless always occupied a significant place in popular Muslim piety. Her importance to ordinary believers, especially women, is "far different and far greater than what these scholarly formulations might suggest."[30] Mary looms large in the consciousness of many Muslim women, some of whom regularly recite Sura Maryam, believing that it confers blessing power (*baraka*) upon them.[31] Others regularly name their daughters after her; Maryam remains one of the most popular names for Muslim girls in Arab countries.[32] Still other Muslims visit Christian shrines devoted to Mary.

While many leaders would discourage Muslims from visiting shrines or asking saints to intercede with God on their behalf, it is nevertheless common for ordinary believers to engage in these practices. After all, it was precisely because so many Muslims were visiting the graves of saints that the medieval Islamic scholar Ibn Taymiyya (d. 1328) felt the need to write a long chapter regulating the practice.[33] Even today there continue to be many aspects of lived Islam that do not accord with orthodox views, and Muslims just like Christians have intraconfessional debates about what is acceptable praxis and what is "innovation" (innovation [bid'a] is frowned upon in Islam). In a recent book about medieval Egyptian Muslims visiting cemeteries to venerate the dead, the author notes that several Muslim friends expressed surprise about his research topic, because, they said, "Muslims do not visit graves."[34] But the reality is that many Muslims did visit graves in medieval Egypt, and many still do today, especially Shi'i and Sufi Muslims.

Indeed, many ordinary Muslims around the world do in fact visit shrines and sometimes even invoke saintly Islamic figures like Mary, Fatima, and others.[35] Visiting shrines and praying to saints are practices especially popular among women, who have traditionally been excluded from more normative Muslim rituals such as Friday prayer at the mosque.[36] Mary is one of the most popular intercessory figures in Islam; some of the most common requests brought before her are for healing, forgiveness, exorcism, and conception. A favorite destination of Muslim women seeking to conceive is often a local Christian shrine dedicated to Mary. It is noteworthy that there are few if any *Muslim* shrines named for Mary anywhere in the world. At first glance, such a lack might seem to confirm the questionable nature of shrines and saint veneration in Islam. But this cannot be the explanation, given the existence of numerous Islamic shrines around the world named after various male prophets (e.g., Prophet Moses Shrine in Palestine or Prophet Hud Shrine in Yemen) and Sufi *shaykhs* (e.g., Shaykh Moinuddin Chishti Dargah in Ajmer, India). There are even Islamic shrines dedicated to holy women, such as the Fatima Masumeh Shrine in Qom, Iran (a Shi'i shrine dedicated to the sister of the eighth imam); the Sayyeda Zaynab Mosque near Damascus (named after the daughter of Fatima and 'Ali);[37] and a stop on the Islamic pilgrimage circuit in Jerusalem honoring the famous female Sufi Rabi'a al-Adawiyya.[38] There is certainly no dearth of shrines devoted to Islamic prophets and saints. However, it seems that there are few if any Islamic shrines devoted to Mary, despite her singular status.[39] Is this because Muslims have been satisfied to visit Christian Marian shrines since Islam's earliest centuries? According to tradition, Caliph 'Umar (d. 644) prayed at the Christian House of Mary in Jerusalem. His prayer gave Mary's House legitimacy, and it was allowed to remain in Christian hands, even as large numbers of Muslims began to visit the shrine in the decades after ʿUmar.[40] In fact, by the eighth century, so many Muslims were visiting the House of Mary in Jerusalem, as well as other Christian shrines in the Holy Land, that legal pronouncements began appearing to prohibit them from doing so.[41] But other laws from the same period explicitly allow Muslims to visit Christian shrines located within Islamic lands, on the grounds that these churches were technically Muslim property.[42]

Today, Christian shrines dedicated to Mary are still visited by Muslims worldwide, including Saydnaya and Soufanieh in Syria; Harissa in Lebanon; Samalut, Assiut, Matariyya, and Zeitoun in Egypt; Kevelaer in Germany; Mariamabad in Pakistan; the Virgin Mary Armenian Church in Iraq; Anjara in Jordan; St. Clement Ohridski Macedono-Bulgarian Orthodox Church in Dearborn, Michigan; Our Lady of Africa in Algeria; and Meryem Ana Evi in Turkey.[43] All these Marian shrines are sponsored by Christians, yet some of them have become so popular with Muslim pilgrims that their Christian hosts have made special accommodations. For example, the Marian shrine at Harissa, Lebanon, is frequented by so many Iranian Shi'ite Muslim women that the Christian rector prepared a chapel especially for them, complete with signs and prayers to the Virgin in Farsi. Meryem Ana Evi in Turkey is divided in two; the "Christian room" is decorated with an altar, statues, and images of Mary, while the "Muslim room" has quotations from Sura 19 inscribed on the walls. Signage at the shrine is in Turkish, English, Arabic, French, and German, and is intended to accommodate the widest range of visitors possible. Pilgrims can also buy souvenirs at Meryem Ana Evi that combine images of the Christian Virgin Mary with the Islamic hand of Fatima.[44]

What pious practices do Muslims engage in when visiting Marian shrines? They light candles, recite Marian suras, take holy water, say informal prayers (*duʿa*), and complete votive rituals. The votive ritual is particularly popular among infertile and infirm Arab Muslims; it involves visiting a Marian shrine to ask Mary to intercede with God, and if God grants the request, the petitioner vows to return to the shrine with an offering to Mary.[45] Christian Marian shrines, as well as the tomb of Fatima in Medina (an Islamic site), are especially popular destinations for infertile Muslim women seeking to perform a votive ritual. Other rituals include the "fast of Our Lady," which is observed by many post-partum women in Morocco; the fast is inspired by Mary's own fast after giving birth to Jesus (Sura 19:26). At Turkey's Meryem Ana Evi, pilgrims write prayers on scraps of fabric and tie them to a large prayer wall outside the shrine. Also at Meryem Ana Evi, some Muslims take holy water for healing purposes.[46] At the House of Mary in Jerusalem, informal prayer (du'a) is "highly recommended" and "it is desirable to recite Sura 19 there and perform sadja, a formal but voluntary prayer."[47] The House of Mary has long been part of an extensive Muslim pilgrim circuit in Jerusalem. A mid-sixteenth-century Muslim pilgrim's guide to Jerusalem lists several Marian stops on the circuit, including Mary's House, Haykal Maryam (Temple of Mary) also known as the Cradle of Jesus (Mahd 'Isa), the Tomb of Mary, the Place of Mary (Maqam Maryam) and the Niche of Mary (Mihrab Maryam).[48]

Here are brief glimpses into the practices of Muslim pilgrims at two present-day shared Marian shrines: the first is a four-hundred-year-old shrine, the Virgin Mary Armenian Church in Baghdad, while the second, Mariamabad, Pakistan, was established more recently (1949).

THE VIRGIN MARY ARMENIAN CHURCH, IRAQ

The Virgin Mary Armenian Church in Baghdad dates to the mid-seventeenth century, and is visited by a variety of local Christians: Assyrians, Chaldean Catholics, Roman Catholics, Armenians, and even Protestants. Muslims, both Sunnis and Shi'i, also come to the church. One of the most popular days to visit is August 15 (Feast of the Dormition for Orthodox, Feast of the Assumption for Catholics). Traditional practices at the shrine for both Christians and Muslims include lighting candles, saying prayers, and distributing meals to the poor.[49] A news reporter who was in Iraq after the most recent war described a young Iraqi Muslim woman's practices at, and views of, this church:

> Twenty-nine-year old Afrar, a Muslim, says she has great faith in Mary. She doesn't think there is a difference between Muslims and Christians. Seated on her haunches, she prays in front of a statue of the Virgin.

She finds comfort in this church, calling it a house of God. She has turned to Mary, begging for the baby that has so far not appeared, and pleading for protection from an uncertain future.[50]

MARIAMABAD, PAKISTAN

The village of Mariamabad (literally, the "town of Mary"), fifty miles from Lahore, Pakistan, has a Marian shrine popular with local Catholics, Muslims, and Sikhs. The town was founded in 1898, the first of several Catholic villages established on two thousand acres of agricultural land given to the Catholic Church of Lahore in the 1890s. Mariamabad's shrine itself was founded in 1949 by a Belgian missionary, Fr. Frank Joseph, OFM Capuchin. The shrine is now visited by a half a million pilgrims annually. Catholics, Muslims, and Sikhs take part in an annual pilgrimage held on the three days surrounding September 8, the Feast of Mary's Nativity. At this time, some Punjabi villagers along the pilgrimage route give out *langar* (the Sikh tradition of offering free meals) to pilgrims.[51] Devotees travel to the shrine by many different modes of transport: some walk 100–200 kilometers or more, others come by push bike, still others by bus or train. As is the case at the Virgin Mary Armenian Church in Baghdad and Meryem Ana Evi in Turkey, infertile women in particular are attracted to Mariamabad's shrine. Many who are successful in getting pregnant return years later with their child to give thanks to the Virgin. People also come to the shrine throughout the year, to pray at its grotto for children.[52]

MARIAN ART IN ISLAM

In addition to popular Marian devotional practices, there is also a long tradition of Islamic Marian art. Despite the religion's general prohibition against images, which intensified in places influenced by eighteenth-century Wahhabi reforms, elsewhere there has been a long and rich pictorial tradition, especially among the Persians, Mughals, and Ottomans. The presence of pictorial traditions within this normally aniconic religion is sometimes justified with a story told by Al-Azraqi (d. 858) in which Muhammad himself is depicted as preserving icons of Jesus and Mary:

> The day of the conquest of Mekka, the Prophet entered the Ka'ba and sent for al Fadl ibn 'Abbas—who brought water from Zemzem, and he ordered him to bring a rag soaked in water and efface the pictures (*suwar*), which he did. They say that the Prophet put his two hands on the picture of 'Isa bin Miryam [Jesus, son of Mary] and His Mother and said: "Efface all these pictures except these under my hands." He then raised his hands from above 'Isa and his mother.[53]

This story was often cited by Muslim rulers who needed justification for patronizing Islamic pictorial art. The Ottoman Emperor Ahmet I (d. 1617) even mimicked the prophet's actions himself by removing all the icons in the Church of Hagia Sophia except the one of the Virgin Mary in the apsidal semidome.[54] Other Ottoman rulers were known to venerate images of Mary, most notably Mehmed II (d. 1481), whom Nicholas of Cusa invited to declare Mary as *Theotokos* (see chapter 4). If Mehmed's veneration of Marian images was so well known that even the German Cardinal Cusa was aware of it, perhaps Nicholas was not so wrong to think that Mehmed might accept his strange invitation.

The Mughals took Marian art one step further than the Ottomans. Jesuit missionaries in India from 1580 to 1620 note the popularity of images of Mary and Jesus among artists patronized by Mughal Emperors Akbar and Jahangir.[55] The images were the result of a new hybrid style that combined classical Persian and Italian Renaissance motifs.[56] The Mughals accorded Mary and Jesus double import. First, their images were used as a form of royal propaganda; Jesus and Mary were seen as stand-ins for the emperor and his mother who represented the royal line (both Akbar and Jahangir had mothers named Maryam). Examples of this include a portrait of Jahangir holding an image of Akbar (his biological father) in one hand, and an image of the Virgin Mary (his spiritual mother) in the other; also, images of Jesus and Mary graced Jahangir's official seal.[57] Second, up to half the miniatures of Jesus and Mary produced by the Mughal art school were made specifically for devotional use by Muslims, according to Jesuit sources.[58] Akbar even commissioned an illustrated life of Christ that includes twenty-seven images of Jesus and Mary (see chapter 6 for more on this topic). Interestingly, the production of these images was an interfaith affair; some of the most famous painters patronized by Akbar and Jahangir were not only Muslims, but Hindus too.[59] Even though Mughal Marian art is based on older Islamic miniature traditions, it must be noted that Akbar and Jahangir were not exactly orthodox Muslims; Akbar founded a new syncretistic religion, Din i Ilahi, in 1583, and encouraged interreligious dialogue between Muslims, Hindus, Christians, and others at his court in Fatehpur Sikri. It is said that members of Akbar's new religion held meetings in rooms adorned with images of Mary and Jesus in the new hybrid art form.[60] Some of the Marian art produced under the Mughals, therefore, was used for rather unique purposes.

Mughal and Ottoman Marian art was rooted in an older pictorial tradition, that of the Persians, who produced miniature images of Islamic personages as far back as the early 1300s. The image of the annunciation gracing a copy of Al-Biruni's *Chronicle of the Nations* (fig. 1), which features an unveiled Mary and Angel Gabriel, was produced circa 1307 in Ilkhanid Iran. Religious themes are infrequent in Persian miniature art, except for Muhammad's night journey to heaven (*isra* and *mi'raj*).[61] But other prophets and holy figures are sometimes depicted, often with their faces covered, possibly as a nod to Islamic iconoclasm. Other times, a subject's special status is indicated by tongues of fire overhead.[62] Scholars have suggested that some of the details found in Persian images of saints (veils, tongues of fire) were influenced by Buddhist iconography, which the Mongol Ilkhanids brought to Iran.[63]

MUSLIM ARGUMENTS AGAINST CHRISTIAN MARIOLOGY

As noted earlier, while Muslims disagree about Mary's precise status, she nevertheless remains an honored figure who is not only praised in Islamic literature but also visited by Muslim pilgrims and depicted by artists. But parallel to the Islamic tradition that praises the Muslim Maryam is an Islamic tradition that

وَفِى الْخَامِسِ ذِكْرَانِ يَسْنَى الْجَاِلَيْنِ أَوَّلَ أَوْرَدَ الْنَصْرَانِيَّة إِلَى خُرَاسَانَ وَفِى الرَّابِعِ وَالْعِشْرَيْنَ ذِكْرَانِ وَجُودَرَاسِ الْمُعَدَّانِ وَمُوسَى رَكَرِيَّا فِى الْيَوْمِ السَّابِعِ كَرَّ أَنَّ الشُّهَدَاءَ الْأَرْبَعِينَ الْمُعَذَّبَيْنِ بِالنَّارِ وَالْبَرْدِ وَالْجَلِيدِ وَفِى الْيَوْمِ الْحَادِى عَشَرَ ذِكْرَانِ سُومِرْسُونِ الْبَطْرِيقِ بَبْتِ الْمُقَدَّسِ وَفِى الْخَامِسِ وَالْعِشْرَيْنَ عِيدُ السَّبَانِ وَهُوَ دُخُولُ جَبْرَئِيلَ عَلَيْهِ السَّلَامُ عَلَى مَرْيَمَ مُبْشِّرًا بِالْمَسِيحِ وَمِنْهُ أَلَى الْمِيلَادِ

تِسْعَةُ أَشْهُرٍ وَخَمْسَةِ أَيَّامٍ وَثَنَى وَمُولِكُ طَبِيعَى لَاسَقَرَ إِنَّ الْمَوْلُودَ فِى بَطْنِ الْأُمِّ وَعِيسَى وَأَنْ عَلِمُ أَبُوةَ الْأَنْسِ وَأَسْدُدُرُوحَ الْقُدْسِ فَلَمْ نَخْلِعْ فِى الْعَالَمِ عَنِ الْقَلْبِ فِى مُوجَبِ الطَّبِيعَةِ فَمَا لَا وَلَى يَمْكِنُ فِى الْبَطْنِ أَنْ يَكُونَ طَبِيعِيًّا أَيْضًا وَمَوْضِعُ الْقَمَرِ الْمُقَوَّمِ لِنِصْفِ نَهَارِ هَذَا الْيَوْمِ بِيْتِ الْمُقَدَّسِ وَهُوَ يَوْمُ الْأَسْنَيْنِ الْخَامِسِ وَالْعِشْرَيْنَ مِنْ آذَارَ سَنَةِ ثَلَثِ وَثَلَثِ يِنَّ الْأَسْكَنْدَرِ فِى قِرْبٍ مِنْ خَمْسَةِ أَسْدَاسِ الدَّرَجَةِ الْأُوَلَى مِنْ بُرْجِ الثَّوْرِ وَنَجَبَ عَلَى مَرْيَدَ هُبَطَ فِى

Figure 1. The Annunciation to Mary, *Kitab al-Athar al-Baqiya* (Chronology of Ancient Nations), Al-Biruni, 14th-century illustration, Or. Ms 161, Edinburgh University Main Library, Folio 141v. Reproduced under a "CC-BY" license.

criticizes the Christian Mary. This criticism emerged early on (seventh century), and was related to broader arguments against Christianity, especially the incarnation and the Trinity, the two doctrines upon which early polemicists focused.[64] While the connection between Mary and the incarnation is obvious, the connection between Mary and the Trinity may be less so, since Christians do not believe Mary is divine, nor do they believe that she is part of the Trinity. Yet the Qur'an in several places (e.g., Sura 5:73–75; 5:116) suggests that Christians do consider Mary to be divine, and as a result, Mary does feature in some early Islamic antitrinitarian arguments as well.[65]

However, the main Muslim quarrel with Christianity has always been about Christ, not Mary. Anti-Marian arguments, therefore, do not feature prominently in historical Islamic polemics against Christianity. Yet, some Muslim scholars still reject what they perceive to be the idolatrous nature of Christian beliefs about, and practices connected to, Mary. Of particular concern is the idea that anyone would pray to Mary (either seeking her intercession, or even invoking her as if she were a goddess), rather than going directly to God. For example, some Muslims today balk at the line in *Nostra Aetate* 3 that suggests that Muslims "call on her with devotion." Of course, many sixteenth-century Protestants had similar complaints about Catholic views of Mary. The last section of this chapter will catalog some historical Islamic arguments against Christian Mariology.

These arguments can be gleaned not only directly from Muslim texts, but also indirectly from Christian theologians writing in response to Muslim polemics. One of the earliest such arguments is that of Anastasios of Sinai (d. 700), whose Greek book *Hodegos* makes explicit reference to Sura 5:116, the qur'anic verse that accuses Christians of idolizing both Jesus and Mary.[66] Not only does Anastasios refute the idea that Christians consider Mary to be divine, but also the related notion that she is God's consort or wife.[67] Before he can begin to argue positively for his own religion, Anastasios feels he must first correct Islamic misunderstandings about Christian doctrine.[68]

Two historical Muslim scholars who weave Mary into their anti-Christian arguments are Abu 'Isa al-Warraq (d. ca. 864) and 'Abd al-Jabbar (d. 1025), both of whom wrote some of the longest and most detailed anti-Christian polemics at the time.[69] Al-Warraq's argument is preserved within the text of a Jacobite Christian philosopher, Yahya ibn 'Adi (d. ca. 974), who quotes al-Warraq at length only to refute him. Al-Warraq's argument is sustained, nuanced (he distinguishes between Jacobite, Nestorian, and Melkite Christians), and focused on the Trinity and incarnation. He brings up Mary when arguing against the Melkites, whom he questions about their doctrine of *Theotokos* (Mary as God-bearer, as contrasted to the Nestorian term *Christotokos*, Christ-bearer):

> Say to the Melkites...part of what is against them is also that if they affirm that the universal human [Jesus] was born of Mary, it must have been her son since it was her child. So the universal would have become son of the individual, and the substance become son to its hypostasis. And if the universal substance was her son and child then all its hypostases and individual beings must have been her sons and children. According to this teaching, Adam and all whom he procreated must have been her sons and children in actuality and through the reality of birth and sonship. It also means that she must have been her own daughter, since according to them she was one hypostasis and one individual of the universal substance. So she must have been her own mother, daughter, parent, and offspring, and one hypostasis was parent, offspring, daughter, mother, father, and son, but not in a comparative or relative manner.[70]

Al-Warraq focuses on the irrationality of a religion that would make Mary both the mother and the daughter of God. His argument is rooted in accurate information about trinitarian doctrine; he uses correct terms such as *substance* and *hypostasis*, and does not bring up the mistaken idea of Mary as a part of the Trinity. His argument is not really about Mary at all, but rather Christology and her role in supporting it. It is clear that al-Warraq respects the person of Mary, for even in this polemical text he follows every mention of her name with "peace be upon her," a phrase normally reserved for prophets or angels.

Another Muslim who refers to Mary in his anti-Christian polemic is 'Abd al-Jabbar, a scholar writing about 150 years after Al-Warraq. 'Abd al-Jabbar's argument focuses more on history than on theology. His main goal is to critique the origins and development of the Christian religion and its Scripture, which he claims were corrupted by Paul and the pagan Romans. Like Al-Warraq, 'Abd al-Jabbar is quite knowledgeable about Christianity; for example, he knows that Christians do not claim Mary to be divine, even though this seems to contradict what the Qur'an itself says in Sura 5:116. He even quotes the Christians themselves on this point: "The Christians say, 'This [Sura 5:116] is a lie for although we said about Christ that he is a god we did not say about his mother than she is a God.'"[71] Since 'Abd al-Jabbar knows that Christians do not believe Mary to be divine, he argues that Muslims are wrong to accept Sura 5:116 as an accurate description of Christian Mariology. Rather, he says the verse is a rhetorical question intended to underscore the true nature of reality according to Islam: that neither Jesus nor Mary are divine. Here, 'Abd al-Jabbar is not concerned about Christian doctrine per se; rather, he wants to defend the veracity of the Qur'an, since he believes the Qur'an could never err in describing Christian doctrine. But then 'Abd al-Jabbar goes on to argue that Christians do not even follow their own doctrine—which in theory denies Mary's divinity—because in practice, he claims, they do in fact worship her. 'Abd al-Jabbar is critical of any and all Christian practices that smack of Mariolatry, listing several:

> [The Christians] supplicate to her and pray to her for abundant sustenance, bodily health, long life, forgiveness of sins, and that she, her son, and the Begetter of her son might be a bastion, a support, a treasure, an intercessor, and a cornerstone for them. Now if a person were to venerate another person one tenth as much as this....then it would be permissible...to say that he had taken [this person] to be as a god.[72]

To prove that Christians do in fact take Mary as a god, 'Abd al-Jabbar quotes a Christian prayer he has heard: "The Jacobites even say, in their intimate prayer to Mary—peace be upon her—'O Mary, O mother of God, be our bastion, support, treasure and cornerstone.'"[73]

The second argument 'Abd al-Jabbar makes in connection to Mary is that the Bible does not prove her purity. In fact, he claims that the Bible leaves Mary open to the charge of fornication:

> According to them Christ did not speak in the cradle and did not declare his mother pure...people thought Christ was the son of Joseph until John baptized him in the Jordan and a voice came from heaven....What stupidity, lowliness, and defamation to the Wisdom of God is this? According to them he is the Lord of the Worlds, yet he allowed his servants to vilify his mother.[74]

Even so, 'Abd al-Jabbar does mention a few Marian doctrines about which Christians and Muslims concur: "Christians agree with Muslims that Christ was born without a male father."[75] But in the end, he concludes that the Bible is wrong about both Jesus and Mary: "Know—may God have mercy on you—that these Christian sects are the most ignorant of God's people regarding Christ, the reports about him, and the reports about his mother."[76]

Whenever 'Abd al-Jabbar brings up Mary, he does so not so much to argue against specific Christian doctrines as to make a case for Islamic scripture and its proper interpretation; all of his discussions of Mary include a defense of the Qur'an and criticism of the Bible. He does not question Mary's purity or her chosenness per se; rather, he questions the Bible's presentation of her purity. He believes that the Bible leaves Mary open to the charge of fornication, and since her purity is unquestionable according to Islam, this means that something must be wrong with the Bible. And in fact, the idea that the Christian Bible has been corrupted is one of the main Islamic arguments against Christianity. Thus, 'Abd al-Jabbar defends Mary by saying that her honor is preserved better by Muslims and their Qur'an than it is by Christians and their Bible.

CONCLUSION

Christians and Muslims agree that Mary is a unique figure worthy of respect and even reverence, because she is the virgin mother of Jesus. They agree about Mary's qualities, too: she is pure, chosen by God, obedient, and faithful. The crucial point of disagreement is really Christology, not Mariology. However, to a lesser degree Christians and Muslims also have some disagreement about the meaning and purpose of Mary's good qualities. For Christians, Mary's virginity is central (although there are intra-Christian debates about whether her virginity was perpetual or not). While Muslims agree that Mary was a virgin when she conceived Jesus, the idea of her *perpetual* virginity would be contrary to the Islamic ideal of women as wives and mothers.[77] For Muslims, the female figure who is more likely to be seen as a role model for actual women would be Fatima: the daughter of the Prophet Muhammad, wife of 'Ali, and mother of two martyred sons.

Nevertheless, Islam has much to say about Mary. A long scholarly tradition has argued about her identity; all acknowledge her uniqueness and sanctity; and some (though only a few) even suggest her to be a prophet. Common people, too, acknowledge Mary as a holy figure, and many visit her shrines and seek her intercession. And as we have seen, despite Islam's general prohibition against icons, there is even a tradition of Marian art, especially among the Persians, Ottomans, and Mughals. Alongside these artistic traditions and popular piety, orthodox Islam affirms, in accord with Sura 5:116, that Mary is only a human being, and as such she should not be worshiped or invoked. In part to counter the Marian devotion of ordinary believers, scholars have attacked what they consider to be Christian Mariolatry. The Islamic argument against Christian Mariology, that Christians believe Mary to be *more* than she actually is, can be seen as the flip side of the Christian argument against Islamic Mariology, that Muslims believe Mary to be *less* than she actually is.

When it comes to Islamic theology, Mary has been seen as a barrier between Christianity and Islam, at least according to most scholars through history. However, when popular Muslim piety and art is considered, she seems to be more of a bridge. Due to Islam's iconoclasm and belief in God's oneness, history has not witnessed Marian images (or indeed any images) raised on Islamic battle standards in wars against Christians, nor has Mary's intercession been sought by Muslim communities fighting the infidel.

Rather, Mary's intercession has been sought by individual Muslims fighting personal infertility or infirmity—not unlike their Christian counterparts, who visit the same shrines. In short, Marian doctrines have traditionally divided believers, but popular Marian devotions have, more often than not, brought them together.

Chapter 4

MEDIEVAL PRAISE OF THE MUSLIM MARYAM

> While gathered [in the mosque], one of the faithful begins to read by heart, without a book, the history of Mary or Joseph or Zechariah, or another lively devotion. And wherever the name of Jesus, Mary, Joseph or Abraham or Muhammad is mentioned, they praise God with sweet whispers and frequently tears....In [their prayer], amazingly, I think, [Muslims] please God and men, if they have true faith.[1]
>
> —Friar William of Tripoli, circa 1270

This vivid description of Muslim prayer comes directly from the experiences of a thirteenth-century Dominican. Such firsthand accounts were relatively rare in medieval Latin writings about Islam, since most Europeans, save Iberians, had never met a Muslim. But William was different; he lived his entire life in the Middle East, and his extant writings not only demonstrate decent knowledge of Islamic doctrine, but also include concrete details of Muslim rituals like this one. What is interesting about

---

A different version of this chapter was published as "Bridge or Barrier? Mary and Islam in William of Tripoli and Nicholas of Cusa," *Medieval Encounters* 22, no. 4 (2016): 307–25. Used with permission.

the complimentary nature of the passage above is that it comes from a book that is mostly critical of Islam. But the presence of contradiction in William's writings is not entirely surprising, given that the Dominican, unlike his confreres back in Europe, did not imagine Muslims as mythical beings from faraway lands, but had to deal with them as real people and everyday neighbors. Familiarity doesn't necessarily breed contempt. Sometimes it breeds a variety of conflicting responses, including admiration, vitriol, and ambivalence—all at the same time.

And William is indeed ambivalent about Islam. But he is not alone in this attitude. Several other medieval Christians also wrote about Islam and likewise vacillated between condemnation and praise. Much of my scholarship has centered on these ambivalent authors, particularly Riccoldo da Montecroce, OP (d. 1320), William of Tripoli, OP (d. *circa* 1273), and Nicholas of Cusa (d. 1464). All three wrote one or more books on Islam that were informed by serious study of Islamic texts or firsthand observation of Muslim praxis, and all their books contain a mix of admiration and criticism.[2] Of these three, William and Nicholas will be the focus of this chapter, since they both wrote extensively about the Islamic Mary, and highlighted her role as a potential link between Christians and Muslims.

Why do William and Nicholas focus so positively on the qur'anic Mary? After all, they were very different churchmen. They were separated not only by centuries, but also by cultural milieux. William was born in the city of Tripoli (now Tarabulus, Lebanon), most likely of French parentage, and became a friar at the Dominican priory in Acre (now Akko, Israel), the Crusader capital.[3] He wrote in Latin, but his works demonstrate some familiarity with Arabic, and much of his knowledge of Islam clearly came from firsthand experience. Two books are associated with William: *Notitia de Machometo* (Data on Muhammad) and *De Statu Sarracenorum* (On the situation of the Muslims—the medieval Latin word for Muslim is *Saracen*). Both books are critical of Islam overall. Yet both also contain sections that portray Muslim practices in a good light. In *Notitia*, William includes many detailed and positive descriptions of fasting, almsgiving, and the veneration of prophets and saints in the mosque as noted previously. What are we to make of William's surprising conclusion that the Muslim devotion to Jesus and Mary proves the efficacy of Islamic prayer? How can we reconcile this with William's statements elsewhere, for example, when he concludes that the Qur'an was written by evil men and demons?[4]

William's relatively positive approach to certain aspects of Islam is mimicked nearly two hundred years later by Cardinal Nicholas of Cusa, an innovative thinker who straddled the medieval and early modern worlds. Although he wrote centuries after William, Nicholas is similar in that his book *Cribratio alkorani* (1460/1) likewise contains a mix of condemnation and praise. For example, in one place Nicholas says that the Qur'an contains many lies and contradictions, yet elsewhere in the same book he also says that "assuredly some fruit can be elicited from [the Qur'an]."[5]

Both Nicholas and William share a sympathetic approach to the Qur'an, but Nicholas's knowledge was gained differently than William's. While Nicholas tried to study Islam as best he could—he consulted the finest Latin sources available and listed them all in the prologue of his *Cribratio*—he was limited by his ignorance of Arabic. Nor did he have any firsthand experience of Muslim praxis; as far as scholars know, the closest Nicholas ever got to the Muslim world was a short trip to Constantinople a few decades before the Ottoman conquest. But despite their differing language abilities and cultural milieux, Nicholas and William shared similar historical circumstances. Both lived at a time when Europeans felt under siege by Islamic entities: William's Crusader State by the Mamluks, and Nicholas's Europe by the Ottomans. Yet even though both lived at a time of intense Muslim-Christian strife, neither man failed to mention positive aspects of Islam, particularly the Virgin Mary.

MAINSTREAM MEDIEVAL CHRISTIAN VIEWS

William and Nicholas's atypically positive views of the shared Mary must be read within the larger framework of a mainstream medieval Christian theology of Islam.[6] By "Christian theology of Islam," I am referring to an internal discussion that seeks to explain Islam systematically using Christian authoritative sources such as

Scripture and Tradition. By "mainstream," I mean that when medieval Latin Christians wrote about Islam, there were certain topics most of them discussed, and certain conclusions most of them reached. These include recognizing Islamic monotheism; criticizing Muslim Christology; condemning Muhammad as a pseudoprophet; determining that the Qur'an is not divine revelation; criticizing the Islamic paradise as entirely physical; and concluding that Islam is a lax, carnal, violent, irrational heresy.[7] Naturally, mainstream medieval Latin views were built on the earlier ideas of Greek-, Syriac-, and Arabic-speaking Christians about Islam, as discussed in chapter 2. Medieval theologians continued to emphasize the same few problems with the Muslim Mary, such as the Mary-Miriam mix-up (the supposed qur'anic confusion between Miriam, sister of Moses, and Mary, mother of Jesus). The Dominican Riccoldo da Montecroce saw this error as an example of Muslim blasphemy, citing it as proof of the Qur'an's mendacity and irrationality.[8] Riccoldo even refers to the Mary-Miriam mix-up in the middle of a prayer addressed to Mary, where strangely he feels the need to clarify her identity: "O Virgin Mary, mother of Christ—not that Mary, sister of Moses and Aaron who became a leper—but you, Mary, virgin daughter of Joachim, who was never a leper nor was ever guilty of sin."[9] Inserting this clarification into his own prayer is odd indeed, since Christians do not normally confuse Mary and Miriam. To whom does Riccoldo direct this clarification: to the Virgin, to Muslim bystanders, or to himself? The latter seems most likely, since at the time he wrote this prayer he was in Baghdad having a crisis of faith, and struggling with questions such as the following: Is the Qur'an the word of God, was Jesus a Muslim, and is Islam superior to Christianity?[10] In any case, many other medieval Christians also mention the qur'anic confusion about Mary, including Peter the Venerable, Petrus Alfonsi, and Ramon Martí. Yet, unlike the rest, William and Nicholas also offer extended, positive comments on Muslim Mariology. It is to these two men we now turn.

WILLIAM OF TRIPOLI

Possibly more than any other European before him, William of Tripoli stresses concord between Christian and Muslim Mariologies.

His book *Notitia de Machometo* consists of fifteen chapters on three topics: Muhammad, the Qur'an, and qur'anic teaching on Christianity. But the book centers as much on qur'anic Mariology and Christology as it does on Muhammad. Chapters 9—12, which in length comprise over half the book, focus exclusively on Mary and Jesus. Chapters 9 and 10 discuss nineteen qur'anic "proofs" or "testimonies" about Mary and Jesus, many of which are long, verbatim quotes from Sura 19 (*Maryam*). In chapter 11, William outlines the Islamic Mariology, and in chapter 12 he presents a Christian response to that Mariology. In short, a Christian-Muslim "dialogue" about Mary (and Jesus) lies at the very heart of *Notitia*. In this dialogue, William tries to avoid putting words into Muslim mouths. This is unusual, given that most medieval texts claiming to be dialogues are not reports of real conversations at all. Rather, they are constructs that put Christian words into the mouths of fabricated Jews or Muslims, and try to mask (rarely successfully) the Christian author's true polemical and apologetic intentions.[11] But William does not write a contrived dialogue here. Instead, at times he allows Islam to speak for itself. For example, chapter 10 consists almost entirely of quotations from the Qur'an, while chapter 11, the so-called Muslim response, is actually a fairly accurate outline of classic Muslim arguments against Christianity: the Bible has been corrupted (a concept known as *tahrif*); Muhammad is the seal of the prophets; the Qur'an corrects all previous scriptures; and "Christians remain in errors and lies [about] Jesus son of Mary, calling him God, crucified, and dead."[12]

In chapter 9, William presents the qur'anic Mary in nineteen points. He is correct in highlighting the points that agree with biblical Mariology: an angel announces that God has chosen Mary above all women, the angel declares that the baby's name will be Jesus, Mary is troubled by the announcement because she is a virgin, and she miraculously conceives. He also notes the points that are unique to qur'anic Mariology: Mary's mother promised her to God before she was born, Mary is accused of fornication by her family, and baby Jesus speaks to prove her innocence. In chapter 10, William further elaborates on these nineteen points, mostly via long quotations from the Qur'an.

But William's chapter 9 is more than a mere reiteration of the qur'anic story of Mary. Rather, by selecting and rearranging the various qur'anic quotes about Mary, William presents an implicit Christian theology of Islam. While doing so, he seems to favor passages that are more aligned with Christian views. He sometimes even omits verses or parts of verses that are blatantly critical of Christianity. For example, he quotes Sura 19:27–33 verbatim, which is a description of Mary's family accusing her of fornication, and of baby Jesus speaking in her defense.[13] But William ends the quote rather abruptly with verse 33, which discusses Jesus coming back at the end of time (a point on which Christians and Muslims agree), while omitting verses 34–35, which dispute Jesus' divine nature and sonship (a main point of Christian-Muslim disagreement). Another of William's omissions is when he offers a verbatim quote of just the first half of a verse: "We sent other messengers to follow in their footsteps. After those We sent Jesus, son of Mary: We gave him the Gospel and put compassion and mercy into the hearts of his followers." (Sura 57:27a).[14] William cuts off the quote right in the middle of verse 27, and omits the second half. Did he exclude the second part of verse 27 because it contains a criticism of Christian monasticism?[15]

These few examples demonstrate that William is not simply quoting the entire qur'anic story of Mary verbatim. Rather, he thoughtfully selects long passages and then rearranges them, deliberately it seems, to suggest a slightly more pro-Christian qur'anic Mariology than is actually the case. William does not offer his Christian readers neutral data about Islam; instead, one might say that he "spins" the verses to present Islam more positively. While other medieval Christians focused mainly on what the Qur'an gets wrong about the Virgin, William focuses on what it gets right. He seems to have been genuinely touched by the parallels between the Muslim and Christian Marys. He expresses surprise in discovering qur'anic verses that honor Christ, Mary, and other shared figures, possibly because he assumed that Muhammad would have been the main focus of qur'anic praise. The quote with which I began this chapter is a case in point. Here, William describes the Muslim devotion to Mary, Jesus, Abraham and others in the middle of a discussion of Muslim prayer: "While gathered [in the mosque], one of the faithful begins to read by heart, without a book, the history of Mary or Joseph or Zechariah or another lively devotion. And wherever the name of Jesus, Mary, Joseph or Abraham or

Muhammad is mentioned, they praise God with sweet whispers and frequently tears."[16] After going on to describe Muslim ritual prayer in great detail, William concludes with the following expression of genuine surprise: "In [their prayer], amazingly, I think, they please God and men, if they have true faith."[17] He is so impressed by the Muslim devotion to Mary and other shared figures (Jesus, Abraham) that he is willing to entertain the possibility that Islamic prayer might be efficacious.

This same praise for Muslim Mariology can likewise be found in another book connected to William, *De statu Sarracenorum*. Scholars disagree whether William or one of his students wrote this book; in any case, its contents are consonant with his thought.[18] Of its fifty-five short chapters, *De statu* devotes twenty to Christ and Mary. Chapters 28—37 mimic *Notitia de Machometo* by recounting the qur'anic story of the Virgin through verbatim quotations from relevant Marian suras. At the very end of a long list of qur'anic quotations about Mary and Jesus in chapters 27—48, a section that contains very little commentary, the author concludes with this rather surprising claim:

> Therefore because Muslims believe in their hearts in the aforementioned proofs [about Mary and Christ]… and because of the Qur'an's lauds and praises of Jesus Christ, his doctrine and his holy gospel, and of blessed Mary his mother…and despite its [the Qur'an's] hidden lies and embellished inventions, it is manifestly apparent that because of their piety [*pia*], they [learned Muslims, *Sarracenorum litterati et sapientes*, according to the title of chapter 48] are neighbors to the Christian faith and near to the way of salvation.[19]

These lines make it clear that the similarity between biblical and qur'anic Mariologies (and Christologies) is the primary reason for William's claim that Muslims are "near to the way of salvation." Of course, the question is, by "way of salvation," does he mean to imply that Christianity alone is salvific and Islam is close to that one true path, or more radically, is he suggesting that Islam itself is salvific?[20] In either case, William's observation is extraordinary for a medieval Dominican missionary living among Muslims.

NICHOLAS OF CUSA

William's positive take on Muslim Mariology is mirrored nearly two centuries later by Nicholas of Cusa, whose anti-Islamic argument is likewise rooted in careful study of the Qur'an.[21] Nicholas's book *Cribratio alkorani* (a "sifting" or "scrutiny" of the Qur'an, written ca. 1460) is notable for interpreting Islamic scripture with both criticism and sympathy. Nicholas's more congenial approach to the Qur'an, which he describes as a reading done in light of the gospel, has been dubbed *pia interpretatio*, a phrase Nicholas himself uses frequently throughout *Cribratio*.[22] *Pia interpretatio* has often been rendered as "devout translation," but "faithful interpretation" has been suggested as an alternative translation, because this implies Nicholas's simultaneous loyalty to his own Christian tradition and his "presumption that it is possible to build bridges to other religious traditions."[23] Nicholas's exegetical approach is significant because he does not dismiss the Qur'an as a book of lies, as so many other Christians did before him. Rather, he read the book with care, noting when he found commonalities as well as differences. When he compared qur'anic and biblical stories of Jesus and Mary, he used the gospel as the measuring stick by which to judge the veracity of the Qur'an. Some have seen this exegetical strategy as a form of "learned ignorance," one of Nicholas's most famous concepts.[24]

Nicholas was not the first to see parallels between the Bible and the Qur'an, but others explained the phenomenon less irenically. For example, Thomas Aquinas noted that "the truths that [Muhammad] taught were mingled with many fables and with the doctrines of the greatest falsity....He perverts almost all the testimonies of the Old and New Testaments by making them into fabrications of his own, as can be seen by anyone who examines his law."[25] Nicholas's comparison of the Qur'an and Bible is not only more sympathetic than Thomas's, it is also more extensive. According to a recent article by José Martínez Gázquez, Nicholas had studied (and glossed) at least two different Latin translations of the Qur'an while writing *Cribratio alkorani*, one in the 1450s, and a second in the 1460s.[26] After such extensive study, and despite his lack of

Arabic, Nicholas arrives at his own unique approach to qur'anic exegesis, which he describes as follows:

> But if we admit that the goal and intention of the book of the Qur'an is, as its followers say, not only *not* to disparage God the Creator, Christ, God's prophets and ambassadors, and the divine books of the Testament, the Psalms, and the Gospel, *but also* to give glory to God the Creator, to praise and bear witness to Christ, the son of the Virgin Mary, above all prophets, and to confirm and endorse the Testament and Gospel...then certainly, when reading the Qur'an with this in mind...some fruit can be elicited from it.[27]

Nicholas's irenic stance toward the Qur'an here is notably similar to William's. In fact, it is very possible that Nicholas's notion of *pia interpretatio* was influenced by William's approach to the Qur'an: Nicholas owned a copy of *Notitia*, which we know he read, since it contains several marginal glosses in Nicholas's own hand.[28] While earlier Latin exegetes studied the Qur'an as carefully as Nicholas, and even more thoroughly due to their knowledge of Arabic (Riccoldo da Montecroce, Ramon Martí), none of them approached the Qur'an as sympathetically as did Nicholas.[29] Some have suggested a connection between Nicholas's unique form of exegesis and his tolerant approach to other religions in general.[30]

Nicholas believed that if Christians would only use *pia interpretatio* when reading the Qur'an, then "it would not be difficult" for them to find "the truth of the Gospel" there.[31] But locating these tidbits of truth might have been more difficult than Nicholas had first assumed; after all, he named his book a "sifting" or "scrutiny" (*cribratio*) of the Qur'an, a word that does not suggest ease. And what was his goal in searching for these bits of truth? One clue comes in book 3, when Nicholas addresses the "Sultan of Babylonia" (the Ottoman Mehmed II) directly, and boldly asks him to compel his Muslim subjects to do two unthinkable things: first to accept Mary as Mother of God, and then to embrace the gospel. Nicholas seemed to think that Mary could easily pave the way to a Muslim acceptance of Christianity, hence his request to Mehmed:

The glorious Virgin Mary asks that you restore to her the honor given by God and declared by emperors (in the third synod under Theodosius, and the fourth under Marcian)....If you order everyone in your empire to believe in the gospel...your command will be just and pleasing to God, Christ, and the undefiled Virgin, and it will bestow salvation and rest to innumerable souls, and immortal praise and eternal life to you. The time must come...when there will be nothing but the faith of Christ. Begin to approach [Christianity], and all the princes of the earth and of that sect [Islam] will follow you![32]

Nicholas's request is odd, but not entirely novel. After all, Pope Pius II—who was then advocating for another crusade against the Turks—wrote a letter to Mehmed in 1461, likewise asking him to convert.[33] Nicholas, a friend and advisor to Pius II, surely knew of this letter, which was written at the very same time as his own *Cribratio*.[34]

It seems that Nicholas makes his strange request of Mehmed for two reasons. First, he tries to convince the sultan to see himself in line with past emperors such as Constantine and Theodosius, who had both temporal and sacral power: "Consider those glorious emperors Theodosius, Marcian, Constantine, etc., who endeavored with the greatest enthusiasm to increase the glory of the virgin and mother of Christ. If you are a prince, pay attention; it is to your honor to act similarly."[35] These emperors had the power and the duty to affirm Christian doctrine, says Nicholas, so why wouldn't Mehmed do the same? (No matter that he is a Muslim!) Nicholas's argument seems to be that Mehmed would legitimize his imperial authority if he mimicked what previous emperors living in the same imperial city (Constantinople turned Istanbul) had done.

But the second reason Nicholas makes this request is that he suspects the sultan is a former Christian who has only recently rejected his former belief in Jesus as son of God and Mary as mother of God. He says to Mehmed,

Once you were Christian, but you denied the Christian faith to be fit for rule....You believed him [Christ] to be the true Son of God; but now you no longer believe this, in accord with the law of the Arabs [Islam]....You believed Mary the mother of Jesus Christ to be *theotokos*, that is, God-bearer; but now you say that the Virgin Mary is the mother of Christ, but not [the mother] of God.[36]

Why would Nicholas think that Mehmed had been a former Christian? In fact, the idea that Muslims were either former or secret Christians was not uncommon among medieval Europeans.[37] Perhaps this was one way Christians could come to grips with the failure of their missionary efforts among Muslims, whom Europeans admired for their philosophical and scientific acumen. What else could explain why Muslim philosophers seemed to reject Christianity, such an obviously rational religion? Another reason for the durability of this idea might have been to legitimize the existence of the Christianity even during times of its political weakness under Islam. Interestingly, there is a similar legend in Islamic literature, where the Byzantine Christian Emperor Heraclius (d. 641) is said to have been a secret convert to Shi'i Islam. This story, which is of medieval Shi'i origin, might also have been told to legitimize Shi'i Islam during a time of political weakness under Sunni rule.[38]

Nicholas's strange request that Muslims accept Mary as *Theotokos* mirrors another concession he asked Muslims (and Jews) to make in an earlier book, *De pace fidei* (On the peace of faith). Written soon after the Ottoman capture of Constantinople in 1453, *De pace fidei* is a thought experiment in which Nicholas hopes to rid the earth of sectarian violence by getting world leaders to agree on a single, common religion. To do so, Nicholas attempts to identify the "lowest common denominators" of this hypothetical religion. He suggests baptism as one common denominator. Why does he think that other religions would accept baptism—which is not only an exclusively Christian sacrament, but also the sacrament most recognizable to outsiders as proof of conversion? Despite all this, Nicholas believes that since both Jews and Muslims already have washing rituals that are at least superficially similar to Christian baptism, it therefore "will not be difficult for them to accept the washing instituted by Christ as their profession of faith."[39] Interestingly, not only does Nicholas expect Jews and Muslims to modify their practices in order to achieve unity, but he also thinks that Latin Christians should do the same. Noting that circumcision is observed among Ethiopian Orthodox Christians, Jews, and Muslims, Nicholas goes on to suggest that maybe Latin Christians, who are in the minority, should accept circumcision as is practiced by the majority, "so that peace might be established."[40] However, the concession Nicholas proposes for Latin Christians (accepting circumcision) is not as difficult as the concession he proposes for Muslims (accepting Mary as God-bearer), since the former is a ritual about which even different Christians disagree, but the latter is a more foundational doctrinal point that separates religions. In trying to figure out how Christians, Muslims, and Jews might come to some agreement about Mary, baptism, and circumcision, Nicholas shows himself to be grappling with one of the most famous lines in *De pace fidei*: "one religion in a variety of rites."[41]

WILLIAM AND NICHOLAS'S MARY: WHAT KIND OF BRIDGE?

This chapter provided a glimpse into the uniquely positive views two medieval churchmen expressed about the shared Mary. Both William of Tripoli and Nicholas of Cusa, thanks to a similarly positive approach to the Qur'an, saw Mary as an interfaith bridge. This was unlike most of their confreres, who saw Mary as an interfaith barrier because they concluded that the qur'anic Mary was not the biblical Mary (e.g., the Miriam-Mary mix-up). But what kind of bridge did William and Nicholas think Mary was? Why did these two swim against the tide, seeming to view the Muslim Mary so positively? Before answering this question, it seems important to state that *positively* is a relative term; medieval Christian writings that spoke well of Islam in one place still contained a great deal of polemic, vitriol, or ambivalence elsewhere. William and Nicholas praised the Mary they discovered in the Qur'an, not because they could affirm her perfect alignment with the biblical Mary. Rather, they praised her because they realized that a shared and truly beloved figure like Mary could perhaps serve as a useful aid in the conversion of Muslims to Christianity. After all, we know that at least William sought converts; at the end of *De statu*, he (or one of his students) boasted that he had succeeded in baptizing over a thousand Muslims.[42] Whether this number is exaggerated, William seemed to believe, despite qur'anic statements to the contrary, that Muslims are fundamentally amenable to Christian doctrines such as the incarnation, virgin birth, and Trinity. For example, he claimed that Sura 4:171 enables Muslims to believe in both the Son and the Spirit.[43] William suggests that this passage reveals the Qur'an's acceptance of the Trinity, even though Muslims are not aware of its true meaning, and he prays that they will make the cognitive leap from implicit acceptance to full and explicit belief in the Trinity.[44] Nicholas, too, is so confident that the Ottoman sultan and his subjects would be willing to accept Mary as the *Theotokos* that he unabashedly invites him to do so.

But perhaps conversion is too utilitarian an explanation. Might there be another reason for William and Nicholas's relatively positive assessment of Mary? The possibility of authentic amazement should not be discounted. For both William and Nicholas express genuine surprise and even delight at the discovery of the qur'anic Mary. After reading verse after verse about her, William concludes that a primary purpose of the Qur'an might be "to praise and glorify Christ Jesus and his mother Mary."[45] Nicholas comes to nearly the same conclusion, admitting that the goal of the Qur'an might actually be to "give glory" to God, Christ, and the Virgin. And after seeing Muslim devotions to Mary in the mosque, William declares, "In [their prayer], amazingly, I think, they please God and men, if they have true faith."[46] Were William's personal observations so compelling that they convinced him of the efficacy of Islamic prayer?[47] Is it possible that William and Nicholas had been genuinely touched, if only for a moment, by what they read about Mary in the Qur'an, or by what they saw Muslims do to honor her? While such emotions are rarely expressed in medieval anti-Islamic polemical literature, every once in a while they do appear, usually in the writings of Christians who gained their knowledge of Islam through personal experiences with Muslims or a serious study of the literature.

In any case, William and Nicholas's relatively irenic approach to Islam was uncommon in the medieval West. Most Dominican missionaries of William's time preferred polemics: first refuting Muslim error, then expounding Christian truth.[48] And most churchmen of Nicholas's fifteenth century were calling for a new crusade against the ascendant Ottomans. But unlike everyone else, William and Nicholas did not engage Muslims with violence or vitriol. Rather, they began with an attempt at rapprochement, no matter how misguided their form of rapprochement might appear to us today. And their "dialogue" was not focused on error, but commonality. That commonality was Mary. It might not seem significant that William and Nicholas viewed the Virgin so positively, given their concomitant desire to criticize other aspects of Islam and lead Muslims to the baptismal font. But theirs was a brief shining moment, because it would be many centuries before Christians would see Mary as an interfaith bridge once again.

Chapter 5

OUR LADY OF VICTORY

Mary, Mother of Mercy, Lover of Piety and Consoler of the Human Race, by her intercession before the throne of God, did not cease to pour forth prayers and supplication for the safety of her people; and by virtue of her prayers and petitions, a decisive victory, which must never be forgotten, was gained over the Turks on October 7, 1571.[1]

—Pope Pius V, *Salvatoris Domini Nostri* (1572), establishing the Feast of Our Lady of Victory

On October 7, 1571, in the waters off southwestern Greece, the Catholic Holy League called on the Virgin Mary to help them defeat their enemy, the Ottomans. And surprisingly, they did. The miraculous naval victory at Lepanto was attributed to the Blessed Mother—not only by the Catholic League's leader, Don Juan of Austria, who kept a statue of Mary aboard his ship and required his troops to pray to her before the battle, but also by Pope Pius V, who thanked members of Rome's Rosary confraternities for their successful prayers.

Almost instantly, "Our Lady of Victory" became the quintessential symbol of enmity between Christians and Muslims—a symbol that has long endured, in part thanks to strong cultural props. Just weeks after the battle, a victory Mass was held at the Roman basilica Santa Maria in Aracoeli, where Pius V announced the commissioning of a new gilt ceiling commemorating Our Lady of Victory's role at Lepanto.[2] Aracoeli's ceiling was one of many new artistic depictions linking the Virgin and the battle, including frescoes in Venice (the ducal palace; Capella del Rosario in SS Giovanni e Paolo) and Rome (Sala Regia at the Vatican; Palazzo Colonna),[3] and paintings by Titian, Tintoretto, and Veronese. Popular images featured a heavenly Mary presiding over an earthly battle or Pope Pius praying the Rosary while receiving a vision of victory at sea. In spring 1572, Pius added "Mary, Help of Christians" to the Litany of Loreto and declared October 7 to be the Feast of Our Lady of Victory.[4] The feast was soon renamed Our Lady of the Rosary, and is still celebrated by the Catholic Church every October.[5] Even in recent years, numerous traditionalist blogs and websites encourage Catholics to "pray to Our Lady of Victory against Islamic terrorists" or "say the rosary to defeat ISIS."[6]

Clearly, the image of Mary battling Muslims has had staying power.[7] The idea of the Virgin as a literal and symbolic barrier between Catholics and non-Catholics burgeoned as the modern period dawned. At that time, Our Lady of Victory was a literal barrier between Christians and Muslims truly at war, her image regularly appearing on the battle standards of Christians engaged in armed struggles against Moors in Iberia and Ottomans in Southeast Europe.[8] But Mary was also becoming a symbolic barrier between Catholics and all non-Catholics: not only Muslims, but Protestants, too. In fact, early modern Catholics often grouped Muslims and Protestants together as a common enemy. Consider the placement of the Lepanto painting in the Vatican's Sala Regia, directly adjacent to the Massacre of the Huguenots. The message is clear: the true faith will vanquish all enemies of the Catholic Church, be they Muslim infidels or Protestant heretics, just like what happened at these two epic battles of 1571 and 1572, respectively.[9] Another example of Catholics pitting themselves against a dual Muslim-Protestant enemy can be found in Antwerp, where a series of paintings were commissioned to commemorate the hundredth anniversary of Lepanto; they depict enemy ships flying both Turkish and North Netherlandish (Protestant) flags.[10] And in a polemical treatise against Protestants, the French Catholic Orientalist Guillaume Postel (d. 1581) listed twenty-eight ways in which Muslims and Protestants agree in error, including their equally insufficient devotion to Mary.[11] Of course, the reverse was also true: many sixteenth-century Protestants also grouped Catholics and Muslims together as a common enemy. A good example is Martin Luther's preface to a book about the Turks, where he accuses both Muslims and "Papists" of privileging works over faith.[12]

This chapter is about the birth and persistence of the idea of Mary as Our Lady of Victory against Muslims. First, we will look at the sixteenth-century factors that contributed to her emergence: the allegorization of the Battle of Lepanto, Pope Pius V's promotion of the Rosary, the rise of Marian sodalities and Rosary confraternities, and Catholic responses to the Reformation. We will then examine some arguments of Catholics against Protestants and Muslims on the one hand, and of Protestants against Catholics and Muslims on the other, with a focus on two Christian Arabists who explicitly brought up Mary in arguments directed against both Muslims and "the other" Christians: the Catholic priest Guillaume Postel and the Anglican minister George Sale. The chapter will end with a discussion of Lepanto's lasting legacy, from the rise of militant Marian devotions at the end of the sixteenth century, to later iterations of Our Lady of Victory such as Croatia's Gospa Sinjska (Our Lady of Sinj) in 1715, to Pope Leo XIII's references to Lepanto and Mary in his Rosary encyclicals, and finishing in the twenty-first century with a nod to her presence on the internet.

LEPANTO, THE ROSARY, AND REFORM

The years between 1570–1580 were key to the development of a new, more militant brand of Marian devotion, which was wielded by Catholics against all enemies, be they Muslims or Protestants.[13] This new image of Mary as Our Lady of Victory, a triumphant military leader, was layered on top of more traditional, more irenic ideas of her as mother, advocate, and queen, and was vigorously promoted after the surprising Catholic League victory at Lepanto. The creation of Our Lady of Victory was also assisted by Pope Pius V's avid cultivation of Marian devotion in general, the Rosary in particular, and other post-Tridentine reforms of early modern Catholicism (formerly known as the Counter or Catholic Reformation).[14]

The backstory to Lepanto began over a century earlier, in 1453, when the Ottomans conquered Constantinople and opened a new chapter of Christian-Muslim relations in Europe.[15] The "Turk" was now the face of Islam for Europeans, and as the late medieval period gave way to the early modern, the Ottomans were seen not only as a religious challenge to Christianity but also as a political and cultural threat to the developing idea of "Europe."[16] Because the Ottoman Empire was physically more proximate to Europe than the faraway Levantine Muslims fought by Crusaders, Renaissance thinkers' views of Islam were "more hostile on the whole" than their medieval predecessors.[17] Islam was not a new enemy, but it was now closer than ever and thus seemed more menacing in the minds of early modern Europeans.

The sixteenth century also gave rise to new foes emerging from within the Church itself. The Reformers and the Roman Church each accused the other of being unfaithful to the gospel, and battles that began as doctrinal became violent in Germany and Bohemia. Mary had no small role in both kinds of battles. Just as Don Juan raised a standard of the Virgin on his galley while fighting the Turks in 1571, so too did the Bavarian Catholic Duke Maximilian I proudly fly Mary on his flag and attribute to her his victory against Protestants at White Mountain in 1620.[18] For Catholics, Mary stood for triumph over the errors of the Reformers. For Protestants, Mary stood for everything that was wrong with the Roman Church. While some early Protestants maintained a certain level of devotion to the Virgin (especially Lutherans), they rejected what they saw as the excesses of Catholic Marian piety, and reframed their own approach to her by rejecting titles like queen, intercessor, and mediatrix, yet still honoring her as a model of Christian faith and recipient of God's grace.[19]

Sixteenth-century Catholics harnessed Mary's power against their enemies by creating Our Lady of Victory. On the eve of Lepanto, forces were already in play to make that happen. The Rosary (from the Latin *rosarium*, rose garden), also known as the *corona* (crown of roses) or Our Lady's Psalter, is a devotional prayer with roots in the late medieval movement known as *devotio moderna*. While tradition says that Christ gave the Rosary to

St. Dominic himself, it was actually fifteenth-century friars in the Low Countries who promoted the prayer at the grassroots level.[20] The first confraternity of the Rosary was most likely founded by the Dominican Alain de la Roche in 1460 in Douai, where he encouraged locals to pray the *corona*. A second more famous confraternity was founded in Cologne in 1475 by another Dominican, Jacob Sprenger.[21] Rosary confraternities quickly spread throughout the Netherlands, Belgium, France, Germany, Spain, and then to Italy; Pope Alexander V first confirmed the idea in 1479 but the Dominican Order had exclusive rights to approve new confraternities until 1569, just two years before Lepanto.[22]

The Rosary confraternities of the late fifteenth century emphasized personal piety. Fast-forward a hundred years to 1575, when the Jesuit Franz Coster founded a related organization: the Marian soldality. Coster's group was also based in Cologne, but the focus was now more on communal practice and corporate life.[23] Actually, the first Marian sodality had been founded a few years before, in 1563 (the same year the Council of Trent ended), at the Jesuit's Roman College by a Belgian named Jean Leunis.[24] The Jesuits worked hard to spread Marian sodalities, and their popularity grew quickly; for example, in 1577 alone, over thirty thousand members joined Rome's Rosary confraternity.[25] By the beginning of the seventeenth century, both Rosary confraternities and Marian sodalities were attracting a diverse crowd: men and women, upper and lower classes, clergy and laity. The foundational prayer of both groups was the Rosary, a versatile devotion that appealed to different kinds of people, could be used in both public and private prayer, and linked ritual and visual culture.[26]

The Marian sodality in particular, which focused less on personal piety and more on reforming society at large, was used to promote a renewed form of Catholicism in the years immediately following the Council of Trent. In fact, in 1577 Peter Canisius told his fellow Jesuit Coster that the main mission of the Marian sodalities was to "preserve the Catholic Church in Germany."[27] Handbooks created for sodalities at that time included not only Marian songs, litanies, and prayers, but also doctrinal polemics to help members counter the arguments of Protestant opponents.[28] Some sodalities required members to wear rosary beads prominently on their person, as a "public testimony" to the wearer's

Catholic identity and doctrinal orthodoxy.[29] And orthodox Catholic doctrine on Marian devotion had just been clarified by the Council of Trent in its very last session of December 3–4, 1563, with the document, "On the Invocation, Veneration, and Relics of Saints, and on Sacred Images." The Catholic approach to Marian devotion outlined in this document found its way into the Tridentine Profession of Faith, which was appended to the Nicene Creed and required believers to state, "I firmly declare that the images of Christ and of the Mother of God Ever Virgin and of the other saints are to be kept and preserved, and that due honor and veneration should be given to them."[30] This Marian doctrine was solidified through concurrent liturgical reforms, including a new breviary stressing Marian devotion, a revival of the Little Office in her honor, and a more elaborate Feast of the Immaculate Conception.[31]

While many early Reformers (including Luther himself) accepted certain mariological doctrines such as the virgin birth and the title *Theotokos*, with a few even promoting Marian devotion, by the end of the century most Protestants became vociferous in rejecting all forms of Marian piety, including the Rosary. For example, Lutheran preachers were critical of the Rosary's central prayer, the Ave Maria, because it calls Mary *gratia plena* (full of grace), which to them implied that the grace is her own, rather than an undeserved gift from God. Luther preferred the term *gratiosa* (enjoying favor) instead.[32] As the century wore on, Protestants became more and more concerned about the Catholic Mary, and raised their voices against her. For example, by the mid-1570s, several Lutheran ministers explicitly preached against the idea of Our Lady of Victory, calling such a moniker a prime example of the Church's misplaced belief in Mary's power.[33] The rising Lutheran chorus against Mary by the end of the sixteenth century may have been a reaction to the growing number of reconversions from Lutheranism back to Catholicism in certain parts of Germany at that time—reconversions that may have been due to the popularity of Rosary confraternities and Marian sodalities.[34]

To accomplish their goal of defeating both Protestant heretics and Muslim infidels, post-Trent Catholics not only created new pious societies but also a more militant image of Mary. They were of course building on the much older idea of *Theotokos* as a guardian against heresy; for example, hymns from the fifth through seventh centuries, including the famous *Akathistos*, depict her as the doorkeeper preventing heresy from entering the Church (as noted in chapter 2, a key doctrinal point separating Chalcedonian and non-Chalcedonian Christians was Mary's identity as *Theotokos*).[35] In fact, some have argued that the acclamations used to praise Mary in the *Akathistos* are modeled after those given to victorious generals in ancient Rome; the hymn expresses the triumph of the Chalcedonians over the non-Chalcedonians, although Mary herself is not praised as the cause of the victory.[36] As already noted in chapter 2, the Byzantines saw Mary as a protectress and a general. But by the seventh century, they also began to embrace the idea of Mary as the mother of defeat; Orthodox Christians in Southeastern Europe came to identify with the mourning Mary, particularly after their lands were overtaken by the Ottomans.[37] But Western Christians preferred to appropriate the Byzantine idea of Our Lady of Victory, and her military might was ratcheted up by Latins beginning in the eleventh and twelfth centuries, when Mary began to take a more active role against the infidel. For example, Mary was tied to Santiago Matamoros ("St. James the Moorslayer") in medieval Iberia, where both were useful mascots in the *reconquista*; King Fernando III (d. 1252) carried an image of "The Virgin of Battles" on his saddle.[38] But the idea of Mary as a warrior truly burgeoned after Lepanto.

Some of the paintings produced immediately after 1571 show Mary directing human wars. In some of these images, she appears to oversee the battles in some way, but remains physically distant from the actual violence. For example, in Paolo Veronese's *The Allegory of Lepanto* (1572), Mary is at the top, observing (and possibly directing) the naval battle raging far below, but she is in heaven, bathed in light and clearly separated from the earthly violence by a line of dark clouds. But later renderings of Lepanto stress Mary's more direct role in the fight against Muslims. One of the most striking examples of the new, militant Mary is a curious image from a seventeenth-century German (Cologne) confraternity pamphlet advertising the Feast of Our Lady of the Rosary. Printed at the top in all capital letters is the line *Triumphus SS.mi Rosarii Mariae* (The triumph of the most holy Rosary of Mary). Just below the title is an image of Mary in the foreground, with the Battle of Lepanto in the background; both are common in depictions of Our

Lady of the Rosary/Victory. What is uncommon is how Mary is portrayed here: she is standing triumphantly over a dead, headless Turk (who is clearly identifiable as such, thanks to his fallen turban). In one hand, she wields a rosary-encircled sword, which also contains the words "shield of Christians" in Latin.[39] In her other hand she embraces baby Jesus, who is holding up the Turk's decapitated, bloody head. Also included at the center is the phrase *Regina Sacratissimi rosarii, pugna pro nobis* (Queen of the most holy Rosary, fight for us).[40] This sword- (or scepter-) toting image of the Virgin, known by a variety of names such as *Mariahilf* in German or *Nuestra Señora la Conquistadora* in Spanish, was (and sometimes still is) carried in religious processions, especially in places that saw inter- or intrareligious strife in the early modern era, such as Germany, Spain, the Balkans, and Mexico. Just a few examples include Our Lady of Victory in Vac, Hungary; Our Lady of Csiksomlyó in Romania; La Virgen de la Victoria in Málaga, Spain; Nuestra Señora la Conquistadora in Puebla, Mexico; and Mariahilf in Passau, Germany.[41] Whatever her name, the Cologne image leaves no doubt that the Mother of God was seen as a powerful military leader who would help Catholics to defeat Muslims, not just through intercession but direct action.[42] In fact, Cologne's unusual image seems to imply that the Mother is more powerful than the Son of God, since she is the one wielding the sword, while baby Jesus is merely holding the decapitated head, the aftermath of her action. In this image more than others, the rosary is a weapon, and the Virgin, a triumphant killer.

At the same time that confraternities and sodalities were gaining traction at the popular level, the Rosary devotion itself was also receiving official sanction. In the 1569 bull *Consueverunt Romani Pontifices*, the Dominican Pope Pius V made his Order's version of the Rosary prayer (15 decades and 150 Hail Marys) standard for the universal Catholic Church. In the beginning of the bull, Pius compares his own sixteenth-century fight against Protestants to St. Dominic's thirteenth-century fight against Albigensians, and repeats the tale (now recognized as legendary) that Dominic was able to defeat the heretics because he prayed the Rosary. As noted earlier, while there are no historical documents linking Dominic to the Rosary before the late fifteenth century, Pius clearly saw a connection between the Rosary, heresy, and

Figure 2. *Triumphus SS.mi Rosarii*, 17th century, Köln, Kölnisches Stadt-museum (RM 1936/1031). Photo: © Rheinisches Bildarchiv Köln, rba_224251. Used with permission.

history: to his mind, Mary had always helped the Roman Church defeat its enemies, and would continue to do so if Catholics would keep asking her.[43] And Pius claimed he had no better proof of this than Lepanto, insisting that the prayers of Rome's Rosary confraternities led directly to the Catholic League's miraculous defeat of the Ottomans.

The links between Mary, the Rosary, and Catholic victory over Muslims and Protestants intensified in the decades following 1571. Almost immediately, innumerable paintings were commissioned that combined images of the Virgin, rosary beads, and battles against various enemies—usually the Ottomans but sometimes also Protestants.[44] The phrase emblazoned on Don Juan's Lepanto galley banner, *Sancta Maria succurre miseris* (Holy Mary, help the wretched!) was in 1572 transferred to the Litany of Loreto as "Mary, Help of Christians." And by the beginning of the seventeenth century, several new churches had been dedicated to this more militant Mary: just a few examples include Rome's Santa Maria della Vittoria, Paris's Notre Dame des Victoires, Lublin's Our Lady Help of Christians, Goa's Nossa Senhora Da Victoria, Prague's Kostel Panny Marie Vítězné, and Augsburg's Maria Hilf. There was a great increase in pilgrimages and dedications to the latter during the Thirty Years War.[45] Our Lady of Victory was celebrated not only in images, litanies, and shrines, but also on stage: for example, the 1617 Jesuit drama *Deiparae Virginis Triumphus*, performed in Dillingen, Germany, featured enemies of Mary such as iconoclast Byzantines, Jews, and Turks, and included a full reenactment of the Battle of Lepanto.[46] The centenary of Lepanto in 1671 inspired a new spate of images, although the Dominicans of Antwerp had already been celebrating the victory for decades with an annual procession.[47] The idea of a militant Mary continued to resonate well into the eighteenth century; in fact, Catholic victories over the Ottomans, such as the one on August 15, 1715, in Sinj, Croatia, and another on August 5, 1716, in Peterwardein, Hungary, encouraged Pope Clement XI to keep Our Lady of the Victory (now Our Lady of the Rosary) alive by extending the feast to the entire Church. The idea of Mary as victor over all Catholic enemies was stressed again and again through art, shrines, dramatic presentations, pious societies, prayers, and liturgical celebrations. The "revolution in iconography" that was Our Lady of

Victory became the ultimate symbol of a Church triumphant in the face of Protestant and Muslim enemies.[48] This new Western Our Lady of Victory trumped the Eastern Our Lady of Defeat, the alter ego embraced by Orthodox Christians of Southeastern Europe. It was the triumphant Mary, not the mourning Mary, who would endure for hundreds of years as the Roman Church faced new enemies such as nineteenth-century modernists, twentieth-century communists, and twenty-first century terrorists.

MARY AND MUSLIMS IN CATHOLIC-PROTESTANT POLEMICS

In their fight against Muslims and Protestants, early modern Catholics not only used Marian images, they also used Marian arguments. Even the Reformers brought up Mary, if only to reject Catholic views of her. In the sixteenth century, detailed Mariologies were presented by both Catholics and Protestants in an attempt to prove their orthodoxy. While both agreed that she is the Virgin Mother of God, each stressed different aspects of her personality. The Catholic Mary was a powerful intercessor and mediatrix whom Bernardino of Siena and other medieval theologians called "the neck of the church," whose image should be venerated.[49] The Protestant Mary was favored by God, an example of faith, and a model Christian who should be respected, not worshiped. Both Catholics and Protestants criticized the other's version of Mary, claiming that it was comparable to or even worse than Muslim beliefs about her; to make their point, they often incorporated arguments against Islam into their intra-Christian polemics.

The next section of this chapter will focus on the writings of the Catholic apologist Guillaume Postel (d. 1581), such as his *Book of Concord between the Qur'an or Law of Muhammad and the Protestants* (*Alcorani seu legis Mahometi et Evangelistarum concordiae liber*), which attacks both Muslims and Protestants as a common Catholic enemy. Postel claims that these two religions share many heretical beliefs and practices, and lists twenty-eight errors, including belief in predestination, a lack of priests or religious, and temples devoid of holy images.[50] Most relevant to the subject at hand is number six on Postel's list, which states that Protestants and Muslims both lack proper devotion to Mary.[51] For Postel, Mary was not only a barrier between Catholics and Muslims, but Catholics and Protestants too. Unlike medieval theologians such as Nicholas of Cusa and William of Tripoli, who saw Mary as a bridge between Islam and Christianity, the early modern linguist Guillaume Postel saw her as a barrier.

Guillaume Postel is known more for his scholarship in Eastern languages and Jewish mysticism than for his writings on Islam or Mariology, yet he wrote a great deal on the latter two subjects.[52] An eccentric and unorthodox character, he remains important in the history of Christian-Muslim relations not only because he studied Arabic and Islam so deeply, but also because he used Mary in his polemical writings against both Muslims and Protestants.

Postel was a polyglot whose first books—*Linguarum duodecim*, a description of Eastern languages, and *Grammatica Arabica*, the first Arabic grammar in Latin—earned him the title "Father of Comparative Philology." His translations include the Hebrew *Zohar*, the Syriac Gospels, and most importantly for the subject at hand, the *Protevangelium of James*, which Postel is credited for translating, naming, and reintroducing the text (not the tradition, which was well known) to Latin Europe.[53] After leaving his position as the first lecturer in Arabic at the Collège de France (1538–42), Postel went on to write *De orbis terrae concordia* (On the harmony of the world, 1544), which discusses Islam, Christian apologetics, and the union of world religions. Also at this time, he wrote *Alcorani*, the book that lists similarities between Muslim and Protestant doctrines. Despite its title, *Alcorani* does not argue primarily against Muslims, but Protestants. In January 1544, Postel entered the Jesuit Order, but was expelled two years later due to eccentric behavior and unorthodox beliefs, both of which would only increase in the years to come. Eventually, Parisian authorities forbade him to preach in public, the Church placed his writings on the Index of Forbidden Books, and the Venetian Inquisition put him on trial, where he was judged not heretical but insane. He spent his last twenty years living under house arrest at the Cluniac priory of St. Martin in Paris.

The eccentric Postel is relevant to this book because he used the Virgin to argue against both Muslims and Protestants. Despite his heterodoxy on certain topics, he had a very traditional Catholic devotion to Mary. Several books defended Marian doctrines like the immaculate conception against Protestant critiques (and Catholic critiques, too, since Catholics disagreed about the immaculate conception at this time).[54] What is interesting about Postel's defense of Mary is the proof that few aside from him—a polyglot—could provide. In one mariological tome, *Du souverain effect de la plus excellente Corone du mond*, Postel cites both Jewish and Islamic texts to support his view of the immaculate conception.[55] But while he uses Muslim texts to justify the Catholic Mary in *Du souverain effect*, in other books he uses Christian texts to criticize the Muslim Mary. For example, in *De orbis* he compares the Marian story in the Gospel of Luke with the Marian story in the Qur'an, only to conclude that the qur'anic account contains the following "lies": Mary giving birth under a palm tree, baby Jesus speaking to defend his mother's purity, and the confusion between Mary and Miriam.

In *Alcorani*, Postel likewise defends the Catholic Mary against Muslim attacks, and brings Protestants into the argument too. He claims that both Muslims and Protestants are wrong to accuse Catholics of idolatry: "Both of them (Muslims and Protestants) assert most falsely that we consider Mary to be like a goddess. But they will never be able to offer any argument to show this to be true."[56] He points out that while in theory Islam and Protestant Christianity reject Marian veneration, in practice, ordinary Muslims and Protestants honor Mary and other saints.[57] Postel then gives evidence for his assertion. First, he says that even though Protestants claim to reject saints, they have created new martyrologies:

> Although many heretics have tried to abolish the memory of those [saints] in the Church whom Christ greatly approves, such that their name and cult is obliterated, [the saints] have [still] crept into their own [Muslim and Protestant] celebrations. Who today is unaware [of the fact] that the Protestants have assembled their own martyrology?...They worship daily the saints enrolled by Luther, such as Jan Hus of Prague.[58]

Second, Postel knows there are Islamic shrines throughout the world, and wonders if their existence proves that Muslims are secretly devoted to Jesus Christ: "If Muslims truly reject the cult of Christ and the saints, [then why do they] everywhere have their own memorials and religious places?"[59] In Postel's eyes, human beings—even heretical Protestants and Muslims—have a natural desire to venerate Christ, Mary, and the saints. This desire is so strong, says Postel, that despite doctrines to the contrary, the hypocritical Protestants and Muslims have still managed to create litanies and shrines to honor saints.

In another text, *De orbis*, Postel has more to say about the Muslim Mary. Like William of Tripoli, he refers to Sura 19; but unlike William, Postel quotes it in its entirety, without editing out the "anti-Christian" parts. Postel's outline of Sura 19 is part of his overall summary of the Qur'an in book 2 of *De orbis*. In this long section (representing over half of book 2), he says he will present the entire Qur'an chapter by chapter, arguing that his treatment will be superior to previous Christians like Nicholas of Cusa or Denys the Carthusian, because he knows Arabic and they did not. Postel's presentation of the Qur'an, unlike William's, contains little spin. Rather, Postel painstakingly goes through the entire book, sometimes quoting verses verbatim, and at other times paraphrasing whole chapters. Postel's love of Mary shines through, for when he gets to the Marian suras, he spends significantly more time on the Marian sections, to the detriment of other topics. For example, Postel takes just twenty lines to quickly summarize the first thirty verses of Sura 3, but then takes triple the space (seventy lines) to treat the twenty-four verses comprising the qur'anic story of Mary and Jesus (3:31–55).[60] Postel's presentation of Sura 19 is no different. He spends the most time discussing Mary (fifty-two lines), and quotes the entire annunciation story verbatim, while ignoring almost all other verses in the chapter, including those about John the Baptist and other prophets.[61] As noted earlier, Postel remains critical of Islamic Mariology, eventually concluding that the Qur'an is not divine revelation. Yet, its Mariology is still very interesting to him and thus worthy of close attention, as *De orbis* makes clear.

Even though Postel wrote *De orbis* to propose a plan for unity among world religions, he did not see Mary as a possible bridge to that unity. For Postel, Mary was not a bridge at all. Rather, she was a formidable barrier between Christians and Muslims, and between Catholics and Protestants. In his view, Mary did have the potential to unify the religions, but only if Protestants and Muslims would imitate Catholics in venerating her. But Postel knew the chances of this were slim, since these religions had either squelched the natural human desire to venerate saints, or redirected it to the wrong saints, like Jan Hus.

Postel is notable in the history of Christians, Muslims, and Mary for his creative use of the Virgin to suit whatever argument he happened to be making at the time. Thus, in some texts (*Alcorani, De orbis*) he used the biblical Mary to argue against Protestant and Muslim views of Mary, yet in others (*Du souverain*) he used the qur'anic Maryam to support Catholic views. Clearly, the Virgin was an especially pliable tool in his hands, given his unique linguistic abilities and wide range of theological interests. But in any case, Postel never saw her as a bridge between religions like William and Nicholas did, which is ironic given that the title and goal of his magnum opus was *concordia orbis*—world harmony.

Catholics like Postel were not the only early modern thinkers to use Mary and Muslims against their fellow Christians. Protestants did the same. While it is important not to generalize, most Protestants held up Mary as a symbol of everything wrong with religion, and not only Catholic religion.[62] Just like Catholics, who accused both Protestants and Muslims of being equally wrong about Mary, so too did Protestants criticize both Catholics and Muslims at the same time. Catholics argued that Protestants and Muslims do not honor Mary enough, while Protestants argued that Catholics and Muslims honor Mary too much.

Martin Luther is a case in point. He wrote two short prefaces against Islam, and while he does not refer to Mary explicitly, he does condemn the veneration of saints among Catholics and Muslims.[63] Luther targeted Catholics, Muslims, and Jews because he knew he could not describe true religion without mentioning all instances of false religion: "As I have written against the idols of the Jews and the papists, and will continue to do so to the extent that it is granted me, so also I have begun to refute the pernicious beliefs of Muhammad."[64] Luther believed that Catholics and Muslims in particular were wrong for stressing "empty rites" such as the veneration of saints and Mary,[65] and contrasted these two false religions with true religion, which is always focused on Christ alone:

> The gospel teaches that the Christian religion is by far something other and more sublime than showy ceremonies, tonsures, hoods, pale countenances, fasts, feasts, canonical hours, and that entire show of the Roman church throughout the world. Indeed, in all these things the Turks are by far superior. Nevertheless, they continue to deny and ardently persecute Christ, no less than our papists deny and persecute him. May they finally then grasp this truth, namely, that the Christian religion is by far something other than good customs or good works."[66]

Like Postel, Luther saw Muslims and Catholics as equal "opponents of the gospel." Actually, Luther thought that Muslims beat Catholics at their own game: "The splendor of your [Catholic] ceremonies is no splendor at all alongside the excellent splendor of the Turks and your customs are clearly an abomination when compared to theirs."[67] Of course, to his mind, both Catholics and Muslims were in the wrong game to begin with, since they focused too much on works. To combat this error, Luther goes on to list the articles of faith, which he calls the "greatest fortification and strongest arms" against false religion:

> These defenses are the articles about Christ, namely, that Christ is the son of God, that he died for our sins, that he was raised for our life, that justified by faith in him our sins are forgiven and we are saved, etc. These are the thunder that destroys not only Muhammad but even the gates of hell. For Muhammad denies that Christ is the son of God, denies that he died for our sins, denies that he arose for our life, denies that by faith in him our sins are forgiven and we are justified, denies that he will come as judge of the living and the dead (though he does believe in the resurrection of the dead and the day of judgment), denies the Holy Spirit, and denies the

gifts of the Spirit. By these and similar articles of faith, consciences must be fortified against the ceremonies of Muhammad.[68]

By calling the articles of faith the "strongest arms" against false religion, Luther uses the language of battle, but stresses spiritual warfare over actual militancy, at least in this text.[69] Furthermore, it is clear that Luther's defense of the true faith is directed not only against Islam but Catholicism too.[70] Even though he explicitly describes all the above denials of Christ as *Muslim* denials ("for Muhammad denies"), Luther is also implicitly suggesting that they are *Catholic* denials too:

> If there are any who deny the articles just asserted, of what benefit is it to them even if they have the religion of the angels, even if they are twice as religious as the Turks? On the other hand, what can harm those who hold on to these articles, even without numerous fasts, prayers, vigils, and abstentions, even without such great modesty in food, dress, gesture, and style of life? The Turks and the papists may be radiant in such matters. At the same time they are void of true faith and filled alike with other most disgraceful crimes, abominable before God and hateful among people.[71]

For Luther, Catholics and Muslims are equally wrong for their focus on "showy ceremonies" like vigils and the veneration of saints.[72]

Two centuries later, the Anglican George Sale wrote more explicitly about Mary's role in false religions like Islam and Catholicism. In the preface to his 1734 English translation of the Qur'an, Sale, an ordained minister and Arabic scholar, states that "Protestants alone are able to attack the Koran with success," because only they follow "rules" of evangelization, such as this: "Avoid teaching doctrines against common sense" like "the worshipping of images and the doctrine of transubstantiation," because these are "great stumbling-blocks to the Muhammadans, and the Church which teacheth this is very unfit to bring those people over."[73] Sale is referring to the Catholic Church here. "Popish image worship" is particularly problematic, says Sale, because it makes Muslims less likely to convert to Christianity, even though true Christianity (meaning Protestantism) rejects image worship.

Sale writes more about the connection between Mary and bad religion in the "Preliminary Discourse," a long, historical introduction he appended to his translation of the Qur'an. He suggests that "the superstitions and corruptions we now justly abhor in the Church of Rome" were established in the "dark ages" of the early Church, and that it was the idolatry of early Christians that helped Islam to spread rapidly in the East.[74] Later, Sale says even more about the relationship between Mariolatry and the rise of Islam. He notes that seventh-century Arabia was a hotbed of heresy, and points to the Kollyridians as especially egregious: "They introduced the Virgin Mary for God, or worshipped her as such, offering her a sort of twisted cake called *collyris*, whence the sect had its name."[75] Furthermore, he argues, early Christian Mariolatry helped strengthen Muhammad's argument against the Trinity:

> This notion of the divinity of the Virgin Mary was also believed by some at the Council of Nice, who said there were two gods besides the Father, viz., Christ and the Virgin Mary, and were thence named Mariamites. Others imagined her to be exempt from humanity and deified; which goes but little beyond the Popish superstition in calling her the complement of the Trinity, as if it were imperfect without her. This foolish imagination is justly condemned in the Quran as idolatrous, and gave a handle to Muhammad to attack the Trinity itself.[76]

Both Sale and Postel were scholars of Arabic and ordained ministers, and both used their linguistic knowledge to criticize Islam. They were also alike in that they both argued simultaneously against Islam and their fellow Christians: Postel against Protestants, and Sale against Catholics.[77] Mary was useful in both men's arguments. They demonstrate how third parties can function in bilateral dialogues, when two temporary "allies" effectively gang up (at least rhetorically) to defeat a third party, the enemy of the other two.[78] We have already seen this in chapter 2, when Jacob of Edessa used the similarities between Christian and

Muslim Mariologies to argue against Jews. It seems that in early modern battles pitting Catholics against Protestants and Muslims, and Protestants against Catholics and Muslims, Mary was also employed as an effective weapon by all sides, against all sides.

LEPANTO'S LEGACY

Although the Battle of Lepanto happened centuries ago, it has remained as a powerful symbol of Catholic victory over Muslims to this day. Long after the Ottomans ceased to be Christian Europe's main foe, Our Lady of Victory has endured in the face of new enemies. Soon after 1571 she was transferred to the Catholic fight against Protestants, as previously discussed, and since then she has been invoked repeatedly: against modernists by Leo XIII in the nineteenth century, against communists by Pius XII in the twentieth century, and against terrorists by bloggers in the twenty-first century. In all cases, the Rosary has been portrayed as an effective weapon for beleaguered believers, and Mary as a powerful general who will fight on "our side" when asked. For those who invoke her in this way, Mary is the ultimate bulwark protecting the Catholic Church from all external threats, including but not limited to Muslims.

The idea that Mary's intercession could guarantee victory over foes was resurrected in the late nineteenth century, when the Catholic hierarchy felt threatened on all sides, by forces including anticlericalism; advances in science, biblical exegesis, and philosophy; church/state political struggles; and increasingly secular societies and academic institutions. In 1868, Pope Pius IX described the scene from his vantage point:

> It is at this time evident and manifest to all men in how horrible a tempest the Church is now tossed, and with what vast evils civil society is afflicted. For the Catholic Church, with its saving doctrine and venerable power, and the supreme authority of this Holy See, are by the bitterest enemies of God and man assailed and trampled down.[79]

The "bitterest enemy" of the Church at this time was not Protestantism, but modernism, "the synthesis of all heresies."[80] The next pope, Leo XIII, would continue to fight the modernists. He asked Catholics to join him in his fight by praying to Mary, and encouraged them by issuing not one but eleven Rosary encyclicals between 1883 and 1898.[81] Leo cited tradition in support of his Rosary strategy:

> It has always been the habit of Catholics in danger and in troubled times to fly for refuge to Mary....This devotion, so great and so confident, to the august Queen of Heaven, has never shone forth with such brilliancy as when the militant Church of God has seemed to be endangered by the violence of heresy spread abroad, or by an intolerable moral corruption, or by the attacks of powerful enemies.[82]

Leo then gave two historical examples where he claimed the Rosary strategy had worked: first, Dominic's fight against the medieval Albigensian heresy and second, the Catholic League's fight against the Ottomans in 1571. Leo devotes an entire section of his encyclical to Lepanto:

> The efficacy and power of this devotion [to Mary] was also wondrously exhibited in the sixteenth century, when the vast forces of the Turks threatened to impose on nearly the whole of Europe the yoke of superstition and barbarism....Therefore, it is clearly evident that this form of prayer is particularly pleasing to the Blessed Virgin, and that it is especially suitable as a means of defense for the Church and all Christians.[83]

Here yet again the Rosary is described as a "means of defense" for the Church against her enemies. And this is not the only time Leo links Mary, devotion, and victory. In another Rosary encyclical, he roots the victory at Lepanto to the ancient Christian tradition of describing Mary's body as a fortress: "We have long desired to secure the welfare of the human race in an increase of devotion to the Blessed Virgin, as in a powerful citadel."[84] Here, Leo is referring to one of Mary's medieval titles, *Turris Davidica* (Tower of David), a biblical image rooted in Song of Songs 4:4 and Psalm 61:3. And in other encyclicals, he says that the Rosary confraternities are "battalions who fight the battle of Christ armed with his sacred mysteries and under the banner and guidance of the Heavenly Queen."[85] Leo's idea of "battalions" is in line with Peter Canisius's original goal for the Rosary confraternities: to fortify the Catholic Church in Germany against Protestant attack.[86]

Pope Leo had help resurrecting Our Lady of Victory. In the 1880s, the German artist Ludwig Seitz painted a modern version of her at the Vatican's Galleria dei Candelabri. Interestingly, Seitz's *Our Lady of Victory* does not possess the usual Marian accoutrements of veil, halo, or baby Jesus. Rather, she is depicted as the winged Roman goddess of victory (and holding the palm of victory, which also doubles as the palm of martyrdom). Before her kneels a Christian soldier who receives the rosary from her as if a weapon of war; in this posture, Seitz's Mary mimics traditional images of Our Lady of the Rosary, who is often seen giving beads to the faithful. In the background, the Battle of Lepanto can be seen, complete with ships and turbaned Muslim enemies. At the top is a quotation from Pope Leo XIII, exhorting believers to pray the Rosary. Seitz's *Our Lady of Victory* is an interesting combination of classical Roman and traditional Christian images, which perhaps makes sense given the Greek and Roman artifacts held in the Galleria dei Candelabri.[87]

Seitz's focus on Lepanto is no coincidence: Pope Leo himself commissioned this painting and several others in the Galleria dei Candelabri during renovations in 1883–87. At the very same time Leo was restoring the gallery, he was writing his Rosary encyclicals. And just as in the Vatican's Sala Regia, where images of Lepanto and the Massacre of the Huguenots are juxtaposed, so too does the Galleria dei Candelabri juxtapose a variety of enemies of the Church. Adjacent to Seitz's new Lepanto are paintings entitled *Defeat of the Errors of the Pseudo-philosophers*, where Muslim philosophers Ibn Rushd and Ibn Sina are depicted along with Protestant heretics (all being defeated by Thomas Aquinas, Leo's hero), and *The Triumph of Truth over Falsehood*, where perhaps modernism is the falsehood being defeated.

Even today, you can find Pope Leo's views of Our Lady of Victory repeated by churches named after her. For example, the website of Our Lady of Victory parish in Aurora, Colorado, includes a history page with language reminiscent of Leo: "How did this extraordinary victory at Lepanto come about? The answer is simple enough: It was obtained—yet again—by the most powerful weapon known to men: the holy rosary."[88] But the Aurora parish's history page does not end with Lepanto, but rather with a few words relating Our Lady of Victory to the present day: "In our times, the threat of Islam is a true and present danger. We must not be complacent but rather we must turn to Our Lady and we must invoke her intercession and use the powerful weapon which is the holy rosary and through which great victories have been obtained."[89] This traditionalist parish (which also rejects Vatican II) proves that at least in some circles, Our Lady of Victory, and the Islamophobia often associated with her, is alive and well in the twenty-first century.

However, despite this long history of referring to Our Lady of Victory as a barrier between Catholics and Muslims, there are have been some cases in which she has changed over time, showing Mary's flexibility as a symbol and her ability to move easily from barrier to bridge and back again. One example of such historical evolution is Our Lady of Sinj (Gospa Sinjska), a figure that emerged soon after the August 15, 1715, defeat of the Ottomans in Sinj, Croatia. Gospa Sinjska has been celebrated in the town of Sinj every Assumption Day since, and due to her resemblances to Lepanto's Virgin, one could even call her the Croatian Our Lady of Victory. However, despite the triumphalist aspects of Sinj's annual Marian celebration, recently Gospa Sinjska has been hailed by UNESCO as a bridge, not barrier, between Catholics and Muslims. How could such an evolution be possible?

Gospa Sinjska is honored for her role in the miraculous Croatian defeat of the Ottomans on August 15, 1715. Her icon had already been venerated in the town for at least a century before that, but soon after the battle, local Catholics added a gold crown to represent the Assumption Day victory attributed to her intercession. Our Lady of Sinj remains one of the most popular pilgrimage destinations in Croatia year-round, but especially during the nine days leading up to the Feast of the Assumption on August 15. Two elements of the Gospa Sinjska celebration are relevant here: (1) Devetnica, the novena of the Assumption (Velika Gospa);

(2) Sinjska Alka, a military tournament held before August 15. The Devetnica is a series of masses (and associated prayers) on the nine days leading up to the Assumption. Some of the prayers in the Devetnica have an anti-Islamic tone. For example, one of the prayers (written in 2009) and posted on the official Gospa Sinjska website includes the following history: "In 1715 your people of Sinj were attacked by the enemy Ottoman army and you heard our prayers.... Your light broke the darkness, and with your Assumption the enemy fled and rays of light entered Dalmatia."[90] The second element of the celebration, the Sinjska Alka, is also held during the Devetnica, and is an interesting addition to Sinj's Assumption festivities because it has nothing to do with the Virgin Mary. Rather, the Alka is a jousting ceremony with clear Turkish roots (including specific words and elements) that is reenacted only in Sinj during the Devetnica.[91] A tourist website explains its meaning: "The Alka tournament is a symbol of victory of the people of Sinj from Turkish attack....In commemoration of their great victory, the people of Sinj instituted the Alka tournament."[92] Interestingly, in stark contrast to this explanation, the official UNESCO website claims, "The name of the tournament derives from this *alka* or ring, a word whose Turkish origin reflects the historical coexistence and cultural exchange between two different civilizations."[93] So which is it? Does the ceremony celebrate the victory of the Croatian Christians over the Muslim Turks, or does it celebrate the coexistence of these two religions in the Balkans? Is Gospa Sinjska a bridge or barrier?[94]

Perhaps these competing interpretations suggest that there has been an evolution of public opinion about the meaning of Velika Gospa. Or perhaps they simply demonstrate divergent views: an "insider" religious Croatian view (Mary as barrier) and an "outsider" secular UNESCO view (Mary as bridge). Of course, a third perspective might be that Gospa Sinjska is neither a bridge nor barrier, but simply a beloved figure who accentuates Croatian Catholic identity as such, with no reference whatsoever, negative or otherwise, to outsiders such as Muslims. This can be seen in diaspora celebrations of Gospa Sinjska, for example, that of St. Jerome Croatian Catholic Church in Chicago; novena prayers for Velika Gospa posted on their website in recent years contain no references to Muslims whatsoever.[95]

In any case, despite the presence of conflicting histories and seemingly polar opposite secular and religious interpretations, there have been some positive religious developments regarding the celebration of the Assumption at Sinj. In 2010, Croatians and Bosnians instituted a joint pilgrimage from Sinj, Croatia to Rama, Bosnia (Rama is the original location of the icon of Our Lady of Sinj, who was formerly called Mother of Mercy in Rama).[96] This new pilgrimage, which begins in Sinj on August 15, the Feast of the Assumption, and ends in Rama on September 8, the Feast of Mary's Nativity, crosses national (Croatia-Bosnia) and religious (Catholic-Muslim) lines. If it ever gains popularity among both Catholic and Muslims, either regionally or internationally, might this pilgrimage express or even help create a new *sensus fidelium*, such that Sinj's Our Lady of Victory will turn decisively from a barrier into a bridge?[97]

Chapter 6

MARY,
TOOL FOR MISSION

A Moor often went to gaze [at an image of Mary] and
thought it over and reasoned to himself that he could
not believe that God would become incarnate....
"However, if God would make one of His manifestations
to me, he would cause me to become a Christian." The
Moor had scarcely uttered this when he saw [Mary's]
breasts turn into living flesh and begin to flow with
milk....When he saw this he wept, called a priest, and
was baptized.[1]

—*Cantigas de Santa Maria*, 46, attributed to King
Alfonso X "the Wise" of Spain

In the story above, a Muslim obtains an icon of Mary as booty
after a war against Christians. He takes the icon home, places
it in a shrine, prays for a miracle, and gets one: the image begins
to lactate! The surprising finale? The Moor is so moved that he
converts to Christianity. Indeed, the illustrated book from which
this story comes, the medieval Iberian *Cantigas de Santa Maria*, is
full of miraculous conversions facilitated by Mary—conversions of
criminals, wayward priests, Jews, Muslims, and others.[2]

95

The idea that the Virgin might ease the conversion of Muslims in particular, due to the respect Islam has for her, has been entertained by Christians for centuries. Certainly this idea is behind Nicholas of Cusa's bold request for Sultan Mehmed to accept Mary as *Theotokos*. Several *cantigas* demonstrate that Iberian Christians were also aware of how similar Muslim Mariology is to their own, perhaps even thinking, as did *cantiga* 46, that it had the potential to lead Muslims to the baptismal font.[3] This idea that Mary could be a "tool for mission" continued to be held for centuries by Catholics in particular: from seventeenth-century Jesuits, to nineteenth-century White Fathers and Pope Leo XIII, to twentieth-century Bishop Fulton Sheen, all of whom actively promoted Mary as a useful means to convert Muslims. Furthermore, beginning with the sixteenth century, a new missionary strategy emerged from Protestants, most of whom saw Mary not as an asset but an obstacle that prevented Muslims from accepting "true Christianity"—meaning a religion focused on Christ and the Bible, not on saints or empty works. Protestant missionaries' use, or more accurately their rejection, of Mary will be discussed in this chapter as well.

This chapter will highlight key moments in history when Christians proffered Mary to Muslims as a bridge to conversion. I say "proffered," because while they have often *put forth* Mary, believing her to be an effective instrument of mission, in reality she has not produced very many conversions at all. Many Muslims do love Mary, but not to the extent that they have decided to become Christian. It seems that honoring the Islamic Maryam—even going to Christian shrines to do so—has been sufficient. Most Muslims have seen no reason to convert.

In this chapter, we will consider how Christians through history have imagined Mary as a tool for mission—or in the case of some Protestants, explicitly rejected her as such. Sometimes she is depicted as converting Muslims through attraction (miracles, visions), but at other times she appears to convert through force (military conquest). Sometimes Mary is a conduit of divine intervention (like the lactating icon responding to the Moor's prayer in *cantiga* 46), while at other times, she is a tool in the hands of Catholic missionaries who employ enticing images or stories of her. And in the case of nineteenth-century American Presbyterians missionizing in Egypt, Mary is used to lure Muslims away from Catholicism and Orthodoxy and toward Protestantism. We will begin with medieval miracle stories from the *Cantigas de Santa Maria* that connect Marian devotion, Muslims, and conversion. This will be followed by medieval pilgrim accounts of shared Marian shrines in the Holy Land—the existence of which have often inspired Christian hope for Muslim conversion. The next part of the chapter will describe seventeenth-century Jesuit missionaries in Mughal India who used novel illustrations and stories of Mary in their proselytism. The chapter will end with a comparison of Catholic and Protestant missionaries in nineteenth-century North Africa: Catholics (White Fathers) used Mary as a tool for mission, while Protestants explicitly rejected her as an obstacle to Christ-centered, Bible-based Christianity. (The recent surge of interest in Mary by some Protestants will be discussed in chapter 8.)

CANTIGAS AND CONVERSION

Written in Galician-Portuguese, and traditionally attributed to King Alfonso X, El Sabio ("the Wise"), the mid-thirteenth-century *Cantigas de Santa Maria* is an illustrated collection of songs praising the Virgin Mary for her intercession.[4] Relevant here are the many *cantigas* that highlight the devotion Iberian Muslims (called *mauros* [Moors] here) supposedly had for Mary. In some *cantigas*, Muslims are depicted as recognizing Mary's help in healing (167), fishing success (183), and defeating enemies (28). In others (28, 46, and 167), Muslims are shown converting to Christianity as a direct result of seeing Mary and recognizing her power.

For example, in both the text and illustrations of *cantiga* 46, we see the growing interest the Moorish protagonist has in Mary: first he takes a Marian icon as booty after warring against Christians, then he puts the image "in a high place" in his home (in this, he mimics the traditional Muslim treatment of the Qur'an, which would also be placed high up, out of respect). Then the Muslim rather furtively goes to gaze at the icon, wonders aloud about the truth of the incarnation, and finally kneels in adoration before the icon when it miraculously turns to flesh and begins lactating. The progression seen in *cantiga* 46's six illustrated panels implies a Muslim proclivity to Marian devotion. For the Iberian illustrator of the *Cantigas*, Mary is clearly a bridge.

Of course, the question is, what kind of bridge is she? If one examines all six panels of this *cantiga*, the Moor's devotion to Mary clearly does not lead to increased interfaith understanding. Rather, it shows her leading him to conversion: in panel 6, the Muslim is baptized, wife and child standing in the wings, waiting their turn at the font. If there were any doubt as to Mary's effect here, the narrative concludes thus: "He and all his followers became Christians, as well as many of his other acquaintances."[5] In *cantiga* 46, Mary is indeed a bridge…to conversion. And Marian devotion is the key to the conversion, because unlike troublesome doctrine (the Moor

Figure 3. A Muslim venerating an image of Mary. Cantiga 46, *Cantigas de Santa Maria*, 13th century, El Escorial Madrid MS T.I.1., folio 68v. Copyright © Patrimonio Nacional. Used with permission.

"simply could not believe that God would become flesh"), devotion smooths the way to acceptance of Christianity, as the Moor himself states: "If God would make one of His manifestations to me, he would cause me to become a Christian."[6] He promises that if God would show him a miracle, he would get over his doubts about Christology and convert. And as previously noted, God does indeed provide a miracle, in the form of a lactating icon. The Moor is so touched by this sight that he begins to weep, and immediately summons a priest. Panel 5 is a split panel; the Marian icon on the right lactates in sync with the Muslim's wife on the left, who is shown breastfeeding her child. The image of the Moorish mother and child also resembles typical Christian depictions of Madonna and child; this idea is repeated in another *cantiga*, 205, where Christians pray that a Moorish woman and her child would be saved from a falling tower, simply because "she looked to them like Mary and Jesus... they and all the other Christians who saw her felt pity and raised their hands to God to save them from death, even though they were pagans."[7] Also, in *cantiga* 205, just like 46, the Muslims convert. Clearly, Iberian Christians were aware of the similarities between Islamic and Christian Mariology, and believed that Mary could attract Muslims to Christianity.

Cantiga 28 presents another Muslim conversion via Mary; here, she uses her mantle to protect the Christian city of Constantinople against early Muslim incursions. According to the text, when the sultan looks to heaven to "pray to Muhammad" for victory, he sees a vision of Mary instead, and is so moved that he converts to Christianity (in secret, however). Thus, *cantiga* 28 is a story of protection by, vision of, and conversion through Mary—all acknowledged by the leader of the Muslim invaders, no less.

Other cantigas affirm the idea that Mary has the power to protect anyone who believes in her—even "infidels." *Cantiga* 183 is a case in point. Like 46, *cantiga* 183 is also about Christians, Muslims, and Marian devotion, but its conclusion is different. Here, the Moors of Faro (a coastal city in southern Portugal) are seen throwing the town's statue of Mary into the sea. The *cantiga* notes that the statue had been placed on the shore by Christians long ago, but now Muslims ruled the town. The Moors resented the statue and threw her into the sea with "great scorn." Why the resentment? Was it because they were offended by the very existence of the image, proof of Christian idolatry? Or was it because they acknowledged Mary's power to intercede for Christians, and hoped to destroy that power? It is only after the Muslims are no longer able to catch any fish (panel 3) that they suspect Mary's intercession might protect not only Christian interests but perhaps even their own. And so the Muslims, possibly with the help of their Christian neighbors (panel 4 is unclear), retrieve the Marian statue from the sea. What is interesting is that the Moors place the image in a more exalted place than it was before: earlier it was on the shore, but now they put it up on the city's walls (panel 5). In panel 6, the Muslims are shown catching abundant fish, clearly thanks to the restored Virgin. According to the *Cantigas*, it appears that the Moors of Faro threw the Marian image into the sea and then retrieved it, not because they considered devotion to her idolatrous, but because they recognized her intercessory power. This story has some parallels to the medieval myth of Jewish host desecration, where Christians claimed that Jews (whom they blamed for the death of Christ) stole consecrated hosts from churches, and then stabbed the hosts with knives. Obviously, to steal and stab hosts would imply that Jews believe in the doctrine of transubstantiation (which they do not). Likewise, for Muslims to throw a Marian icon into the sea and then retrieve it would seem to demonstrate a belief in her intercessory power (which Islam condemns, at least in theory). Both stories are cases of wishful thinking: where medieval Christians imagined Jews and Muslims to be more sympathetic to Christian doctrine than they really were.

What is also interesting about *cantiga* 183 when compared to others (28, 46, 167) is that at the end of the story, the Muslims of Faro appear to remain Muslims, even after the Marian miracle; no conversion to Christianity is depicted here. Nor are the Muslims shown as defeated in any way, as opposed to *cantiga* 99, where a group of marauding Muslims are thwarted by Mary in their attempt to destroy a church and its icons. Rather, it seems that 183 portrays Mary as the patron saint of the town of Faro—a patron shared by both Christian and Muslim residents. Might Mary be a true bridge here? After all, the narrator claims that the miracle story is shared; he says *both* "Moors and Christians told me the tale."[8]

The idea of Mary as a shared saint is repeated elsewhere in the *Cantigas*, for example in 181: "This is how Abouycaf was

Figure 4. The Muslims of Faro throw a statue of Mary into the sea. Cantiga 183, panel 2, *Cantigas de Santa Maria*, 13th century, El Escorial Madrid MS T.I.1, folio 242r. Copyright © Patrimonio Nacional. Used with permission.

routed in Marrakech by the banner of Holy Mary. The Virgin will aid those who love her, although they may be of another faith and disbelievers....Thus Holy Mary helped her friends, although they were of another faith, to defeat their enemies...in that way her mercy was made manifest to all."[9] These lines clearly state the possibility that Mary could intercede for non-Christians who are devoted to her. Panel 4 shows Christians and Muslims marching together under the Virgin's banner, and the text describes the first group of Muslims (under the Marian banner) defeating a second group of Muslims (without a banner).[10] Clearly, the source of the first Muslim group's victory is Mary. Iberian Muslims seem to think that her mercy is wide and available to all, even to "disbelievers."

Cantiga 181 shows that medieval Iberian Christians were aware that some Muslims had a devotion to Mary. Other *cantigas* demonstrate that Iberians knew concrete information about

Muslim Mariology, too. For example, *cantiga* 329 (which is unillustrated) acknowledges that Muslims revere Mary and believe in the virgin birth, and that the Qur'an contains verses about her.[11] Muslim Marian devotion is actually depicted in the illustrations of *cantiga* 165; one panel shows a group of Muslims in a church offering gifts to a Marian icon, while another panel shows a sultan opening the Qur'an and pointing to Sura 19 (Maryam).[12]

King Alfonso X, who authored or at least oversaw the creation of the *Cantigas*, not only influenced its content but also its use. Alfonso's will stipulated that the *Cantigas* were to be sung in the Seville cathedral for all Marian feasts, which was done until the sixteenth century.[13] The location of the performance of the *Cantigas* is important not only because the cathedral is a former mosque now dedicated to Mary, but also because the city of Seville maintained an interreligious population even after the expulsion of Jews and Muslims at the end of the fifteenth century, and well into the sixteenth century.[14] The hybrid nature of the society in which the *Cantigas* were created (thirteenth-century Reconquista Iberia) and of the place in which they were later sung (a mosque-turned-church, with a multifaith audience) should not be neglected when considering the different kinds of Christian-Muslim relations depicted therein.[15] Most stories had a proselytizing bent, but as we have seen, a few acknowledged that the Muslim reverence for Mary did not always lead to conversion.

PILGRIMS, SHARED SHRINES, AND CONVERSION

Medieval accounts of shared Marian devotion are not only found in the *cantigas*, but also in pilgrim itineraries, both Christian and Muslim. Some of the oldest and most popular shared shrines in the Holy Land for which we have accounts include Saydnaya in Syria and the House of Mary in Jerusalem. In their writings, pilgrims describe seeing Christians, Muslims, and even Jews gathering at Marian shrines to pray together. Once again, Mary is seen as a bridge between religions—in this case, a bridge to shared devotional rapprochement.

One of the earliest Latin descriptions of shared Marian devotion can be found in the 1175 *Itinerarium* of Burchard of Strasbourg.[16] Burchard describes two shared Marian shrines he visited during his travels: Matariya near Cairo, and Saydnaya near Damascus. He says of Saydnaya, "During the feast of the Assumption of the Virgin and the feast of her birth, all the Saracens of this province come to this place, together with the Christians, to pray. And the Saracens offer their ceremonies with great devotion."[17] Our Lady of Saydnaya became known in medieval Europe as Our Lady of Sardonay, in part thanks to the Knights Templar, who popularized devotion to her.[18] Her cult is mentioned in *cantiga* 9, which describes the Sardonay icon as having flesh and oozing oil. In this detail, *cantiga* 9 matches Burchard, who makes the same claim:

> In this church...I saw a wooden panel...a likeness of the Blessed Virgin...now wondrous to relate, the picture on the wood has become incarnate, and oil, smelling sweeter than balsam, unceasingly flows from it, by which oil many Christians, Saracens, and Jews, are often cured of ailments.[19]

The miracle of Sardonay's icon turning to flesh and oozing oil also mimics the miracle in *cantiga* 46, where Mary's breasts became flesh and began to lactate.

Burchard's account of Saydnaya describes devotions common to Muslims, Christians, and Jews. Furthermore, these three religions share not only devotion to Mary, but also belief in her intercessory power, such that devotees are healed. But while the account describes both Jews and Muslims as visiting the Christian shrine, it seems that the Muslims were more devoted than the Jews, since Burchard specifically notes that only Muslims came on Marian feast days like the Assumption and Nativity of Mary, and that these Muslims were very reverent when performing their devotions.[20]

Shared shrines elsewhere in the Holy Land are mentioned by other medieval Christian pilgrims, including the Florentine Dominican Riccoldo da Montecroce (d. 1320) and the German Dominican Felix Fabri (fl. 1480s). The shrines in question are the House of Mary and the Tomb of Mary, both in Jerusalem. Like Burchard, both Riccoldo and Felix are impressed by the great devotion Muslims have for Mary. Riccoldo observes, "We entered the beautiful tomb of the Virgin which the Saracens have illuminated with many lamps and protect with great reverence."[21] His description here is short but telling; he calls the shrine "beautiful" and notes, perhaps surprisingly, that the Muslims themselves have adorned the shrine by adding "many lamps." He also says that Muslims guard the tomb with "great reverence." These details suggest great Muslim investment in the tomb, if not actual ownership (it is unclear whether it was then a Muslim shrine or a Christian shrine under Muslim guardianship). It is also unclear whether Riccoldo visits two separate Marian locations in Jerusalem (house and tomb) or one.[22]

Felix also visits the House of the Virgin in Jerusalem: "We came to another place…where tradition says that the house of the blessed Virgin stood, in which she lived a domestic life for fourteen years….This place is remarkable for being held in great reverence both by all Christians and by many Saracens."[23] Felix knows that not all Muslims are devoted to Mary, for he explicitly states that "all Christians" venerate Mary, while only "many Saracens" do. However, Felix's account goes a step beyond description. He doesn't just record shared devotional practices like Burchard and Riccoldo. Rather, Felix ends with a theological prediction: the Muslim devotion to Mary will lead them to convert. He concludes this after hearing a story about the Franciscans asking the sultan for permission to build a chapel at the House of Mary (when Felix visited, he says there was only a single, unadorned wall at the site). After hearing that the sultan agreed to the Franciscan plan, Felix concludes that the sultan is assenting because "he is inclined to our faith."[24] Then Felix adds, "Nor do I doubt that were some sage, eloquent, and powerful Christian to direct toward him that prayer to which the venerable Master Nicholas of Cusa addresses him in [*Cribratio alkorani*],…he would turn himself to the better way. Christians ought to pray for [the sultan]."[25] Apparently, both German ecclesiastics, Felix and Nicholas, saw the Muslim devotion to Mary as "preparation for the gospel"—in other words, both were expressing an early "Christian theology of Islam."[26] But what's more, Felix also unwittingly describes a *Muslim* theology of Christianity here, one in which the Christian veneration of Mary is recognized as legitimate by Islam, such that Muslim leaders allow Marian shrines to be built, protected, and even adorned.

The House of Mary was also acknowledged by medieval Muslims as a pilgrim destination. In fact, not one but three places connected to Mary in Jerusalem were visited by Muslims in the Middle Ages: Mihrab Maryam, the Church of Mary, and the Tomb of Mary. It is unclear whether the Mihrab Maryam or the Tomb of Mary is the same place as the House of Mary described by Felix. Early Islamic tradition attests to the existence of Mihrab Maryam in Jerusalem, located at the southeast corner of Haram, just inside the Gate of Repentance, and scholars claim that this Muslim shrine was built at this spot due to an earlier Christian tradition.[27] The word *mihrab* has many meanings, including a prayer alcove; a private seclusion cell (perhaps referring to Mary's seclusion before the annunciation [Sura 3:37], or her confinement "in a remote place" while pregnant [Sura 19:22]); a mosque or place of worship; a shrine; a place where kings sit; and the *qibla* (direction of prayer in a mosque).[28] The second Marian site, the Church of Mary, also known as Kanisat Maryam, is described in seventh- and eighth-century Islamic sources as being regularly visited by Muslims, including the early caliphs Mu'awiya and 'Umar al-Khattab, both of whom were rumored to have prayed two *rak'ahs* (a *rak'ah* is one cycle of Islamic prayer movements) at this church.[29] Elad notes, "It was not unusual in the early period, and later as well, for Muslims to visit and pray in Christian churches in Jerusalem and elsewhere in the Muslim world."[30]

Yet documents from this same time also show evidence of intra-Islamic debates about whether it is acceptable for Muslims to enter and pray at the Church of Mary. Some scholars including al-Wasiti (c. 710) and Yazid (c. 770) forbade Muslims from entering Christian churches in general.[31] Yazid specifically mentions the Church of Mary in his prohibition: "Do not come to the Church of Mary, or approach the two pillars, for they are idols. Whoever goes to them, his prayers will be as naught. Cursed be the Christians for not seeing the things to come."[32] Another important legal scholar, Ibn Hanbal (d. 855), describes a variety of scholarly opinions on visiting churches, including one that allows it, one that forbids it, and another that distinguishes between praying in a church with images (not allowed) and praying in a church without images (allowed).[33] But despite these reservations, there were never any laws prohibiting Muslims from entering churches, and so ordinary believers continued to pray at the Church of Mary well into the fourteenth century, and beyond.[34]

The third Marian site in Jerusalem visited by medieval Muslims is the Tomb of Mary. This shrine is mentioned in a mid-sixteenth-century guide for Muslim pilgrims by Nasir al-Din Muhammad b. Khidr al-Rumi. Nasir describes the Tomb of Mary as follows: "The Muslim pilgrim leaves the Haram through the Gate of the Tribes arriving at the Tomb of Mary. He enters through the gate and descends the stairs within the church towards the tomb, which is in a small room."[35] Were medieval Muslim pilgrims visiting one or several different Christian churches dedicated to Mary, plus the exclusively Muslim shrine, Mihrab Maryam? Again, the sources are unclear as to how many Marian sites were being visited by medieval pilgrims to Jerusalem. What is clear is that Mary featured prominently in both Christian and Muslim itineraries.

As this section shows, not only are there multiple Christian shrines to Mary in the Holy Land (Saydnaya, House of Mary), but also at least one *Muslim* shrine to Mary (Mihrab Maryam). We know that Muslims have always visited the Christian shrines to Mary, but have Christians ever visited Muslim shrines to Mary? If not, why not?

For much of history, Christian pilgrims such as Felix Fabri witnessed the Muslim devotion to Mary and hoped that it might lead to their eventual conversion. Muslims witnessed the same devotion among their coreligionists, but they worried about it, as is evidenced by the Islamic scholars who explicitly forbade Muslims from visiting Christian churches—especially Marian churches, which were mentioned by name. Yet despite the warnings, ordinary Muslims continued to visit Marian shrines anyway, to the extent that some shrines were even recommended by Muslim guidebooks for pilgrims. Clearly, both sides saw the conversion potential inherent in the Muslim devotion to Mary. The Christians were pleased with the possibility, but Muslim leadership was not. Not only were they worried about Muslims converting to Christianity, but they were also concerned that Muslims might engage in heterodox practices such as praying to saints or venerating icons. Due to these dangers, mainstream Islam has almost always been suspicious of Marian devotion, even while it has been practiced by many grassroots believers (as already noted in chapters 2 and 3).

JESUIT MISSIONS AND MARY

The medieval *Cantigas* and pilgrim accounts showcase miraculous conversions; that is, they describe cases when devotion to Mary has led Muslims to the baptismal font, due not to human intervention but divine power. In this section, we will discuss more intentional uses of Mary as a tool for proselytism. In the sixteenth century, missionaries from new or reformed religious orders like the Jesuits, Capuchins, Discalced Carmelites, Mercedarians, and Trinitarians began targeting Muslims, joining Franciscans and Dominicans who had already been working as missionaries in the Middle East since the mid-thirteenth century.[36] This section will focus on writings by and about Jesuit missionaries, some of whom used Mary as a tool for mission among the Mughals in India. The fact that these Jesuits connected Mary, Muslims, and mission is not too surprising, given that their founder's autobiography includes the famous story of Ignatius trying to convince a Moor that Mary was a perpetual virgin. Yet some Reformers objected to how the Jesuits used Mary in their missionary efforts; for example, the Dutch Protestant Ludovico De Dieu wrote an extensive critique of the life of Christ written by the Jesuit Jerome Xavier for the Mughal context, which De Dieu said contained many errors about Christ and Mary.

Jesuit missionaries in India from 1580 to 1773 thought that the Mughals would be more open to conversion than the Ottomans.[37] Early on, they targeted Emperors Akbar and Jahangir, both of whom who sponsored interreligious discussions at court and seemed genuinely interested in learning about Christianity. The Jesuits had good reason to use Mary as a conversion tool, since both emperors possessed and even venerated icons of Jesus and Mary.[38] Akbar celebrated the Feast of the Assumption with the Jesuits in 1590 and wore a reliquary with an image of the Virgin on it.[39] Jahangir's desire for Christian pictures "became almost embarrassing," according to one Jesuit source, and his official seal featured an image of Mary and Jesus.[40] As noted in chapter 3, both emperors patronized a hybrid art studio that produced devotional images of Mary and Jesus for wider Muslim consumption, and both decorated their palaces with Christian iconography. Yet it is important to note that despite their interest in Marian images, Akbar and Jahangir wanted to learn about all religions, not just Christianity. In the end, neither converted. They both remained marginal Muslims at best; some have argued that they rejected orthodox Islam altogether.

The heterodox emperors were not the only Mughals who expressed interest in the Marian images offered by the Jesuits. According to an account by the Jesuit Fernam Guerriero, a Marian icon displayed at Christmas in 1602 attracted both rich and poor Muslim visitors; he claims that nearly ten thousand Muslims per day visited the icon, many of whom wept at the sight: "Truly, even to these infidels, the Virgin showed herself a mother of consolation, seeing how consoled, contrite and touched by the sight they were."[41] Guerriero goes on to say that the Jesuits took advantage of the chance to tell visitors about Mary; apparently, the Muslims "listened to it all, and took it very well, and showed a high opinion of our [Christian] faith."[42] Here we have a concrete example of the Jesuits using Mary as a tool for evangelization among ordinary Muslims. However, while many seem to have genuinely appreciated the Marian icon, there is little evidence that anyone converted, at least in Mughal India.[43] Jesuits in other locations, however, would have some success in using Mary as a tool for mission; for example, Baldassarre Loyola Mandes (d. 1667), a Muslim who converted to Christianity and became a Jesuit, used Mary in his own mission work among Muslim slaves in Genoa and Naples, and also spoke very explicitly about her influence on his own conversion.[44]

Yet a lack of converts did not stop the Jesuits, who continued to try many different methods of missionizing in India. In addition to promoting Marian icons, they also wrote apologetic texts expressly for the Mughal context, some of which focused on saint veneration in general and Mary in particular. For example, Jerome Xavier (d. 1617), the great-nephew of the famous Jesuit missionary St. Francis Xavier, wrote *The Truth-Revealing Mirror* (1597), which is styled as a dialogue among a Muslim, Christian, and philosopher, and includes a polemic against Islam and an apology for Christianity.[45] It also contains an entire chapter about venerating icons, including descriptions of the faces of Mary and other saints, which resemble the verbal descriptions of Muhammad's physical characteristics common in Islamic tradition.[46] Clearly, Xavier was attempting to show parallels between the Muslim veneration of Muhammad and the Christian veneration of Mary, and then to use this to entice Muslims to Christianity.[47]

Xavier wrote another book with a Marian emphasis: *The Mirror of Holiness* (*Mirat al Quds*, also known as *Dastan-i Masih* or *Deeds of the Messiah*), an illustrated life of Christ commissioned by Akbar himself.[48] This book, possibly the first biography of Christ written by a Christian at the behest of a Muslim, includes twenty-seven illustrations of Mary and Jesus.[49] The book's first section is entitled "On Christ's Infancy," but it could have been called "On Mary's Infancy," because there are more details about Mary's birth and childhood than Jesus'. Of twenty pages, ten are exclusively about Mary, and an additional three pages describe her postpartum virginity.[50] Included in this section are accounts of the annunciation to Anne, Mary's birth, her seclusion in the temple as a young girl, and her virginity (Xavier notes with painstaking detail that after giving birth, she "remained intact without any opening being made...without tearing anything").[51] Furthermore, the book contains numerous images of Mary; nine of its twenty-seven extant illustrations center on her, including "The Birth of Mary," "Mary Ascends the Steps of the Temple," "The Annunciation," "Mary and Joseph Travel to Bethlehem," "Simeon Kneels in front of Mary and Jesus," and "The Inn at Bethlehem." The last illustration is unusual in that it does not feature the typical nativity scene, but rather, it shows a pregnant Mary cleaning the stable before giving birth! The odd subject matter of this painting, created by a Muslim artist unfamiliar with traditional Christian iconography, nevertheless corresponds with Xavier's text: "Noticing the ruination and smallness of the stable...they swept out the place, cleaned it up, and put the chamber in order."[52]

Xavier's 1602 life of Christ, just like his earlier book *The Truth-Revealing Mirror*, also contains a long written description of the physicial and moral characteristics of Mary, taking up an entire column in the translated text. Here is an excerpt:

> Mary was a girl of middling height and olive complexion, with a long face. Her eyes were large and tending

Figure 5. The Inn at Bethlehem, *Mirat al-Quds* (Mirror of Holiness), Jerome Xavier, 17th century, inv. no. IS 170-1950. Copyright © Victoria and Albert Museum, London. Used with permission.

to blue. Her hair was of a golden color. Her hands and fingers were long and well-formed. In every feature she was well proportioned. Her speech was extremely soft. Her gaze was modest and unassuming. The words from her lips were humble and pure, but so much greatness and magnificence were apparent in her countenance that any distressed sinner who chanced to gaze at her face would pull himself together and become a different person in righteousness.[53]

Elsewhere in the text, Xavier says that anyone who gazed at her face would be converted. For him, Mary, even while alive, was a miraculous icon full of power and worthy of veneration. It seems that he included this section on Mary's appearance for two reasons. First, as noted earlier, he is consciously mimicking the Muslim tradition of *hilya* (describing Muhammad's physical characteristics) for his audience. But second, he seems to be capitalizing on the love Mughals had for Mary—in particular Akbar's, which was well known among the Jesuits.[54] A final observation is that Xavier's Mary, with her olive complexion, blond hair, and "eyes tending to blue" seems to be a physical hybridization combining European and Indian ideals of beauty. After all, this syncretic Mary had to appeal to both Iberian Christians like Xavier and Indian Muslims like Akbar.

But in his quest to capitalize on Akbar's love of Mary, Xavier might have taken things too far. In a few places, he "spins" the biography of Christ to appeal to his Muslim audience's Maria-philia. For example, at least twice Xavier modifies the words of the gospel to add mention of Mary. Quoting the prediction made to Simeon in Luke 2:26, Xavier adds "the Virgin" to it : "You shall see before your own eyes the Virgin and the Christ before you die." There is no mention of Mary in the original verse from Luke.[55] In another section of his life of Christ, Xavier makes what seems to be an even bolder change to the gospel by amending the resurrection story to say that the Virgin Mary was the first to see the risen Christ: "When he rose, the first person who saw him was Blessed Mary....When the mother apprehended her son, she took his foot and worshiped him as her God."[56] This is contrary to all four Gospel accounts, none of which name his mother as the first. (However, the idea that the Virgin Mary saw the risen Christ first can be found in a few early apocryphal texts, as well as in some medieval sermons, *vitae Christi*, and iconography, any of which Xavier might have relied upon to write his *Mirat al Quds*).[57] Finally, Xavier adds another detail that is not found in any Christian texts, biblical or extrabiblical: he claims that several important Marian feast days (including September 8, her birth, and November 21, her presentation in the temple) occurred on a Friday, which is the day Muslims attend communal prayer at the mosque.[58] Xavier's presentation of Christian Mariology to a Muslim audience seems reminiscent of what William of Tripoli did three centuries earlier: he "spins" scriptural Mariology for a particular audience, but in reverse. That is, William modified verses of the Qur'an to present a more positive Mariology to Christians, while Xavier modified verses of the Bible to present a more positive Mariology to Muslims.

Interestingly, the very same year Akbar received the completed life of Christ from Xavier (1602), he issued an imperial decree protecting Christian converts in his empire. Did Akbar see a connection between this book and its images, and conversion to Christianity? The Jesuits did, of course, since one of their main goals in writing this book was to convert the emperor. Why not use the book Akbar himself commissioned to help accomplish their goal? Xavier hoped his book would reach a wider audience, and it did, as it was used by Jesuit and non-Jesuit missionaries throughout the subcontinent.[59]

Protestants, however, were critical of Xavier's book and Jesuit missionary methods in general. A Latin translation of Xavier's text (along with the original Persian) was published by the Protestant Orientalist Ludovico De Dieu in 1639.[60] Subtitling the text *Contaminata*, De Dieu makes it clear what he thinks of Xavier's life of Christ. Furthermore, De Dieu's translation, which is over six hundred pages long, includes a one-hundred-page section at the end entitled "Animadversus," in which he takes issue with many aspects of Xavier's life of Christ, particularly its overemphasis on Mary, and its use of extrabiblical sources. In the preface, De Dieu claims that in their Mughal mission, "the Jesuits preach Mary more than Christ."[61] He is more critical of what Xavier has to say about Mary than anything else. Even though the section on Mary is just one-fourth of Xavier's book, De

Dieu's argument against it takes up half the "Animadvertus." He calls the establishment of Mary's birth as a feast day on September 8 (which Xavier describes in detail) an unacceptable innovation of the Roman Church. He disputes Xavier's claim that the presentation of Mary in the temple on November 21 was on a Friday, asserting that neither the date nor the day can be found in Scripture or even in extrabiblical sources such as the *Protevangelium of James* (which De Dieu criticizes as *mendacissimum*—exceedingly deceitful). De Dieu is so shocked with the liberties he believes Xavier has taken with Scripture that he interjects insults throughout: calling his book nonsense, accusing him of impiety, and even questioning his belief in God.[62] De Dieu ends his "Animadversus" with a condemnation of Xavier's Marian "idolatry."[63] As we have already seen with Postel and Luther in chapter 5, Catholic-Protestant arguments can often be found in books ostensibly about Christian-Muslim topics.

NINETEENTH-CENTURY MISSIONS IN NORTH AFRICA

Fast-forward a few centuries, and Mary reemerges as a tool for mission: this time in the burgeoning mission fields of nineteenth-century North Africa, which was attracting Catholics and Protestants alike. The famous American missionary Samuel Zwemer (d. 1952) asserted that the history of Christian mission to Muslims only began in the early nineteenth century with the Anglican Henry Martyn (d. 1812), whom Zwemer called "the first modern missionary to the Mohammedans,"[64] claiming a five-hundred-year "neglect" of mission to Muslims between Martyn and Ramon Llull (d. 1316).[65] Of course, both Catholics and Protestants had been working among Muslims continuously during these supposedly neglected centuries, although missionary activity did slow somewhat in Ottoman lands, where proselytism was illegal.[66] But in Zwemer's eyes, Martyn represented the dawn of a new missionary era, and his approach, which has been called "the first literary response to arise out of direct encounter with Muslims since the Jesuits at Akbar's court,"[67] coincided with other factors aiding

Christian missions at this time, such as expanding colonialism and the initiation of a concerted missionary movement in both Britain and the United States.[68]

The final part of this chapter will discuss the ramped-up efforts at mission to Muslims in the nineteenth century, focusing on Presbyterians in Egypt and Catholic White Fathers in North Africa. Mary was a key aspect in both Catholic and Protestant missionary strategies, but for opposite reasons. Naturally, the Mother of God played a positive role in the work of the White Fathers, whose patron saint Our Lady of Africa symbolized their aspirations for the entire continent. But she also played a role in the missionary strategy of some Protestants, such as the Presbyterians, albeit mostly a negative one.[69] Presbyterian missionaries in Egypt mentioned Mary in their missionizing only to argue against her, not only when they were evangelizing Muslims, but also Eastern Christians such as Copts and Armenians. Indeed, Eastern Christians—not Muslims—were the main focus of the Presbyterians' North African mission for much of the nineteenth century.[70] Again and again, the Presbyterian missionaries brought up Mariolatry as a prime example of bad religion, whether expressed in Orthodoxy or Islam, for they saw devotion to Mary and the saints as one of the main obstacles to the spread of "true Christianity."[71]

PROTESTANTS IN EGYPT: MARY, THE ANTITHESIS OF BIBLE CHRISTIANITY

As noted in chapter 5, Protestants had been equating the "empty rites" of Catholics and Muslims since the sixteenth century. Therefore it is not surprising that nineteenth-century Protestant missionaries in Egypt would likewise contrast their own religion, what they called "Bible Christianity," with what they saw as Catholic and Orthodox idolatry. Protestant missionaries considered Eastern Christians such as Copts and Armenians as much targets for mission as Muslims, not only because they believed Orthodoxy was corrupt, but also because they thought the errors of these local Christian groups might be preventing their Muslim neighbors from embracing true Christianity. The missionary W. A. Essery (d. 1905) stated as much: "These Oriental Churches are among the greatest obstacles to the conversion of their Mohammedan neighbors."[72] Most Protestant chroniclers describe Oriental Christians as "degraded forms of Christianity" and bastions of darkness longing for the true light of Christ.[73] And nearly all missionaries explicitly mention Mariolatry as one of the greatest sins of Oriental Christians.[74]

The Presbyterian minister Giulian Lansing wrote about Mariolatry, but was less polemical than others. In his 1864 book *Egypt's Princes*, he describes a dialogue between himself and Coptic Christians, in which he affirms that Mary is the mother of God and worthy of praise, but corrects the Coptic practice of seeking her intercession:

> While saying all this [praise] concerning her, we said nothing *to* her, that as she is in heaven and we on earth, she could not hear us, nor should we address her.... Therefore we never prayed to her nor sought her intercession, as we know that the Son was the only intercessor and mediator between God and man.[75]

Lansing tells his readers that the Coptic priest did not like what he said, but the simple people did. But unlike other Protestant missionaries who moved the focus quickly from Mary to Christ, Lansing stayed with Mary in order to appeal to the Coptic women: "I closed with an application to the women, telling them that Mary was a poor humble *fellaha* [peasant] such as they were, and that they too should strive to please God."[76] Most Protestant missionaries, however, totally condemned devotion to Mary and the saints and promoted Bible study instead; their ultimate goal was to convince Muslims that the Protestant focus on Scripture and denial of images made them more like Muslims than the Orthodox. Sometimes they succeeded too well in convincing locals of the evils of saint veneration. In one famous incident, a newly converted Protestant youth broke into a Coptic church in Assiut, Egypt (the city where the Presbyterian Mission was located), and single-handedly destroyed all the icons of Mary, Jesus, and other saints.[77]

There were, however, some Protestants who refused to see Mary as an obstacle in their outreach to Muslims. Samuel Crowther (d. 1891), the first native African bishop in the Anglican Church, worked among Christians and Muslims in Sierra Leone and Nigeria, where he sought common ground by highlighting shared figures like Mary, Jesus, and the Angel Gabriel, which he used to spark conversation, not debate. Crowther pioneered a Christian approach to Islam that was sensitive to the interreligious context of West Africa; his approach differed from other Protestant missionaries at the time, who often forced neophytes to make a choice between the Qur'an and the Bible. Crowther "avoided posing that choice. He began with acceptance of what the Qur'an said about Jesus, and founded the body of debate on that premise."[78] Crowther, like William of Tripoli and Nicholas of Cusa before him, saw qur'anic Christology and Mariology as useful bridges to dialogue and friendship, if not conversion.

Despite the reservations many Protestants had about Mary in the past, today some are using her as a tool for mission among Muslims. One recent and controversial idea among evangelicals is the so-called C.A.M.E.L. method, which is an acronym for the Christian teachings considered most amenable to would-be Muslim converts (two of the five relate to Mary): (1) Mary was *Chosen*, (2) the *Angel* Gabriel spoke to her, (3) *Miracles* were performed by Christ, who is the way to (4) *Eternal* (5) *Life*. One can see the affinities of this method to Nicholas of Cusa's *pia interpretatio* (reading the Qur'an in light of the Bible), in that both focus on similarities between the religions, not differences. However, the C.A.M.E.L. method has been criticized by other evangelicals as deceptive.[79]

THE WHITE FATHERS AND "OUR LADY OF AFRICA"

In many ways, the missionary approach of Cardinal Charles Lavigerie (d. 1892) mimicked that of Bishop Samuel Crowther's: both men lived in Africa (North and West, respectively), and understood that missionaries needed to adapt their evangelization strategies to specific cultural contexts. However, the Catholic Lavigerie was different from the Anglican Crowther in one key way: he put the Virgin Mary at the very center of his evangelization campaign.

Cardinal Lavigerie is best known for founding the Missionaries of Africa order (aka the White Fathers), and also for leading a worldwide antislavery campaign in the 1880s.[80] A native of France, he was appointed archbishop of Algiers in 1868, after having learned Arabic while serving in Lebanon and Syria. Lavigerie was convinced that his North African mission could only succeed if the following principles were followed: language study, medical care, catechesis, and evangelization by Africans themselves. In this, Lavigerie was an early proponent of enculturation, warning his missionaries to "Christianize, not Europeanize." He said, "In North Africa they must accept the externals in the people's way of life in order to win over their hearts....The perfect approach for these Latin missionaries in the East therefore will consist in their becoming Orientals themselves, adopting the dress, language and liturgy of the Oriental clergy."[81] These principles earned Lavigerie respect as "the most outstanding Catholic missionary strategist of the nineteenth century."[82]

Lavigerie was also devoted to the Blessed Mother, and this devotion was evident in many aspects of the two orders he founded, not only the White Fathers, but also the White Sisters, whose full title is "Missionary Sisters of Our Lady of Africa." The habit for both orders consisted of two key elements: a large rosary and an Algerian white cloak (from which they get the nicknames White Fathers/Sisters). Lavigerie wanted his missionaries to adapt their clothing to the local situation as much as possible, but he was adamant about wearing the rosary: "With regard to their habit, they are free to modify the one they wear in Algiers...but I do not want them to leave off the Rosary, which is the protective shield of our little Society."[83] In this outfit, therefore, we can see the order's attempt both to enculturate (Algerian white cloak) yet remain distinct (French Catholic rosary).

Lavigerie considered Mary, in the form of Our Lady of Africa, the patron saint of his order, not only for protection (which they needed, since twenty-three out of fifty-one missionaries were violently killed between 1878 and 1888), but also for overall success.[84] Indeed, Lavigerie attributed all the order's achievements to the Virgin Mary. In a circular letter sent to all White Fathers in 1876, he wrote, "We have never been able to do any good except through the intercession and special protection of Our Blessed Lady....The Missionaries of Algiers will never accomplish anything except with her help."[85] In Lavigerie's eyes, Our Lady of Africa was a powerful tool for mission, and he required his missionaries to pray daily to her. In this, Lavigerie agreed with the pope at that time, Leo XIII, who likewise linked Marian devotion and mission: "It is mainly to expand the kingdom of Christ that we look to the Rosary for the most effective help."[86]

Cardinal Lavigerie also consecrated his basilica in Algiers to Our Lady of Africa in 1872, although her cult in that city was founded decades earlier by some French priests and two laywomen, Agarithe Berger and Anna Cinquin.[87] The basilica, which had formerly been a mosque, was converted into a church in 1832.[88] The previous bishop of Algiers, Louis Pavy, OMI, created a shrine to Our Lady of Africa there in 1854, the same year the dogma of the immaculate conception was promulgated. Pavy noted that within just a few years, local Muslims were flocking to the Marian shrine.[89] Perhaps this experience made Pavy consider Mary as a potential tool for mission among Muslims, for in 1858, he established a prayer group with the express goal of converting Muslims; by 1863, his group had sixty thousand Christian members across Europe praying daily to convert Muslims, and their prayer ended with these words: "Our Lady of Africa, pray for us and for the Muslims."[90] This is the very same Marian prayer Lavigerie asked all his missionaries to recite daily.[91]

CONCLUSION

As this chapter has shown, Christians have long considered Mary a tool for mission to Muslims, from thirteenth-century Iberia, to seventeenth-century India, to nineteenth-century North Africa. Lactating icons of Mary miraculously swayed the hearts of Moors in the *Cantigas de Santa Maria*, while Jesuits in India encouraged the Mughals' Marian devotion through art and books. Catholic missionaries in North Africa prayed to Mary for success, while Protestant missionaries encouraged would-be converts to reject Mary and embrace Christ and the Bible instead.

Yet despite the deep desire of both Catholics and Protestants to convert Muslims—either with or without Mary's help—none of the missionaries ever gained more than a tiny number of converts.[92] Here is just a small sampling of Protestant records from

Egypt: in 1900 there were 6 Muslim converts to Christianity; in 1901, 6; in 1902, 8; in 1903, 14; in 1904, 12; and most of these converts were not from Islam, but from Coptic Christianity.[93] Catholics did not fare much better among the Muslims of North Africa: while Lavigerie had baptized survivors of an 1867 famine and settled them in several Christian towns in Algeria, by 1906 there were still only 360 Christians in 36 families.[94] Even the missionaries themselves acknowledge the difficulty of their work among Muslims: for example, the seventeenth-century Jesuit Nicolo Pallavicino remarked, "The conversion of a Turk is almost impossible."[95]

Clearly, Mary has not been the effective tool some Christian missionaries imagined her to be. Yet, conversions have sometimes happened, but of an unexpected kind. For indeed, both the proselytizers and the proselytized would change due to their encounters with each other, but rarely by switching religious affiliation.[96] Rather, it has often been the case that Christian missionaries themselves, thanks to direct and sustained exposure to Muslim people, the Qur'an, and Islamic languages such as Arabic, Persian, and Urdu have been "converted"—not into Muslims, but into linguists, scholars of Islam, and advocates for interfaith dialogue. Indeed, many prominent Protestant missionaries working in North Africa went on to become great scholars of Islam. One of the best examples is Samuel Zwemer, "the apostle to the Muslims," who later taught at Princeton Theological Seminary and founded the academic journal *Muslim World*. On the Catholic side, White Fathers Robert Caspar and Joseph Cuoq, scholars and missionaries both, were among the key framers of *Nostra Aetate*; a few decades later, the White Father Michael Fitzgerald would serve as the head of the Pontifical Council for Interreligious Dialogue. Sometimes, what started out as a "bridge to conversion" became a "bridge to dialogue and friendship," after Christians and Muslims actually encountered each other in the flesh.

The Virgin Mary continues to bring ordinary Christians and Muslims together, even in former mission lands. The shrine of Our Lady of Africa in Algiers, originally built for Catholics, has drawn Muslim visitors since the beginning, and today receives about forty thousand visitors per year, of which 95 percent are non-Christian.[97] The prayer used by Pavy and Lavigerie, both of whom sought to convert Muslims, is written inside the apse of the shrine: "Our Lady of Africa, pray for us and for the Muslims." The goal of this prayer can be interpreted in a variety of ways: conversion, dialogue, friendship?[98] Perhaps all of the above.

Chapter 7

MERYEM ANA EVI, POPULAR DEVOTION, AND VATICAN II

I have seen [Muslim devotion to Mary] with my own eyes in the city of Ephesus, in a place called Panaga Kapulu, namely the "House of Mary"—*our* lady Mary. Here for ten years, we have seen 100,000 Muslims annually and the same number of Christians... venerate together the Virgin Mary, the mother of Jesus!...If a heavenly dialogue has happily already begun with the Blessed Virgin Mary and Muslims, why would we not express hope for an earthly dialogue with them?[1]

> —Archbishop Joseph Descuffi, CM, of Turkey at Vatican II Council, September 29, 1964

There is a site near Ephesus which a venerable tradition holds to be the "Home of Mary," the place where the Mother of Jesus lived for some years. It is now a place of devotion for innumerable pilgrims from

---

A different version of this chapter was published as "Meryem Ana Evi, Marian Devotion, and the Making of *Nostra aetate* 3," *Catholic Historical Review* 103, no. 4 (Autumn 2017): 755–81. Used with permission.

all over the world, not only for Christians, but also for Muslims.

—Pope Francis at Turkey's Presidential Palace,
November 28, 2014

What is so special about the House of Mary (Meryem Ana Evi in Turkish) that it was mentioned at the Second Vatican Council in 1964 and again by Pope Francis fifty years later? Actually, several other popes besides Francis (Leo XIII, Pius X, Pius XII) have referenced this Marian shrine near Selçuk (Ephesus), Turkey, which is popular among both Christians and Muslims. Other popes have also visited (Paul VI, John Paul II, Benedict XVI).[2] And not one but three Vatican II Council fathers mentioned it while debating a draft of the document *Nostra Aetate* on September 29, 1964. The bishops who spoke that day listed several places with Marian shrines shared by Christians and Muslims, including India, Pakistan, Mozambique, Egypt, Iran, and Turkey,[3] but Meryem Ana Evi is the only site named by all three.[4] Soon after these speeches, the next draft of *Nostra Aetate* was expanded to include this line: "They [Muslims] honor Mary, his virgin mother; at times they even call on her with devotion." The fact that ordinary Christians and Muslims throughout the world travel to and pray at Marian shrines seems to have impressed popes and Council fathers alike, which in turn has influenced the Catholic Church's official view of Islam, as well as grassroots interfaith dialogue.

Meryem Ana Evi (referred to by the Council fathers as *Panaga Kapulu*, "Doorway to the All Holy") is now visited by nearly one million people a year. Some visitors are tourists, but many are pilgrims, mostly Christians and Muslims who come to honor the Virgin and ask her to intercede on their behalf. While Christianity and Islam disagree about Mary's precise identity vis-à-vis Jesus, they do agree that she is a virtuous virgin favored by God. And just as different Christian denominations disagree about Mary, so too do different Muslims disagree about who Mary is, or whether she—or any other saint (*wali*, "friend of God") for that matter—could intercede on someone's behalf. For example, while it is common for South

122

Asian Muslims to visit shrines associated with different martyrs, Sufi masters, or saints like Mary, this practice is condemned by other Muslims, who say it encourages praying to people rather than to God, which is considered *shirk* (associating partners with God), one of the greatest sins in Islam. In fact, the same Muslims who are critical of Marian shrines might also take issue with the line in *Nostra Aetate* that suggests that Muslims "call on Mary," saying that true Muslims invoke no one but God.

Despite these concerns, hundreds of thousands of Muslims do visit the House of Mary every year. Some Turkish Muslims even go so far as to say that three visits to Meryem Ana Evi are equivalent to the *hajj* (pilgrimage to Mecca).[5] What is so attractive about this site? Many pilgrims are Muslim and Christian women who come with petitions related to childbearing. They light candles in the shrine, drink holy water from the spring, and attach strips of cloth with prayers to a nearby prayer wall. The shrine itself reflects the dual identity of Mary's devotees: one room is decidedly Christian, complete with an altar, statue of Mary, icons, candles, and sanctuary lamps, while an adjacent room is adorned more simply, with verses from Sura 19 (Maryam) of the Qur'an.

The devotion shared by ordinary Christians and Muslims at Ephesus and at other shrines around the world captured the imagination of Council fathers as they deliberated *Nostra Aetate* in 1964. At the time, Catholics were beginning to see the Virgin Mary more as a bridge than a barrier, but Catholics disagreed about what kind of bridge. There were two possibilities (not necessarily mutually exclusive): was she a bridge to conversion, or a bridge to dialogue and friendship? The first idea, that Mary could be a one-way bridge to conversion from Islam to Christianity, has a long pedigree in the Christian tradition, as chapter 6 has shown. This idea remained strong in the 1950s, the "Marian decade," during which the Virgin was implored in Catholic efforts to convert all manner of infidels, from Muslims to communists. Perhaps the best expression of the "Mary as bridge to conversion" idea can be found in the writings of the popular media personality Bishop Fulton Sheen, who devoted an entire chapter of his 1952 book, *The World's First Love*, to the topic "Mary and the Moslems."[6] The belief that Mary could help convert Muslims to Christianity endures even today among some traditionalist Catholics.[7]

The second idea, that Mary could be a two-way bridge to dialogue and friendship, was also expressed during the fifties, in particular by the French Catholic Islamicist Louis Massignon and his students, two of whom were among the framers of *Nostra Aetate*: the Dominican Georges Anawati, and the White Father Robert Caspar. Given the longer pedigree of the "Mary as bridge to conversion" idea, it might seem surprising that "Mary as a bridge to dialogue" would be stressed more at Vatican II. Yet dialogue is indeed emphasized by *Nostra Aetate*, including the line about Marian devotion, which is featured in a list of commonalities between Islam and Christianity. There is no mention of conversion in this document.[8]

This chapter centers on the years leading up to *Nostra Aetate* ("On the Relation of the Church to Non-Christian Religions"), the text that articulates the first official Catholic teaching on Islam at the highest level of church authority—an ecumenical council. First, the preconciliar context will be discussed, particularly regarding two groups writing about Mary and Islam during the 1950s: those who saw her as a bridge to conversion (Bishop Fulton Sheen), and those who saw her as a bridge to dialogue (Louis Massignon and the framers of *Nostra Aetate*). The blossoming of the shared Marian shrine Meryem Ana Evi in the 1950s will also be described, along with its connections to *Nostra Aetate*. Finally, the development of *Nostra Aetate*'s theology of Islam as it pertains to Marian devotion will be considered.

One caveat: this chapter distinguishes between "bridge to conversion" and "bridge to dialogue" because each of the two groups mentioned above stressed one over the other in their writings. However, it is important to note that conversion (mission) and dialogue are related. In fact, the 1991 Vatican document *Dialogue and Proclamation* attempted to clarify the correct relationship between the two, especially among those who misread *Nostra Aetate* as replacing mission with dialogue. *Dialogue and Proclamation* states that the two are not in tension, but rather are "both authentic elements of the Church's evangelizing mission. Both are legitimate and necessary. They are intimately related, but not interchangeable."[9]

BEFORE THE COUNCIL

Catholics often refer to the 1950s as the "Marian decade."[10] It began with the November 1, 1950, proclamation of the dogma of the assumption of Mary, but the entire decade was marked by Marian devotional practices such as sodalities, rosaries, processions, novenas, scapulars, shrines, and May crownings. Some of these rituals had already been popular for decades or even centuries, but they reached a zenith in the mid-twentieth century. Pope Pius XII (d. 1958) observed that "piety toward the Virgin Mother of God is flourishing and daily growing more fervent."[11] In fact, Pius claimed that it was the vitality of grassroots Marian devotion that moved him to write a letter to the world's bishops, asking them to confirm the *sensus fidelium* regarding Mary's assumption.[12]

Mary was not only at the center of this decade, but also in the forefront of the mind of Pius, whom some have called "the most Marian pope in Church history."[13] During his tenure, not only did he issue several Mary-centric encyclicals, but he also declared 1954 a "Marian Year" to mark the one-hundredth anniversary of the dogma of the immaculate conception.[14] The year was filled with special prayers, papal radio messages, pilgrimages, and an encyclical instituting yet another Marian feast day, the Queenship of Mary.[15] Furthermore, during this year, Catholics were encouraged to visit local and international Marian shrines such as Lourdes, and to seek Mary's intercession on behalf of persecuted Christians in communist countries.[16] Mary was once again seen as a weapon against a powerful non-Christian enemy.[17] In the past, that enemy was Islam; in the 1950s, the enemy was communism.[18]

Also during the Marian year, Pius XII did two things to demonstrate his recognition of the special connection between Christians, Muslims, and Mary. First, in a *L'Osservatore Romano* article, he explicitly referred to the House of Mary in Turkey as a pilgrimage site shared by Christians and Muslims: "The holy House should be a Marian center which is unique throughout the world, a place where Christians and Moslems of all rites and denominations and of all nationalities can meet each other to venerate the Mother of Jesus, and make true the prophecy, 'All generations will call me blessed.'"[19] Second, he commissioned a mosaic of Pius V (d. 1572), the pope who instituted the Feast of Our Lady of Victory after Lepanto. The mosaic, which was installed in 1954 at the Church of St. Pius V in Rome, features the Virgin Mary and Pius V holding a rosary in the foreground, and sinking Turkish ships at the Battle of Lepanto in the background. These two acts of Pius XII during the Marian year are noteworthy for capturing the tension between the ways Christians, Muslims, and Mary have related throughout history: is Mary a barrier (as highlighted by his commissioning of the Lepanto mosaic), or is she a bridge to either conversion or dialogue (as highlighted by his recognition of Meryem Ana Evi)? Does Pius contradict himself, or is he accurately expressing the paradox inherent in Catholic doctrine on this subject?

With the overall Marian context of the 1950s clear, we can now turn to the two champions of the idea of Mary as bridge at this time: Mary as bridge to conversion (Bishop Fulton Sheen) and Mary as bridge to dialogue (Louis Massignon).

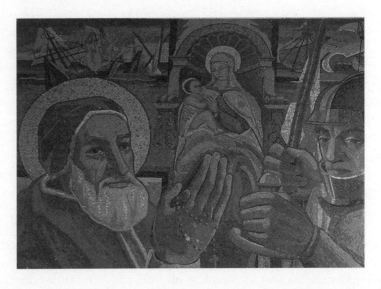

Figure 6. Mosaic of Pius V, Mary, and Lepanto, by Joseph Strochata, 1954. Chiesa di Papa Pio V, Rome. Photo courtesy of David Collins, SJ.

FULTON SHEEN: MARY AS BRIDGE TO CONVERSION

The idea of Mary as a one-way bridge to conversion is not new, as chapter 6 has shown. This old idea is given new life in the mid-twentieth century by the popular American Catholic media personality Fulton Sheen (d. 1979). His 1952 book, *The World's First Love: Mary, Mother of God*, includes a chapter on Mary's potentially powerful role as an evangelizer of Muslims. In it, Sheen encourages Christian missionaries to foster Marian devotion among Muslims, for the express purpose of converting them:

> It is our firm belief that Moslemism [*sic*] will eventually be converted to Christianity—and in a way that even some of our missionaries never suspect. It is our belief that this will happen not through the direct teaching of Christianity, but through a summoning of the Moslems to a veneration of the Mother of God....Because the Moslems have a devotion to Mary, our missionaries should be satisfied to expand and to develop that devotion, with the full realization that Our Blessed Lady will carry the Moslems the rest of the way to her Divine Son.[20]

In this passage, Sheen is describing a reality most Catholic missionaries in Asia and Africa already knew: that many ordinary Muslims revere Mary. Sheen was simply asking the missionaries to harness this devotion as a tool for mission. He believed that the Muslim devotion to Mary could be used as a stepping-stone to their conversion. This type of missionizing might be criticized as disingenuous today.

The fact that Sheen wrote an entire chapter about mission, Muslims, and Mary is not surprising given his evangelizing bent. For in addition to his popular TV and radio shows, Sheen was national director for the American Society of the Propagation of the Faith from 1950 to 1966. In 1951, he created a "World Mission Rosary," with sections color coded according to the continents: yellow is Asia; white is Europe; red is the Americas; blue is Oceania; and green is Africa. Sheen said that green represented Africa for two reasons: first because of its forests, but second because green is the color of Islam, the special target of missionaries on that continent. Sheen had personally visited Kenyan and South African missions in 1960, and perhaps it was then that he first saw shared shrines to Mary, or at least heard about them from locals.[21] Such shrines were not only present in Africa; Sheen soon learned from missionaries in India, Nepal, and Pakistan that some Asian Muslims (and Hindus) also have a devotion to Mary. In a different chapter of the same book, *World's First Love*, Sheen shares the following account:

> Our missionaries report the most extraordinary reaction of these peoples as the Pilgrim statue of Our Lady of Fatima was carried through the East. At the edge of Nepal, three hundred Catholics were joined by three thousand Hindus and Moslems, as four elephants carried the statue to the little Church for Rosary and Benediction....At Karachi an exception was made by the Moslems to favor her; whenever the Christians there hold a procession, they are obliged to cease praying whenever they pass a mosque. But on this occasion they were permitted by the Moslems to pray before any mosque along their way.[22]

Clearly, the evangelization strategy Sheen was suggesting—using Mary as a tool for mission among Muslims—was influenced by knowledge of lived religion that was shared with him by his missionaries throughout the world.

But Sheen's use of Mary as a mission tool was not unique to him; rather, it was representative of broader Catholic views at the time. During the 1950s, Mary was seen as a weapon against all the "godless," be they Muslims or communists. In fact, Sheen wrote a 1951 article about the twin communist-Muslim threat, expressing concern that "Communism and Moslemism may unite against Christianity."[23] But eventually, Sheen came to believe that certain Islamic doctrines (e.g., monotheism, Virgin Mary) made Muslims less of a threat to Christians than communists, although Muslims still remained a target of his evangelizing efforts.[24] Indeed, Sheen came to believe that these common beliefs made Muslims better (meaning easier) candidates for conversion to Christianity than communists. In any case, Sheen's recognition of the Virgin as a key part of his mission strategy was thanks to his colleagues in the field, who shared with him their firsthand knowledge of Islam as a lived religion. If the missionaries had not told him about their experiences, Sheen most likely would never have known that Mary is revered by many African and Asian Muslims.

LOUIS MASSIGNON: MARY AS BRIDGE TO DIALOGUE

At the same time the American bishop Fulton Sheen was writing about Mary as a tool for mission, the French scholar Louis Massignon was presenting a somewhat different image of her as a bridge to dialogue and friendship. Massignon was an Islamicist whose encounter with Muslims had had a profound effect on his own spiritual life.[25] As a young man traveling in the Middle East, his personal interactions with Muslims and his study of Islam impressed him so deeply that he had a conversion experience. But surprisingly, his conversion was not to Islam, but rather back to his own Catholic faith, from which he had strayed.[26] Massignon's encounter with Islam thoroughly revitalized his practice of Christianity, and he eventually became a priest of the Arabic-speaking Melkite Catholic Church. He also cofounded in 1934 (with the Egyptian Christian Mary Kahil) the Badaliya society, a group originally comprised of Arab Christians who wished to pray for and offer their lives as "substitutes" for Muslims (*badaliya* means "substitution" in Arabic). The language of Badaliya's founding documents is somewhat ambiguous but does suggest a hope for conversion.[27] But by the 1950s, Badaliya had become more genuinely interfaith; its members, which now included both Christians and Muslims, gathered regularly to pray, converse, and pilgrimage together.[28] Dialogue, not conversion, had become their main goal.

Massignon's personal faith journey also affected the direction of his scholarship. As the years went by, he focused more and more on "crossover" figures that he believed connected Islam and Christianity in some way. First among these was the subject of his dissertation: the Christlike Mansur al-Hallaj (d. 988), a Sufi mystic who was crucified. Other crossover figures included Fatima, the daughter of Muhammad, and the Seven Sleepers of Ephesus, whose story is found both in the Qur'an and in early Christian tradition. Later in his career, Massignon became increasingly fascinated by shared figures and their associated shrines (Our Lady of Fatima in Portugal, Shrine of the Seven Sleepers in France). By the 1950s and 1960s, the bulk of his scholarship centered on them.[29] It must be noted that many of the crossover figures so attractive to Massignon, like Fatima and Hallaj, were more important to minority Muslim communities such as Shi'i and Sufis than to Sunni Muslims, and therefore some of Massignon's ideas regarding these figures were considered marginal or suspect by mainstream Sunnis.

While Louis Massignon is still relatively unknown in the Anglophone world (most of his scholarship remains untranslated from the French), he had an enormous influence on the development of the Catholic theology of Islam in the twentieth century, especially as it is articulated in *Nostra Aetate*. Even though he died on October 31, 1962, just days after the Second Vatican Council opened, many scholars consider his influence to have been significant. Several of Massignon's colleagues and protégés were active participants at the Council, including bishops, *periti*, and even Pope Paul VI himself.[30] In fact, the two *periti* most responsible for writing *Nostra Aetate*'s section on Islam, Georges Anawati and Robert Caspar, had been Massignon's students, and both explicitly declared the Frenchman's direct influence on their own thinking.[31] Pope Paul VI, who promulgated *Nostra Aetate* in October 1965, had a long association with Massignon stretching back to the 1930s.[32]

While a few scholars have questioned the extent of his influence,[33] most have affirmed what Anawati, Caspar, and others have concluded: Louis Massignon had a singular effect not only on the Council, but also on twentieth-century Catholic views of Islam more broadly.[34] Andrew Unsworth calls the theology of Islam found in *Nostra Aetate* a "paradigm shift" in how the Catholic Church viewed Islam,[35] a shift that paralleled the evolution of Massignon's own views. While his earliest scholarship expressed the traditional Catholic theology of Islam (see, for example, in his 1914 article in the journal *Moslem World*), over the years his position changed dramatically such that it became quite distinct from the traditional view. By the end of his life, Massignon's novel ideas had not only been accepted by a small group of progressive Catholic scholars of Islam, but amazingly, by 1965, "the Council too had adopted his vision."[36]

What Massignonian language can be seen in Vatican II documents—not only *Nostra Aetate* 3, but also *Lumen Gentium* 16, which discusses the salvation of non-Catholics? According to Unsworth, the three most important Massignonian *theologoumena* found in these documents are that Muslims can achieve salvation; that Christians, Muslims, and Jews believe in the same God; and that Abraham is the common father of Judaism, Islam, and Christianity.[37] All three claims have become significant aspects of the developing Christian theology of Islam, although all have been contested at various times since Vatican II.[38] The third claim has been particularly influential, spreading far beyond Christian circles. In the last fifty years, it has become common parlance among scholars and laity to call Judaism, Islam, and Christianity the "Abrahamic faiths," and many books and articles have been written to support, challenge, and further nuance the term *Abrahamic*.[39] In any case, the idea of a shared spiritual (if not genetic) patrimony in Abraham most likely originates with Massignon, who was using the term as early as 1949.[40]

One additional Massignonian *theologoumenon* present in conciliar documents that Unsworth does not mention but that is equally significant to the development of a Christian theology of Islam can be found in the line that inspired this book: "They [Muslims] honor Mary, his virgin mother; at times they even call on her with devotion."[41] Given *Nostra Aetate*'s focus on commonalities, and Massignon's preference for crossover figures, it is not surprising that it would mention Mary, one of the most important shared saints between Christians and Muslims.[42] The mere presence of this line cannot, of course, be attributed solely or even mainly to Massignon. After all, Council fathers such as Maronite Patriarch Sfair and Archbishop Descuffi argued that the Virgin Mary should be mentioned in *Nostra Aetate* on doctrinal grounds.[43] However, the emphasis on *devotion* to Mary—rather than on *doctrines* about Mary—does suggest some Massignonian influence.[44] For in the 1940s and 1950s, Massignon wrote several articles highlighting the similarities between the Christian devotion to Mary and the Muslim devotion to both Fatima and Mary.[45]

In one of these articles, Massignon emphasized the parallels he saw between the Muslim devotion to Fatima, Muhammad's daughter, and the Catholic devotion to Mary, Jesus' mother. In 1955, Massignon wrote about a Shi'i festival, *Mubahala*, which is connected to Fatima. Massignon entitled the article "La Mubahala de Medine et L'Hyperdulie de Fatima."[46] The choice of the French word *hyperdulie* here is significant, because its Latin equivalent, *hyperdulia*, has traditionally been used by Catholics to refer to the special veneration reserved for the Virgin Mary. *Hyperdulia* is higher than *dulia* (standard veneration of saints), but less than *latria* (worship of God alone). By calling the Muslim devotion to Fatima *hyperdulie*, Massignon was implicitly connecting it to the special devotion Christians have for Mary. But the Mary-Fatima connection is not only implicit in the article title, for in the text itself Massignon explicitly states that Fatima and Mary are not only comparable but complementary: "Fatima consists of the human guarantee of divine inaccessibility; [she is the opposite of] Mary, the superhuman hostess of divine immanence."[47] He then goes on to contrast the divine fiat given to Mary at the Annunciation with a similar fiat given to Fatima on the "Night of Power" (*laylat al qadr*), the holiest night of Ramadan. In these few lines, Massignon suggests that Mary and Fatima are complementary. Was he attempting a synthesis between Islam and Christianity? If so, he would have gone even beyond comparative theology (which aims at gaining "fresh theological insights" by studying another tradition), a field that did not yet exist in the 1950s.[48]

Massignon also wrote two articles in 1956 that both explicitly connect the Muslim devotion to Maryam and Fatima to the Christian devotion to Mary. The first article, "La notion du voeu et la dévotion musulmane à Fâtima," focuses on the Shi'i Muslim devotion to Fatima, and the fact that some Shi'i Muslims (especially pregnant women) call on Fatima to intercede for them in the same way they call upon prophets, Sufi masters, or imams for assistance.[49] Once again, Massignon's article title is significant for its use of the word *devotion* to describe how some Muslims approach Fatima. It should be noted that in mainstream Islam, the only acceptable "devotion" is to God alone; the praise given to human beings such as prophets (even Muhammad) should be of a lesser order, if given at all. Intercession (*shafaʿa*) is generally discouraged, but nevertheless is still widespread at the popular level. Clearly, popular devotion to Fatima, Mary, and other saintly figures remains a contested point.[50]

Massignon's second article discusses Fatima's connection to the Al-Aqsa Mosque in Jerusalem.[51] Interestingly, he begins with a quote from Fulton Sheen: "Just as Esther was a 'figure of Mary' for Israel before the First Coming [of Christ], Fatima might be a 'figure of Mary' for Islam before the Second Coming."[52] Massignon elaborates on Sheen's idea in the third section of his article (entitled "Practical Devotions Dedicated to Mary and Fatima"), by noting that the Shi'i literature recommends both *ziyarat* (lesser pilgrimages) to shrines associated with Fatima, and prayers to her. He notes that Shi'i prayers describe Fatima using phrases reminiscent of those used by Christians for Mary such as "queen of women," "virgin mother," and "unpolluted."[53] One particular Shi'i prayer, observes Massignon, "is like the *Stabat Mater*."[54] He also claims that the Qur'an calls both women prophets, without mentioning that Muslims disagree on this point, with most denying it, as noted in chapter 3.[55] He concludes the article by saying unequivocally that "Fatima was, for the Shi'ites, a figure of Mary."[56] With statements like this, it's no wonder that some accuse Massignon of Orientalism.[57]

Nevertheless, Massignon's focus on shared Christian-Muslim devotion to Mary in the 1950s influenced the direction of his students' scholarship, as well as their activism. For it was during this same decade that one of Massignon's students, Archbishop Joseph Descuffi of Turkey, began promoting the shared shrine that was to be mentioned by several bishops at Vatican II: Meryem Ana Evi.

CREATING MERYEM ANA EVI

As noted at the beginning of the chapter, no less than seven popes have either visited or mentioned Meryem Ana Evi in the last century. Yet despite all this attention from twentieth- and twenty-first century pontiffs, were it not for two nineteenth-century religious women—the German mystic Anna Katharina Emmerick and the French nun Sr. Marie de Mandat-Grancey—it is doubtful that any popes or bishops would have known about the House of Mary, and thus the line on Marian devotion might not have made it into *Nostra Aetate* at all.

The establishment of Meryem Ana Evi began with a popular book from 1880, *The Life of the Blessed Virgin*, which recounts the private revelations of Anna Katharina Emmerick (d. 1824). One chapter includes a detailed description of the House of Mary in Ephesus, possibly the first modern reference to such a house in this city. After reading Emmerick's book, Sr. Marie de Mandat-Grancey (d. 1915), a Daughter of Charity stationed at a French Naval Hospital in Izmir, Turkey, convinced two local Lazarist priests to help her find the house, financing the expedition with her personal family fortune. They eventually found the house in 1891. The next year, Sr. Marie purchased the property in her own name (with the permission of her order), and went on to restore, develop, and promote the shrine after that.[58]

The foundations of the House of Mary were being laid at the very same time that Pope Leo XIII was promulgating his series of Marian encyclicals. As Leo stated repeatedly in these encyclicals, Catholics believed the Virgin would help Christians to defeat the Ottoman "menace," just as she had done at Lepanto in 1571. It is likely that the Vincentians stationed in Turkey at this time, including Mandat-Grancey and the Lazarists, shared Leo's vision. When these French Catholic missionaries founded the House of Mary, they probably never dreamed that Muslims would someday visit the shrine. However, from the start, the House of Mary was an ecumenical destination: Armenians, Catholics, Greek Orthodox, and Protestants came early on.[59] In fact, decades before Sr. Marie "rediscovered" the house, there had been a tradition of local Orthodox Christians (called Kirkindje, after their village) pilgrimaging there every Assumption Day (August 15).[60]

Initially, the Turkish government opposed the creation of the House of Mary.[61] They forbade Sr. Marie from building a church, school, or shrine at the site. But eventually a small shrine was built, only to be abandoned during the two World Wars. Then in the years immediately following World War II, interest in the House of Mary was revived. This was due to two factors: first, the Marian decade already discussed, and second, the nationalization of the site. In 1953, the government replaced the shrine's old Greek name with a Turkish one, *Meryem Ana Evi*. With the support of both the government and local church authorities like Archbishop Descuffi (also a Vincentian), the site developed rapidly. Another champion of the new shrine was Massignon himself. In 1952 in Paris, he founded the *Association des Amis d'Éphèse et d'Anne-Catherine Emmerick* and encouraged people to call the shrine "Our Lady of Ephesus."[62] With this moniker, Massignon wanted to emphasize the shrine's provenance in Ephesus, a city important to the history of Mariology: it was here that the Council of Ephesus (431 CE) defined Mary as *Theotokos* (God-bearer). Massignon also claimed that certain patristic theologians had identified Ephesus as the place of Mary's dormition.[63] Despite all these reasons, the choice of Ephesus as the location for a shared Christian-Muslim shrine remains somewhat ironic, since the Council of Ephesus's title for Mary, *Theotokos*, emphasizes the aspect of her identity about which Muslims and Christians most fundamentally disagree.

Given that one of the stated goals of Massignon's *Association des Amis d'Éphèse* was to "orient thoughts and pilgrimages towards the holy saints of Ephesus," it is likely that he also wanted to stress the name "Our Lady of Ephesus" because he hoped to connect Meryem Ana Evi to other Christian shrines in the area such as the sixth-century Basilica of St. John and the Cave of the Seven Sleepers. The story of the Seven Sleepers had become a major crossover point for Massignon, who wrote several articles about its importance to Christian-Muslim relations.[64] He was probably aware that archaeologists had recently discovered the ruins of a mid-fifth-century church under the Ephesian Cave of the Seven Sleepers; this church had been popular both as a pilgrimage destination (attested to by medieval Latin and Greek accounts), and as a burial site (attested to by the archaeological evidence).[65] Massignon seemed anxious for pilgrimages to return to Ephesus; he did this by stressing connections between all the Christian shrines in the region.[66]

In any case, because of their enthusiastic promotion of the House of Mary throughout the 1950s, Descuffi and Massignon have been called "entrepreneurs of pilgrimage."[67] Pope Pius XII even wrote Descuffi a letter in 1957, commending him for his work in developing the site.[68] His work paid off, for by the late 1950s, Christians were indeed flocking to Meryem Ana Evi, reportedly

Figure 7. Multilingual signage at the shrine of Meryem Ana Evi, Turkey. Photo courtesy of Flo Merkl-Deutsch.

as many as one hundred thousand a year.[69] It was also during this same decade that a "massive and spontaneous influx" of *Muslim* pilgrims began to visit the shrine, too.[70] Rome did not oppose them. In fact, Pope Pius XII explicitly declared the House of Mary "open to all people, even non-Christians, who have a special devotion to the Virgin Mary."[71] Perhaps Pius's invitation can be taken as evidence that he saw mission and dialogue as complementary—an idea in line with the 1991 document *Dialogue and Proclamation* discussed earlier.

The House of Mary rapidly evolved into a popular pilgrimage destination thanks to a complex mix of historical, theological, and political factors.[72] Popes such as John XXIII and Paul VI, who mourned the decimation of Christian communities in Turkey earlier in the century, surely welcomed the presence of a new Christian shrine in that country. Turkey's secularist government (*laiklik*) has also been influential; it encouraged the growth of the site in the 1950s, and today has officially sanctioned it as an *interfaith* destination by placing a multilingual placard out front. The placard, written in Turkish, English, French, and German, lists qur'anic verses associated with Mary so that all visitors, be they religious pilgrims or secular tourists, will know Mary's significance to Christians and Muslims.[73] Foreign policy considerations may have also played a role, plus the approbation of local ecclesiastical authorities such as Descuffi, and the compelling ideas of Louis Massignon.[74] Together, all these factors helped to create Meryem Ana Evi as an interfaith pilgrimage destination.

THE MAKING OF *NOSTRA AETATE* 3

The development of the House of Mary in the 1950s influenced the development of *Nostra Aetate* in the 1960s. The link between the shrine and the document can be seen when the *Acta Synodalia*, the official written records of the Second Vatican Council proceedings, are examined. At General Congregation 90, held September 28–29, 1964, the Council fathers deliberated the text that was to become *Nostra Aetate* (at this time, it was called *De Iudaeis et de non-Christianis*, "On the Jews and Non-Christians"); the September 1964 draft was the first to include a reference to Islam.[75] The reference is brief. After discussing Judaism at length, the draft goes on to affirm a few key elements of Islamic doctrine and practice:

> We also and above all embrace the Muslims, who worship one personal and recompensing God, and who come near to us in religious feeling and many aspects of human culture.[76]

This passage affirms that Muslims worship one God and rather vaguely acknowledges Muslim piety ("religious feeling"). Furthermore, the phrase "above all" suggests that in the eyes of the Church, Islam is closer to Christianity than any other religion (except

Judaism, which is discussed at much greater length). But nothing specific is said about shared beliefs or practices, and there is no mention of Christ, Mary, or devotion.

Two bishops from Muslim-majority countries, Sfair (Syria) and Descuffi (Turkey), responded to the draft at length, encouraging the addition of key theological points, including the qur'anic understanding of Christ as "Word and Spirit of God" (Sura 4:171), and the acknowledgment of Islam as an Abrahamic religion. But what is most pertinent to this book is that three bishops (Sfair, Descuffi, and Yves Plumey, OMI) mention shared Marian devotion as further proof of the affinity between Christianity and Islam—and all three of them name Meryem Ana Evi as a concrete example of this shared devotion.[77]

Yves Plumey, OMI, a French missionary stationed in Cameroon, was the first Council father that day to expand on doctrinal points related to Muslim Mariology: "The Muslims, more than all other non-Christians, understand the mystery of Christ. Heirs of Abraham, they fully recognize Jesus as first in holiness among the prophets, virginally born of the Blessed Virgin Mary, and Mary herself as the greatest daughter of Abraham. They fervently uphold both Mary's virginity and Jesus' virginal birth."[78] Plumey then goes on to describe Muslim devotional practices related to Mary:

> [Muslims] piously visit Marian sanctuaries, take part in processions honoring her, devoutly honor her images, often name their daughters after her, and implore her protection everywhere: these things are very frequently reported in India, Pakistan, Mozambique, Egypt, Iran, Turkey, and most especially in Ephesus, where the government kindly approves and allows the opportunity.[79]

Why does Plumey—a missionary living in Africa—mention a shrine in faraway Turkey? The connection appears to be Massignon, with whom Plumey, a fellow Frenchman and Breton, corresponded before the Council. Plumey wrote Massignon a letter dated August 10, 1962, because he was interested in learning more about the joint Christian-Muslim pilgrimage Massignon had founded at Vieux Marché in Brittany, and hoped to replicate it in Cameroon, where Plumey says Christian-Muslim relations were strained at the time.[80] Massignon replied to Plumey on September 2, 1962, a few weeks before the Council began. In that letter, Massignon manages to touch on every major crossover point, not only the Vieux Marché pilgrimage, but also the Seven Sleepers, Abrahamic faiths, interreligious hospitality, and the House of Mary.[81] Plumey was not a scholar of Islam, but as a missionary in Cameroon, a country with a significant Muslim population, he evidently cared greatly about local Christian-Muslim relations, and therefore it is not surprising that he was interested in learning more about rituals that might bring Christians and Muslims together in positive ways. After learning about the House of Mary from Massignon, it seems that Plumey began to see Mary as a possible bridge to dialogue and fraternity in Cameroon. This was the opposite of Sheen, who, though likewise influenced by the stories of missionaries on the ground, nevertheless chose to see Mary mainly as a bridge to conversion. While the post–Vatican II Church came to understand dialogue and proclamation as complementary, as previously noted, Sheen's writings stress only the pre–Vatican II, nondialogical view: conversion, and conversion alone.

The final speech of the September 29 session was given by Archbishop Joseph Descuffi. In it, he repeats and expands upon the theological points already brought up by Sfair and Plumey. But Descuffi adds the testimonial with which this chapter begins, stating that he has personally witnessed a decade of Muslims and Christians sharing Mary at Meryem Ana Evi. It would seem from this speech that Descuffi provided the Council with a glimpse of the *sensus fidelium* at work, for he cites his own experience: "I have seen with my own eyes." It is not surprising that Descuffi would mention Meryem Ana Evi, since the shrine is in his diocese. But it *is* surprising that two other Council fathers also referred to the Turkish shrine—including Bishop Plumey, who was stationed in faraway Cameroon. Why didn't any of them (especially Sfair, who was born in Syria) mention other shared shrines such as Our Lady of Saydnaya in Syria, given its longer tradition of shared popular devotion? Descuffi and Massignon had been promoting the House of Mary in Ephesus among the laity for a decade; were they now promoting the shrine at the Council?[82]

It seems that the bishops' speeches on September 28–29 were compelling, for the next draft of *Nostra Aetate*, discussed in

November 1964, was greatly expanded. A few lines were added on Hinduism and Buddhism in section 2, but the Islamic section was expanded to two full paragraphs.[83] Several *periti*—all Francophone churchmen and Islamicists—were highly influential in expanding section 3 on Islam.[84] These *periti* included Robert Caspar, Joseph Cuoq, Jean Lanfry (all White Fathers), Georges Anawati, OP, and Jean Corbon.[85] The amended text of November 18, 1964, looks very similar to the final version of *Nostra Aetate* promulgated in 1965. Both outline key aspects of the Islamic doctrine of God; praise, prayer, fasting, and almsgiving; and distinguish clearly between the Islamic Jesus and the Christian Christ.[86] But most relevant to our discussion here is the addition of the following line: "They also honor Mary, His Virgin Mother; at times they call on her with devotion."[87] Overall, the expanded draft of *Nostra Aetate* 3 benefitted from the scholarly knowledge of the *periti*, as well as the theological points made by the bishops in their discussion of the draft. But the inclusion of the line on Marian devotion seems to have been influenced at least partly by the three bishops' speeches on September 29, all of which referred to popular Marian devotion in general and Meryem Ana Evi in particular.[88] Even the same Latin word, *devote*, "with devotion," was used in both Plumey's speech and the subsequent draft.

Could it be argued that the addition of *Nostra Aetate*'s line on Marian devotion is an example of the *sensus fidelium* at work? Bishops Plumey, Descuffi, and Sfair all mentioned shared Marian devotion in their speeches, and made a direct link between popular piety on the ground, and what they believed *Nostra Aetate*'s theology of Islam should be. There is a long tradition of the Church relying on the *sensus fidelium* to confirm doctrine—particularly mariological doctrines. A recent Vatican document mentions four cases in history where Mariology was influenced by the *sensus fidelium*: Mary's perpetual virginity, Mary's divine motherhood, the immaculate conception, and the assumption.[89] Could the shared Marian devotion of Christians and Muslims also be added to this list?

It is plausible to conclude that the speeches of Plumey, Descuffi, and Sfair expressed the *sensus fidelium* of ordinary Catholics at the time, as it pertained to shared Christian-Muslim devotional practices at Marian shrines. Of course, this idea had to be affirmed by other bishops, which it was.[90] However, it must be noted that the three speeches were rather one-sided, in that they only focused on Marian devotions promoting *positive* Christian-Muslim relations. The bishops ignored the other side of the tradition, for example, Our Lady of Victory (invoked *against* Muslims since the 1571 Battle of Lepanto), or Croatia's Gospa Sinjska, whose intercession is believed to have led to the miraculous defeat of Ottoman forces on August 15, 1715, and is still celebrated in Sinj annually on the Assumption. Did the bishops, and therefore does *Nostra Aetate*, present an incomplete or imbalanced *sensus fidelium* that sees Marian devotion only as a way to bring Muslims and Christians together? What about those instances in history when Marian devotions and shrines have been used expressly to increase divisions between Islam and Christianity?

CONCLUSION

The twentieth century shows us yet again that the history of Christians, Muslims, and Mary is complicated. This can be seen even during the Marian decade of the 1950s, when some Catholics stressed Mary's role as a bridge to conversion (Sheen), while others stressed her role as a bridge to dialogue (Massignon). Pope Pius XII clearly saw her as both, as is evidenced by his positive comments about Meryem Ana Evi, on the one hand, and his commissioning of the triumphalist Lepanto mosaic, on the other. It seems that the tensions between dialogue and mission, between bridge and barrier is expressed well in Pius's actions here. This tension, and this complicated history, should not be ignored or minimized. While *Nostra Aetate* "urges all to forget the past," history must still be taken into account, and revisionist histories in particular must be avoided, even as today practitioners of dialogue promote Mary as a bridge to understanding.[91]

Nostra Aetate's line on Marian devotion may very well express the *sensus fidelium* during the 1950s. And the continued popularity of Meryem Ana Evi, Saydnaya, and other shrines suggests the longevity of this kind of shared devotion. It will be interesting to see how current changes in Catholic praxis (e.g., a decline in Rosary use in certain circles) will affect shared shrines particularly, and

Christian-Muslim relations more generally, going forward.[92] Even though pro-dialogue Muslims today often promote Mary as a bridge, what about younger Catholics, or other Christians, who do not have a devotion to Mary at all? Just as the *sensus fidelium* seems to have influenced the Catholic theology of Islam in 1965, how might a changing *sensus fidelium*, which today in some quarters deemphasizes Marian devotion, affect the Christian theology of Islam and interfaith dialogue, now and into the future? The final chapter will attempt to answer these questions.

Chapter 8

MODEL OF DIALOGUE?

Contemporary Challenges

> Addressing the Archangel Gabriel, she asks, "How can this be?" Mary, a model for Muslims and Christians, is also a model of dialogue, because she teaches us to believe, not to close ourselves up in certainties, but rather to remain open and available to others.[1]
>
> —Bishop Miguel Ángel Ayuso Guixot, March 25, 2014, Eighth Islamic-Christian Prayer Meeting, Lebanon

Lebanon is unusual among Middle Eastern nations for its high percentage of Christians, as well as for its overall religious diversity, which includes Shi'i Muslims, Sunni Muslims, Maronite Catholics, Orthodox Christians, Protestants, and Druze.[2] Also unique to Lebanon is the fact that March 25, the Feast of the Annunciation, has been a national holiday since 2010. Several Christian-majority countries have declared the Feast of the Assumption (August 15) a public holiday, including Chile, Croatia, Spain, and Poland, but no other country except Lebanon officially observes the annunciation. This makes sense, given Lebanon's unique 62:38 ratio of Muslims to Christians, and the fact that the annunciation can be found in both the Bible and Qur'an—unlike the assumption, which is found in neither. The idea to make the annunciation a national holiday was the brainchild of a Sunni Muslim, Sheikh Mohamed Nokkari, who also created the day's motto: "Together around Mary, Our Lady."[3]

Not only do Lebanese Muslims and Christians celebrate the annunciation together, but they also share the shrine of Our Lady of Lebanon in Harissa, near Beirut. Muslims visit this Christian church in great numbers, and it is not uncommon for imams to preach there on Marian feast days. As the country's unofficial patron saint, Our Lady of Lebanon could be seen as parallel to the medieval Our Lady of Faro, who also seems to have been accepted by Muslim and Christian residents alike.

Choosing the country of Lebanon and the date of March 25 to host a Christian-Muslim dialogue would thus make perfect sense. And it was at just such a dialogue in 2014 that Bishop Ayuso, secretary of the Vatican's Pontifical Council for Interreligious Dialogue, observed that Mary should be a "model of dialogue." His idea, and Lebanon's shared annunciation feast, will serve as the backdrop for this last chapter, which shifts the book's focus from historical accounts of Mary as bridge and barrier, to questions about her role in interfaith relations today.

As we move from past to present, it is worth revisiting the book's four central questions as found in the introduction: (1) In what sense can Muslims and Christians say they "share" Mary? (2) When and by whom has she been seen as a bridge, when and by whom has she been seen as a barrier, and why? (3) How has the shared figure of Mary, as seen by believers at different times and places, influenced the development of a Christian theology of Islam, and popular devotion? (4) How can knowledge of this history shape interfaith relations today? These questions will frame our discussion in this chapter.

QUESTION 1. THE SHARED MARY: OUR LADY OR YOURS?

Chapter 1 explored the idea of a shared Mary by comparing passages in both Christian and Islamic scriptures. Beginning with a reminder that the Muslim Maryam and the Christian Mary should not be seen as entirely equivalent, and noting distinctive Christian and Islamic theological emphases, the chapter nevertheless identified several Marian qualities that both religions have consistently stressed: her chosenness, responsiveness to God, purity (both physical and spiritual), and unique motherhood. These qualities have not only been highlighted in the most authoritative scriptures of both traditions, but they have also been mentioned frequently by prominent Christian and Muslim thinkers throughout history. Therefore, these four Marian qualities can and should serve as a basis for theological conversations between Christians and Muslims today.

Another way in which Christians and Muslims have shared Mary is through devotional practices. As we have seen, there are interesting parallels between how Marian doctrine and devotion have developed in Islam and Christianity. For both religions, there has always been some tension between orthodox Marian doctrine and popular Marian piety. On the one hand, Muslim leaders have traditionally stressed Islam's focus on one God and have decried the veneration of saints; yet on the other hand, ordinary Muslims have always visited saints' graves and Marian shrines. Similar tensions around Mary arose for Christians in the sixteenth century, when Protestants condemned what they saw as Catholic excesses in Marian doctrine and devotion. But as early as the third century, Christians were already disagreeing about Mariology; for example, the Marian devotion of the heterodox Kollyridians was considered suspect. In short, both Islam and Christianity have had as many *intra*religious debates about Mary as they have had *inter*religious debates about her. In both religions, Marian doctrine and devotion have sometimes been associated with heterodoxy. And in both religions, she is embraced by the masses even while she is looked upon with suspicion by the elite. There is one final parallel. In both religions, Marian doctrine and devotion seem to have emerged partly due to the principle of *lex orandi, lex credendi*, not only in Christianity but even in Islam. For all these reasons, and despite Jon Levenson's caveat about shared religious figures, there is some warrant for Christians *and* Muslims to call Mary "Our Lady" (not just "your lady"), as the Lebanese do.[4] A December 2016 op-ed in *The New York Times*, written by a Muslim, suggested as much, arguing that Muslims would not be offended if Christians wished them a Merry Christmas, in large part due to the shared Mary.[5] A Senegalese

Muslim religious order, the Layenne, actually does celebrate Christmas, and some of its female leaders claim to have visions of the Virgin.[6]

One final caution: while this book has grappled with the question of a shared Mary, and noted the need to nuance any descriptions of her as such, it also is important to keep in mind another related issue. The question is not only *whether* Muslims and Christians can say they share Mary. But also, *should* they? Sometimes it is appropriate for Christians to revel in the Christian Mary as Christians, without reference to other religions. Likewise, Muslims may want to reflect on the Islamic Maryam in a similarly exclusive manner. One goal of this book has been to describe shared shrines and beliefs about Mary, while keeping distinctiveness and difference ever in mind. After all, the vast majority of believers love Mary not for her resonances with other religions, but for her centrality in their own.

QUESTION 2. BRIDGE OR BARRIER?

Much of this book has centered on the "bridge or barrier" question, by considering how Christians at various times and places have connected Mary and Islam. As suggested in the introduction, it seems that Mary's role as a bridge or barrier has always been in flux, depending on her polemical or irenic usefulness at a particular time and place. Our brief look at the last fourteen hundred years has borne this observation out, as we have seen Christians constantly vacillating in their views of Mary and Islam: from seventh-century Byzantines in Constantinople (barrier), to ninth-century Arabophone Christians in Iraq (bridge and barrier), to thirteenth-century Latins in Iberia (bridge to conversion and dialogue), to sixteenth-century Catholics in Western Europe (barrier), to seventeenth-century Jesuits in Mughal India (bridge to conversion), to twentieth-century Protestant (barrier) and Catholic missionaries (bridge to conversion), to *Nostra Aetate* (bridge to dialogue), to twenty-first-century bloggers (barrier). In the final analysis, no clear arc of history has emerged; whether Christians have seen Mary as a bridge or barrier depends greatly on the circumstances of time and place.

The two earliest Christian groups to write about Islam—the Byzantines and the Arabophones—were distinguished by culture, geography, government, and language, and these differences affected how they interpreted Mary vis-à-vis Islam. Early Byzantine Christians saw Mary primarily as a barrier. Because Islam was entirely extrinsic to their culture, they needed Mary's help to deter Muslim invasions. Not only did they see the Virgin's mantle as protecting Constantinople from the attack of "infidels," but they also saw Mary as a general who actively took part in battles. Even when the Ottomans eventually took much of southeastern Europe, the Byzantines still needed Mary to be a barrier—one who also stood at their side, comforting them as "Our Lady of Losers." In either victory or defeat, Mary was a barrier between Muslims and Byzantine Christians. However, for the Eastern Christians who lived in Islamic lands and became Arabicized in language and culture, the picture was more complicated. For them, Mary was both a bridge and a barrier. The unique situation of Arabophone Christians meant that their dialogue with Islam was internal to their own culture, and therefore required simultaneous accommodation and resistance, as Sidney Griffith has noted. These Eastern Christians often began theological debates with Muslims by stressing similarities between Christian and Muslim Mariologies, and from this common foundation moved into arguments about christological differences. While early Arabophone Christians saw Mary as both a bridge and barrier, they often chose to emphasize her role as a bridge. As such, she has tended to function differently than Christ, since as a topic of dialogue he has always been the greater theological barrier. This is perhaps best illustrated by the fact that Arabic speakers of this time used two different names for Jesus (*Yasu'* for the Christian Jesus and *'Isa* for the Muslim Jesus), but never used two different names for Mary, to the best of my knowledge. For Arabic-speaking Christians and Muslims alike, she was and is simply Maryam.

The Eastern Christian idea of Mary as a bridge would transfer to the medieval Latin West, but only for those who tried to study Arabic and Islamic literature. But only a few medieval Europeans succeeded in this. (Things would change in the sixteenth century, when there was a renewed interested in Arabic philology.) And for those who did study Islamic texts, such as William of Tripoli and Nicholas of Cusa, Mary turned out to be a surprising commonality.

However, the vast majority of medieval Latins were ignorant of Islamic literature and doctrine (important exceptions include Petrus Alfonsus, Peter the Venerable, Riccoldo da Montecroce, Ramon Martí, and Ramon Llull). The result of this ignorance was that most Latin Christians who wrote against Islam during the medieval era were entirely unaware of the Marian connection and thus were silent about her, focusing instead on issues that Christians and Muslims have always argued about: prophethood, scriptural integrity, Christology, and heaven. Practically speaking, during the medieval period, Mary was a barrier between Islam and Latin Christianity, albeit an invisible one, simply because so few Christian theologians knew the Muslim Maryam even existed.

But the situation was different when it came to praxis. Not only did medieval Latin Christians observe and even visit shared Marian shrines such as Saydnaya in Syria and the House of Mary in Jerusalem, but they also told stories of shared devotion, real or imagined. As the Iberian *Cantigas de Santa Maria* show, Mary was seen as a bridge to conversion, as evidenced by the Moor in *cantiga* 46, who venerates a Marian icon and then accepts baptism. However, other *cantigas* suggest her to be a different kind of bridge, perhaps a bridge to neighborliness, as seen in *cantiga* 183, which shows the Muslims and Christians of Faro retrieving a statue of Mary from the sea, and reestablishing her as the shared patron saint of the city. In *cantiga* 183, there are no conversions. When devotion was involved, the medieval Latin Mary leaned toward being a bridge.

In the early modern period, Christian Europe felt threatened by a new Islamic foe, the Ottomans, and the old Byzantine image of Mary the protector was resurrected and amplified to become Our Lady of Victory, who was now implored via a new prayer, the Rosary. The sixteenth-century Catholic Our Lady of Victory fought Muslims, but she also fought a new enemy, the Protestants. Sometimes she even battled "infidels" with a sword, as in the violent *Triumphus Rosarii* image from Cologne, but at other times she enticed them to convert with her virtue and beauty, as seen in the hybrid Mughal image of Mary sweeping the stable before giving birth. A few centuries later, American Presbyterians in North Africa used the Virgin in their missionizing, too—but to repel, not attract. They held up Mary as proof of what was wrong with Catholic and Orthodox Christianity, and to show would-be converts that Protestantism was more similar to Islam than those other forms of Christianity, especially in terms of its iconoclasm, *sola scriptura*, and direct access to God.

Moving into the twentieth century, Mary was once again held up by Catholics as a bridge between themselves and Muslims. While the 1950s television evangelist Bishop Fulton Sheen stressed the traditional notion of Mary as a bridge to conversion, the French Islamicist Louis Massignon retrieved the ancient idea of Mary as a bridge to dialogue and fraternity—an idea hinted at but not fully developed in the writings of early Arabophone Christians like Jacob of Edessa and medieval Latins like William of Tripoli and Nicholas of Cusa. This history of Mary as a bridge, plus the knowledge of shared Marian shrines such as Meryem Ana Evi in Turkey, did have some influence on the Catholic theology of Islam articulated in Vatican II's *Nostra Aetate*—a theology that noted differences but minimized them, choosing instead to stress commonalities such as belief in one God, ascetic practices like prayer and fasting, and Marian devotion. Since *Nostra Aetate*, it might appear that the arc of theological history is moving toward seeing Mary as a bridge, thanks to Catholics who have received Council teachings, Protestants who are part of the recent Marian revival, and Orthodox who have always accepted Mary. At the official level, a preference for Mary as bridge certainly appears to be the case. However, even today there remains a small but vocal "Mary as barrier" camp: for example, traditionalist Catholics who call upon Our Lady of Victory to fight against terrorism. Their hateful anti-Islamic rhetoric, which often includes prayers to Mary and images of Lepanto, abounds on the internet. Thus, it appears that both strains of the tradition, Mary as bridge *and* Mary as barrier, are alive and well in the twenty-first century.

QUESTION 3. THE SHARED MARY: INFLUENCES ON THEOLOGY AND PIETY?

How has the shared Mary influenced the Christian theology of Islam? As chapter 7 has shown, three Vatican II Council fathers spoke about shared Marian shrines around the world, especially Meryem Ana Evi in Turkey, and their interventions helped shape the theology of Islam articulated in *Nostra Aetate* 3. In this case, popular Marian devotion did have some effect on doctrine. Since then, has popular praxis continued to influence the development of a postconciliar Christian theology of Islam, or has *Nostra Aetate*'s theology impacted praxis? Or both? To answer these questions, this section will review major developments in the Christian theology of Islam since the 1960s.

For Catholics, Vatican II offered the first explicit theology of Islam at the highest level of church authority, an ecumenical council. The document *Nostra Aetate* lists several areas of Muslim-Christian agreement: doctrine of God (God as one, Creator, Revealer, merciful, Judge), eschatology (judgment, resurrection of the body), and praxis (prayer, fasting, almsgiving).[7] Abraham is acknowledged, though equivocally, as a possible but not definite connection between Christians and Muslims. Christology is the only difference noted in *Nostra Aetate* (Muhammad and the Qur'an are not mentioned at all), and after naming Jesus, the document pivots to another similarity, Jesus' mother, declaring that Muslims honor her as a virgin and "at times even call on her with devotion." In so doing, *Nostra Aetate*'s approach mirrors that of early Arabophone Christians, whose writings likewise linked mariological similarities and christological differences.

The Catholic theology of Islam has not developed much since the Council, at least at the magisterial level.[8] Only one major curial document on Islam, *Guidelines for Dialogue between Christians and Muslims* (1970; revised in 1981 and 1990), has been issued by the Secretariat for Non-Christians (now the Pontifical Council for Interreligious Dialogue).[9] More progress has been made through papal actions and addresses.[10] For example, John Paul II, the first pope to visit a mosque, also gave speeches affirming Islam as an Abrahamic faith, something *Nostra Aetate* 3 suggested only vaguely. As early as 1979, he told Turkish Christians that "they [Muslims] have like you the faith of Abraham," while in Casablanca in 1985, he assured his Muslim audience that "we are brothers and sisters in the faith of Abraham."[11] This repeated and explicit affirmation of Islam as an "Abrahamic faith" is arguably the single most important development in the official Catholic theology of Islam since Vatican II.

While the magisterium has moved slowly, several individual Catholic and Protestant theologians have made greater strides in advancing the theology of Islam.[12] The two most popular topics discussed are the very ones left unnamed in *Nostra Aetate*: Muhammad and the Qur'an. Some Catholics have argued that while they cannot call Muhammad "the seal of the prophets," nevertheless they might be able to accord him some privileged status due to his "prophetic charisma" and "authentic witness."[13] Protestants seem more willing to label Muhammad a bona fide prophet. For example, the Anglican bishop and Islamicist Kenneth Cragg suggested that the proper Christian response to his prophethood must be a reserved yet "positive acknowledgement of its significance."[14] Cragg has also affirmed the Qur'an's revelatory status, recommending that Christians reconsider the idea of the "closing of the canon," since such a doctrine is "not inclusive" of other religions; he has also suggested that Christians use scriptures like the Qur'an during their own liturgical services.[15] Other Protestants who seem willing to accept the Qur'an as revelation include theologians involved in the World Council of Church's (WCC) ongoing Christian-Muslim dialogue, some of whom suggest that it might be possible for Christians "with a more dynamic understanding of revelation" to accept the Qur'an as divine revelation.[16] But these WCC theologians are in the minority; most other Christians, including Catholics, do not affirm the Qur'an's revelatory status. Only a few individual Catholic theologians, such as the Dominican Claude Geffré and the White Father Robert Caspar, have gone a step further by calling the Qur'an "*a* word of God" (as distinct from "*the* Word of God," Jesus himself).[17]

But what about Mary? Does she fit into the postconciliar Christian theology of Islam at all? Do Vatican or WCC documents include Mary in lists of suggested topics for Christian-Muslim dialogue? Strangely, her name is rarely found in any of these documents. The 1990 Vatican *Guidelines* mentions Mary briefly, but only in relation to Jesus, and she is not included at all in its last section, "Potential Areas of Religious Agreement." A 1977 WCC report says Christians "acknowledge the special esteem and honor in which Muslim tradition holds Jesus and the Holy Family" but it does not name Mary explicitly.[18] Edited scholarly volumes such as *Christian-Muslim Encounters* (1995) and *Islam and Christianity* (1998)—both of which include chapters by famous Protestant, Catholic, and Muslim academics—hardly mention Mary at all, and here too she is absent from lists of dialogue topics, which include monotheism, scripture, proselytism, secularism, prayer, Abraham, and Jesus.[19] The same is true of more recent books on Christian-Muslim relations. One book devoted to prayer in Islam and Christianity mentions the Rosary in passing but says nothing about Marian devotion or shared shrines, while another, an overview of Christian-Muslim relations, omits Mary from the index altogether (but Jesus and Muhammad have substantial entries).[20] A 2014 book entitled *The Qur'an in Christian-Muslim Dialogue*, which could easily have included a substantive section on Sura 19 (Maryam) or the Qur'an's two annunciation stories, mentions Mary only briefly, as she pertains to the incarnation.[21]

In short, overall development in the Christian theology of Islam since the 1960s has been slow, and Mary's role has been small. Perhaps this is partly due to a "plateau" in the theology of religions project, coupled with an increased interest in interfaith social cooperation beginning in the 1990s.[22] Joint documents from this time, like the WCC's "Striving Together in Dialogue: A Muslim-Christian Call to Reflection and Action" (2000), stress interfaith work over interfaith talk, and Mary rarely figures into interfaith work. But even in the arena of interfaith talk, Mary continues to be neglected. Despite the perennial emphasis on Christ as a key locus for Christian-Muslim dialogue, as seen in a recent spate of books focusing on the Muslim Jesus, Mary has been ignored.[23] She is largely absent from official Church documents and joint Christian-Muslim statements. Muslims have ignored her, too. Their landmark document, *A Common Word* (2007), which centers on the two commonalities of love of God and love of neighbor, still manages to mention contentious topics like Jesus, Muhammad, Trinity, and Scripture. But it does not mention Mary, even in passing. The document's Muslim authors were probably trying to be sensitive to ecumenical differences among their Christian (and Muslim) readers, many of whom consider Mary as marginal to their faith, but perhaps they missed an opportunity?

Possibly more surprising is the fact that Mary has been neglected even by Catholics writing about Islam since the Council. She has only been mentioned by Church leaders a few times: by popes visiting shared Marian shrines (John Paul II, Benedict XVI, Francis); in a 1988 Ramadan greeting from the Pontifical Council of Interreligious Dialogue; and in remarks given by Cardinal William Keeler ("How Mary Holds Christians and Muslims in Conversation," December 8, 1995) and Bishop Ángel Ayuso Guixot ("Mary as Model of Dialogue," March 25, 2014). In short, Mary remains a largely untapped resource for the Christian theology of Islam. This might be expected of Protestants, but it seems also to be the case among Catholics.

Despite Mary's absence from higher-level theological reflections, her popularity remains strong at the grassroots devotional level. As has been noted repeatedly throughout this book, shared shrines such as Our Lady of Africa in Algeria; Our Lady of Saydnaya in Syria; Mariamabad in Pakistan; Our Lady of Lebanon in Harissa; St. Clement Ohridski Macedono-Bulgarian Orthodox Church in Dearborn, Michigan; Meryem Ana Evi in Turkey; Our Lady of Kevelaer in Germany; the Virgin Mary Armenian Church in Iraq; and other places around the world continue to be frequented by both Muslims and Christians. Catholics are well known for having visions of Mary, but in places like Zeitoun, Egypt, and Cambérène, Senegal, Muslims have seen her too.[24] Shared shrines have brought Christians and Muslims together in unexpected ways, and as such have become unintended bridges. Sometimes places or prayers that began as barriers have become bridges. One example is the annual assumption celebration at Our Lady of Sinj in Croatia, which has traditionally commemorated the Christian defeat of Muslims on August 15, 1715, but now also includes an interfaith pilgrimage from Sinj to the city of Rama in Bosnia. Another example is Cardinal William Keeler's story of how the Grand Mufti of Syria gave him a copy of the Hail Mary in Arabic, which Keeler later used to pray for the mufti when he was in the hospital. Given the Rosary's history as a weapon of war against Muslims, the fact that Keeler used the Hail Mary as an instrument of healing for a Muslim friend is remarkable indeed.

Jesus Christ and his mother Mary are among the most important figures shared by Islam and Christianity. Historically, Christians and

Muslims have always spent more time discussing Christ, because calling him prophet or son of God determines religious identity. Thus, it would only make sense that when it comes to Christ, there is more interreligious disagreement than intrareligious. Christ unites Christians but divides religions. When it comes to Mary, the opposite is true. There seems to be less *inter*religious disagreement about her, and more *intra*religious disagreement, because devotion to Mary does not function as an identity boundary the way belief in Christ does. This might be why Mary can serve as an effective bridge between Islam and Christianity in ways that Christ cannot, even while she often remains a barrier between factions *within* each religion.

An example of Mary functioning in this dual way can be seen in recent cases of mosques being named after her. Muslims in suburban Melbourne chose to call their new place of worship the Virgin Mary Mosque to serve as a bridge to their Christian neighbors. To best communicate the idea of a shared Mary, they opted for an English title over the less recognizable Arabic, Masjid Maryam. In Tartous, Syria, another mosque was named Al-Sayyida Maryam. Like the Australians, the Syrians chose this name in hopes of reaching out to their non-Muslim neighbors. But they also had a second goal: to distinguish themselves from other, less tolerant Muslim groups. A government minister said, "The mosque's construction symbolizes the openness of Islam, in stark contrast to the 'deviation' being seen today thanks to *takfiri* extremists. Naming the mosque after al-Sayyida Maryam is an expression of belief in the Holy Qur'an's verses that bring people together and do not divide them based on religion or sect."[25] The Syrian Muslims thus see their new mosque as serving two functions, one interreligious and the other intrareligious: connecting themselves to non-Muslims and distinguishing themselves from some other Muslims.

The existence of mosques named for Mary in both Syria and Australia highlights one of the main points of this book, which is that time and place matter. In twenty-first-century Melbourne, for example, Muslims think it is important to cultivate Christian allies, thus shaping the theological meaning given to Mary by this community, at this moment in time.

QUESTION 4. INTERFAITH RELATIONS TODAY: MARY AS MODEL OF DIALOGUE?

Mary's greatest promise for Christian-Muslim relations today may not be doctrinal, but devotional and dialogical. Given the long history of Christians and Muslims affirming Mary as a shared figure, and sometimes approaching her together in devotion, it seems like she would be an obvious starting point for dialogue, despite her history as a barrier. And indeed, Muslims are often the first to bring up Mary in interfaith conversations. But sometimes Christians are reluctant to mention her, due to concerns related to feminism, ecumenism, and violence—all of which could potentially keep Mary in her age-old role as a barrier to Christian-Muslim understanding.

BARRIER 1. MARY AND FEMINISM

Muslims involved in interfaith dialogue with Christians will often point out that "Muslim women wear a veil just like Mother Mary did." They take pride in this commonality, as is evidenced by the Australian and Syrian mosques named after her. Therefore, it is somewhat ironic that at the same time Muslims are promoting Mary, many Christians (particularly women) are rejecting her for being irrelevant, uninteresting, or damaging to the feminist cause. Furthermore, many baby boomer, Gen X, and millennial Catholics—not only women but men too—no longer participate in traditional Marian devotional practices such as saying the Rosary or visiting Our Lady shrines.[26] Mary cannot serve as a bridge between Christians and Muslims if most Christians (and even Catholics!) see her as marginal or antithetical to their faith. Therefore, feminist critiques of Mary need to be considered if she is to be an asset to Christian-Muslim dialogue today.

This is not the place for a comprehensive review of the contemporary feminist critique of Mary.[27] Briefly, feminist theologians have argued that the traditional picture of Mary as gentle, submissive, and sinless—not to mention her extraordinary identity as Virgin Mother of God—tends to disempower ordinary women and reinforce structures of patriarchal oppression. One example of this can be found in traditional views of the Virgen de Guadalupe, whose "sacred duty, self-sacrifice, and chastity" support an idealized form of Mexican womanhood called *marianismo*, which, along with its alter ego *machismo*, serves to disempower women (and misinform men) in traditional Mexican culture.[28] Christian men of many cultures have often idealized this chaste and subservient Mary, but Christian women have sometimes felt alienated by her. The dichotomy between how men and women relate to Mary still plays out in today's college classrooms, where some professors have observed a stark distinction between rosters: courses entitled "Mariology" are full of young men, while courses entitled "Feminist Theology" are full of young women.[29]

Yet feminist theologians do not want to give up Mary, not only because she is a central figure in the Christian story, but also because she may have the potential to empower women. But for Mary to do this, theologians must rethink Marian imagery. The last chapter of Elizabeth Johnson's most recent mariological study focuses on previously ignored descriptors of Mary such as "Friend of God" and "Prophet" (interestingly, both titles have Islamic resonances).[30] Another way to do this is to retrieve unexplored aspects of the Marian story from Christian history and tradition; recent studies such as Amy Remensnyder's *La Conquistadora* and Bissera Pentcheva's *Icons and Power* have done this. But as some scholars have noted, these studies tend to privilege Our Lady of Victory over Our Lady of Defeat, despite the prevalence of the latter in middle Byzantium, for example.[31] The fact that some scholars today are emphasizing Mary's strength is not surprising if traditional images of her as docile and submissive are to be countered. But perhaps we have failed to fully appreciate Mary's subversive power, which is already intuitively recognized by grassroots believers who love Poland's dark, scarred, and defeated Our Lady of Czestochowa, or Cuba's *mulata* Cachita (Nuestra Señora de Caridad).[32] Indeed, liberation theologian Dorothee Sölle has warned, "Let us not be too hasty to abandon Mary to our patriarchal opponents. The millions of women before us who have loved Mary were not simply blind or duped. They too sensed her subversive power and offered resistance from which we can learn."[33] Some liberation, *mujerista*, and womanist theologians suggest that it is Our Lady of Defeat, not

Our Lady of Victory, who represents the most authentically Christian Mary fighting on behalf of society's "least"—the least being not only women but also people of color and other traditionally marginalized groups.[34] For example, Angela Polite, a black actress and member of First AME Bethel Church in Harlem, wrote an off-Broadway, one-woman play called *Mary Speaks*, which ties the suffering Mary to black mothers likewise grieving over their murdered sons.[35] While we should not ignore the long history of Our Lady of Victory in interfaith relations, perhaps today's Muslims and Christians could spend more time thinking together about what Our Lady of Defeat might mean for women and others who have traditionally been disenfranchised by the patriarchal structures operating in both religions.[36]

BARRIER 2. MARY AND ECUMENISM

Another potential problem with making Mary an interfaith bridge is that many Christians simply do not relate to her—especially Protestants, whose famous aversion to her has roots in the Reformation. It must be noted, however, that Protestant approaches to Mary are as varied as the denominations themselves. Lutherans and Anglicans have traditionally had more affinity for Mary than Presbyterians, Pentecostals, or Evangelicals. Also, race and ethnicity can play a role in how Protestants view her. White European Protestants have had problems with Mary since the beginning (although recent scholarship shows that views differed even among sixteenth-century German Lutherans).[37] However, Protestants from the Middle East and Latin America may have fewer reservations about Mary, with many proudly affirming that "we embrace our brown Mama."[38] Furthermore, there has been a renaissance in Marian studies among Protestant scholars recently; just one example is *Blessed One: Protestant Perspectives on Mary*, which features eleven different Protestant views of Mary.[39] Contributors to this compendium are critical of the traditional Protestant silence on Mary, which they say can have negative consequences for theological thinking about women, motherhood, and Christian theology more generally.[40]

While Mary has caused difficulties between Christians in the past, today she presents opportunities for both ecumenical and interreligious dialogue. And indeed, some have begun to capitalize on those opportunities. In 2004, an international Anglican-Catholic commission wrote a joint document focused exclusively on Mary, "Mary: Grace and Hope in Christ," which states that "progress in ecumenical dialogue and understanding suggests that we now have an opportunity to re-receive together the tradition of Mary's place in God's revelation."[41] And not only Anglicans and Lutherans, but also Evangelicals are considering Mary's ecumenical potential; two examples include a friendly conversation between two laymen in the book *Mary: A Catholic-Evangelical Debate*, and the more academic discussion in *Mary for Evangelicals*.[42] A 2016 editorial in the Protestant magazine *Christianity Today* was entitled "What Evangelicals Can Love about Mary: What Protestants Can Affirm in the 'Hail Mary,' What Luther Thought about the Mother of God, and Why Christmas Shouldn't Be the Only Time Protestants Give Her Some Love."[43] This recent "re-reception" of Mary by Protestants has renewed ecumenical dialogues, so why couldn't Mary also be reintroduced into interreligious dialogues between Muslims and a wider range of Christian denominations?

Another important locus for ecumenical conversations about Mary vis-à-vis Islam is the Holy Land, where Catholic, Protestant, and Orthodox Christians interact in unique ways. After all, the Holy Land is one of the few Christian pilgrimage destinations in the world visited by Evangelicals and other Protestants. Of course, most Protestants do not have an interest in Mary on her own, but they do visit sites mentioned in the Bible or otherwise included in Holy Land tours, such as the Church of the Annunciation in Nazareth, Mary's Well in Nazareth, the Church of the Nativity in Bethlehem, Cana, the Via Dolorosa station where Jesus and Mary met, the Church of the Holy Sepulchre, and Mary's Tomb in the Kidron Valley. Furthermore, local Palestinians, be they Orthodox, Catholic, Protestant, or Muslim, all feel a sense of ownership in these holy sites. After a 2002 battle that damaged the Church of the Nativity, *The New York Times* reported that local residents of all denominations hurried to "their" church to assess the damage, including Sayeeha Khamees, a Muslim who "came to thank the Virgin Mary for protecting [her son] and to ensure that the 'church is safe.'"[44] Displays of gratitude to Mary like this one often span denominational lines in Palestine; Sayeeha is not alone among her neighbors in feeling personally connected to a Marian church or thanking Mary for her protection. However, it must also be noted that Mary can divide believers in the Holy Land too; for example, some local Christians have "refused to share their Mary with Muslims" and explicitly reject the qur'anic Mary as "not our Mary."[45]

BARRIER 3. MARY AND VIOLENCE

Violence is the last barrier to consider when thinking about Mary as a bridge in Christian-Muslim relations. It is a barrier due partly to ignorance about Mary's historical connections to violence, and partly to the inability of some Christian devotees to accept any link whatsoever between their beloved Mary and violence. While Mary is commonly known as the Queen of Peace and Mother of Mercy, this book has highlighted multiple historical depictions of her as a general, *conquistadora*, or Our Lady of Victory fighting Muslims. Yet the idea of a militant Mary is still difficult for some Christians to accept, especially those who prefer her *Salve Regina* descriptors: clement, loving, and sweet. Yet recognition of Mary's simultaneous gentleness and strength is present throughout the tradition.

Today it is common for Christians to accuse Islam of being a violent religion, yet Christians themselves have long used the language of war to describe their own ideological and actual battles with enemies, Muslim or otherwise. For example, the titles of the following traditional hymns employ military language: John Wesley's "Soldiers of Christ, Arise" and Isaac Watts's "Am I a Soldier of the Cross." During the medieval period, coercion and conversion were often connected; consider the title of Ramon Martí's anti-Jewish polemic, *Pugio fidei*, "The sword of faith."[46] Pope Urban II's 1095 call to arms at Clermont, France, used the language of "holy war" against Muslims (*Deus vult*, "God wills it"), and the Crusades produced military religious orders such as the Knights Templar and Hospitallers. The very context out of which the *Cantigas de Santa Maria* was written, thirteenth-century (*re*)*conquista* Spain, was war; even *cantiga* 46, which depicts a Moor sweetly venerating a Marian icon in the privacy of his own home, begins with violent images of interfaith warfare. In fact, it is only because of the war that the Moor obtained the Marian icon in the first place. While some might argue that full-fledged religious wars like the Crusades and the Spanish *reconquista* are a thing of the past, the rhetoric of holy war has never gone away.[47] It can still be seen today, not only in theories such as Samuel Huntington's "clash of civilizations," but also in the language used by reporters and politicians to describe relations between Islam and "the West" (a dichotomy that ignores the fact that many Muslims live *in* the West).[48]

Apropos of chapter 6 ("Mary, Tool for Mission") is the fact that Christian missionaries often explicitly linked mission and war in their evangelizing rhetoric. There are many examples of this, from seventeenth-century Jesuit missionaries like Possevino (d. 1611), who wrote an anti-Islamic polemic entitled *Il soldato Cristiano*,[49] to nineteenth-century popes like Leo XIII, whose encyclicals describe the Rosary as "a most powerful warlike weapon" to be used as a "means of putting the enemy to flight."[50] Leo also connects the Rosary, warfare, and mission: "It is mainly to expand the kingdom of Christ that we look to the Rosary for the most effective help."[51] The pope was not alone; Protestant missionaries also used military language to describe their missionary efforts. For example, the great Presbyterian "apostle to the Muslims," Samuel Zwemer, described Christian attempts at evangelizing Muslims as "a mighty conflict" and encouraged missionaries to engage in a new holy war, explicitly echoing Pope Urban II's Crusader call: "God wills it. Let our rallying cry be: 'Every stronghold of Islam for Christ!' Not a war of gunboats, or of diplomacy, but a Holy War with the Sword of the Spirit."[52]

Christianity does not lack for violent words or images when it comes to its relations with Islam, yet one of the most enduring stereotypes about Islam is that Muhammad was a warlike man who spread his religion by the sword. This stereotype has been repeated by Byzantine, medieval, and modern-day Christians; consider the controversial Danish cartoon depicting Muhammad with bombs in his turban. But most Christians today are unaware of how Mary, mission, and violence have also been linked in their own tradition.

The "Islam is violent" stereotype convinced me to reconsider this book's cover image. I had originally planned a split cover with two images of Mary, one Islamic and one Christian. The Christian image was to be a violent Our Lady of Victory from the Lepanto period, while the Muslim image was to be the irenic annunciation from Al-Biruni (see figure 1 in chapter 3). My goal was to shake up readers' assumptions. But after having a conversation about religion and violence with a colleague, and considering the resurgence of Islamophobia in the United States today, I began to wonder if putting Lepanto on the cover might appear to encourage triumphalism and affirm the Islamophobia prevalent among some extremist Catholics today.[53] So I chose another historical image instead: a sixteenth-century Islamic image of Mary and Jesus used in popular piety, which I hope will be amenable to Christians and Muslims alike.[54] Recent years have seen the proliferation of interreligious violence—both real and rhetorical—and while my book does discuss a Christian history replete with images of violence, I did not want the cover to glorify violence, or to suggest that the weight of history could be reduced to this stereotype, because the reality is more complicated than that.

Another issue related to violence is triumphalism, a phenomenon highlighted by Scott Alexander in a new book on the role of triumphalism in Christian-Muslim relations.[55] And indeed, as my own book's review of the history of Christians, Muslims, and Mary has shown, there appears to be a strong link between Mary, violence, and triumphalism, at least in the Christian tradition. At times, Mary has indeed been used by certain Christians in their quest for victory against all kinds of "godless" enemies, from the Avars and Arabs in the eighth century, to Ottomans and Protestants in the sixteenth, to modernists in the nineteenth, to communists in the twentieth, to terrorists and secular liberals in the twenty-first. A prime example of Marian triumphalism against "godless liberals" in the United States can be found in the recent internet acrostic "T.R.U.M.P.," which stands for "Trump Rules Under Mary's Protection."[56] Shocking as this may be, it squares neatly with the Marian triumphalism of earlier times. An antidote to such triumphalism can be found in Matthew Milliner's forthcoming study of the seventh-century Byzantine Our Lady of Losers, who possesses subversive, not brute power. While recent historical studies focusing on Mary's military strength can serve as a feminist critique of the submissive Mary, perhaps a second critique can come from the subversive power of Our Lady of Defeat. Is not one of the main points of Christianity to turn symbols of power on their head? Is not this the true power of Christ and his resurrection? And thus, is not this also the true power of Mary, the one who "stood with" Christ at the foot of the cross, a la the medieval hymn, *Stabat Mater*? Do those who revere the various Our Lady of Mourning icons of Southeastern Europe, for example, in Studenica, Serbia, or Ohrid, Macedonia, where Orthodox Christians were long ruled by the Ottomans, have something to teach those who embrace the more triumphalist Our Lady of Victory of Sinj, Croatia, where Catholic Christians never experienced that kind of defeat?

To conclude, let us return to the question posed in the introduction: Is Mary a bridge or barrier in interfaith relations today? For those Christian-Muslim dialogue groups who know about the shared Mary and discuss her, it would seem yes, she is a bridge. But other dialogue groups do not focus on her. This might be because some groups are more involved in social action, while others prefer to engage in religious experiences (although shared Marian shrines might be appealing to them). Yet, there are dialogue groups focused squarely on theological questions that are silent about Mary. Perhaps the participants of such groups include Protestants or Muslims who find Mary problematic or irrelevant. And even if some members are Catholic, there is no guarantee that Mary will be discussed; according to a recent study, 88 percent of American Catholics are unaware that Muslims honor Mary.[57] Or, it could simply be that their theological interests lie elsewhere.

Today, the interfaith movement has embraced commonalities as a key route to harmony between religions (while still respecting differences).[58] But commonalities in and of themselves are not enough to achieve this goal. For there is nothing inherent in commonalities that inevitably leads formerly warring groups toward peaceful rapprochement. Rather, as the history of Christians, Muslims, and Mary has shown, believers always have agency over how common symbols are used. And sometimes it is not common symbols that come first, but a common cause. Often, alliances between two religions against a third have spurred the use of shared symbols like Mary: for example, the Eastern Christians who allied themselves with Muslims to denounce Jews, or the Protestants who said that Muslims are bad but Catholics are worse, or the Syrian Muslims who named their mosque for Mary to show unity with Christians over fellow Muslims they saw as intolerant. In the end, believers must recognize that they have agency over religious symbols that are fundamentally ambiguous. The Virgin Mary has always been a flexible tool with the *potential* to be a bridge in Christian-Muslim relations, but only when and where believers choose to embrace her as such.

EPILOGUE

Sayyidatuna

A common title for Mary in Arabic is *Sayyida Maryam*, "Lady Mary." If the first-person plural possessive suffix is added, *Sayyida* becomes *Sayyidatuna*, equivalent to "Our Lady" in English. This book is a reminder that while Christians and Muslims "share" Mary in many ways, and thus some might even feel comfortable calling her *Sayyidatuna*, the history of this sharing is complicated. Those engaged in Christian-Muslim dialogue today need to have a nuanced understanding of that history, since Mary is a flexible symbol, functioning as either a bridge or barrier, or both, or neither—depending on time and place.

Christians have yet to fully explicate Mary's place in their theology of Islam. Furthermore, it would be good to hear what contemporary Muslim scholars have to say about how she figures into an Islamic theology of Christianity.[1] Luckily, interfaith relations can be furthered not only through theology, but also dialogue. The Vatican has described four interrelated forms of dialogue (dialogue of life, action, theological exchange, and religious experience), a schema that encourages everyone to get involved, not just experts.[2] While in the past Christ has been suggested as a model for dialogue, this epilogue will consider Bishop Ayuso's proposal of Mary as such.[3] What follows are some practical ideas about Mary as both a *topic* for and *model* of interfaith dialogue today.

MARY AS TOPIC

The all-women interfaith group from St. Fabian's Catholic Church and the Mosque Foundation in Bridgeview, Illinois, has been meeting monthly for nearly twenty years, and has devoted at least one of their dialogues to Mary. On a day dedicated to discussing holy women in each tradition, the group declared their mutual admiration of Mary's character and faith and affirmed her as a "righteous woman," but they did not feel the need to discuss her much more beyond that.[4] Why not? Did the group feel obliged to discuss the shared Mary at some point, even though members did not really relate to her? Furthermore, why is Mary often relegated to all-female dialogues or discussions of "women's issues"? Jesus, Muhammad, and Abraham are held up as examples for both men and women, so why shouldn't Mary likewise be held up as an example for all believers, regardless of gender? It seems that any Christian-Muslim dialogue group could benefit from reflecting more deeply on the meaning of Mary. For example, an all-male dialogue group could discuss Mary as a model of purity for themselves. Muslim scholar Mona Siddiqui seems to agree:

> There needs to be a "resurrection" of Mary in Muslim theology beyond debates around gender, virtue, and female piety. This has already happened among some Christian theologians who have wished to promote Mary as an image of liberation of women from poverty and injustice. But in Islam, Mary has no such role, for the Jesus story pales her own significance. Yet further reflection on her unique nature may well open up new questions and lead to new engagement in the virtual impasse that is the divine/human nature of Jesus for many Christians and Muslims.[5]

It would also be interesting for dialogue groups today to discuss the subversively powerful Mary claimed by Christian liberation theologians, to see if there has been any similar evolution in Muslim descriptions of Mary beyond her traditional qualities of purity, chosenness, and obedience. While Siddiqui is correct that in traditional Islam, "Mary has no such role" as a liberator, neither did she have such a role in Christianity until recently. Would a liberator Mary be an attractive figure for Muslim and Christian men and women to consider together?

Another possibility for dialogue would be a joint scripture study of Marian stories in the Qur'an and Bible, a format that may be more amenable to Protestants. But dialogue participants should be prepared for the possibility that some of their interlocutors (as well as their coreligionists) might use passages about Mary to confirm traditional gender roles, while others might use the same passages to challenge such roles. The Lutheran theologian Anne Hege Grung, a participant in a Norwegian Christian-Muslim scripture study group, observes that sometimes scripture is used "to confirm and not challenge...the patriarchal heritage of a tradition, with a double legitimization from two traditions, not merely one."[6] To account for a greater diversity of perspectives both between and within religions, Grung suggests calling such dialogues "transreligious" rather than "interreligious." Transreligious dialogues pay more attention to the diversity within each tradition, which "opens up spaces for identifying challenges across religious affiliations and for critique and self-criticism."[7] Is not Mary—a figure long popular among grassroots and heterodox Muslims and Christians, a figure who sometimes causes more intrareligious strife than interreligious—an especially appropriate topic for "transreligious" dialogues, scriptural or otherwise?

Mary has great potential not only as bridge between religions or denominations, but also between factions within a single denomination. For example, so-called liberal Catholics are more likely to engage in interreligious dialogue than traditional Marian piety, while so-called conservative Catholics are more likely to engage in traditional Marian piety than interreligious dialogue. Could an interreligious dialogue focused on Mary bring these two groups of Catholics together?

MARY AS MODEL

As has already been noted, Mary is not just a *topic of* dialogue. She is also a *model for* dialogue. But can Muslims and Christians today accept her as such? It depends. The answer will always vary based on the culture, language, history, geography, religion, and preferences of those involved. For those willing to give Mary another look, she does seem to offer a concrete example of the attitudes necessary to build real-life relationships between Christians and Muslims. Furthermore, this dialogical attitude has the potential to bridge all kinds of longstanding, seemingly intractable boundaries between people: not only religious boundaries, but also racial, ethnic, gender, socioeconomic, and political. In the United States today, a dialogical attitude is sorely needed.

Those who choose to accept Mary as a model for dialogue might find it useful to return to chapter 1 and review the annunciation conversation between Gabriel and Mary. What Marian attitudes do the Qur'an and Bible emphasize? Are there any significant differences between the stories? Several aspects of the annunciation exchange seem relevant to interfaith dialogue today. Obviously, there is not an exact parallel between the Gabriel-Mary conversation and a Muslim-Christian one. Nevertheless, it may be helpful for modern-day interlocutors to pay attention to Mary's attitudes and actions in both accounts. Here are some key similarities: Mary doesn't immediately respond. Rather, she listens and reflects on what is said. Despite confusion and possibly fear, she does not run away from the stranger who appears at her door; instead, she welcomes him into her home. Gabriel tries to put her at ease, then proceeds to give her some information. Mary still does not understand, so she asks follow-up questions. The angel offers more information. Only at the very end of the dialogue does Mary assent. Hers is not a quick assent; rather, it comes after much reflection. In fact, the Gospel of Luke paints Mary as a woman of contemplation, someone who regularly "ponders" and "treasures" experiences in her heart. Mary is described as a contemplative not only at the annunciation, but also after Jesus is born (Luke 2:19), and when she finds her twelve-year-old son teaching in the temple (Luke 2:51). A similarly inquisitive and courageous Mary can be seen in the Qur'an, when she questions how she can be pregnant (Sura 19:20), and even tells the angel to go away (Sura 19:18). In sum, a modern interfaith encounter inspired by the annunciation Mary might look like this: welcome the stranger into your space, listen first, reflect, ask questions, listen some more, respond with conviction, and later (hopefully) treasure the experience in your heart.

Even if some believers are ambivalent about Mary as a topic of dialogue, they can hardly go wrong accepting her as a model of dialogue. And not only women, but also and especially men, who have often neglected Mary, seeing her only as a paragon of ideal womanhood rather than an example they could imitate too. While there will always be contextual realities and personal preferences that make Mary unappealing to some, nevertheless, scriptural and historical sources, as well as the *sensus fidelium* of ordinary Christians and Muslims, encourage us to embrace her as a model of dialogue. Those who wish to build bridges instead of barriers would do well to follow Mary's lead.

NOTES

PREFACE

1. The following are some examples of magisterial speeches relating Mary and Islam: Cardinal William Keeler, "How Mary Holds Muslims and Christians in Conversation" (1996); Miguel Angel Ayuso, Secretary of the Pontifical Council for Interreligious Dialogue, "The Virgin Mary and Islamic-Christian Dialogue" (2014); Cardinal Francis Arinze, President of the Pontifical Council for Interreligious Dialogue, "Message at Ramadan" (1988). At the first papal visit to a mosque in Damascus in 2001, Pope John Paul II said, "As we make our way through life toward our heavenly destiny, Christians feel the company of Mary, the mother of Jesus; and Islam too pays tribute to Mary and hails her as 'chosen above the women of the world' (Qur'an, 3:42). The virgin of Nazareth, the Lady of Saydnaya, has taught us that God protects the humble and 'scatters the proud in the imagination of their hearts' (Luke 1:51). May the hearts of Christians and Muslims turn to one another with feelings of brotherhood and friendship."

2. William of Tripoli, *Notitia*, chap. 12 in *Wilhelm von Tripolis: Notitia de Machometo et De statu Sarracenorum*, ed. (Latin) and trans. (German) Peter Engels (Würzburg: Echter, 1992).

3. Guillaume Postel, *Alcorani seu legis Mahumeti et evangelistarum concordiae Liber* (Paris, 1543), 21–22. Chicago, Newberry Library, Special collections, Case C 5238.706.

4. Number 6 reads, "Mariam non debere coli aut honorare." Postel, *Alcorani seu legis*, 21.

5. The Christian theology of Islam seeks to explain Islam systematically vis-à-vis Christianity. It is primarily an internal discussion that draws upon authoritative sources such as Scripture and tradition. The development of a Christian theology of Islam is a subset of the

171

larger project of the Christian theology of religions, a discrete theological topic that has burgeoned in the years following Vatican II's *Nostra Aetate* (1965), a document that remains the Catholic Church's official theology of religions, and that spurred statements by other Christian denominations. In the 1990s, Francis X. Clooney and James Fredericks suggested a moratorium on the Christian theology of religions project, favoring comparative theology instead. Many scholars today engage in both.

CHAPTER 1

1. Jon D. Levenson, *Inheriting Abraham: The Legacy of the Patriarch in Judaism, Christianity, and Islam* (Princeton, NJ: Princeton University Press, 2012).

2. Timothy Winter, "Pulchra ut Luna: Some Reflections on the Marian Theme in Muslim-Catholic Dialogue," *Journal of Ecumenical Studies* 36 (1999): 439–69.

3. This orthodox christological language is rooted in Scripture but was expressed more fully in the Nicene-Constantinopolitan Creed (written in 325, expanded in 381), and continued to be refined until the Council of Chalcedon (451), when the language was set. Also, another layer of complexity involves the differing emphases various Christians accord Mary; Catholics and Orthodox (both Eastern and Oriental) have more developed Mariologies than do Protestant Christians, who are critical of what they see as Marian excesses.

4. Aliah Schleifer, *Mary the Blessed Virgin of Islam* (Louisville, KY: Fons Vitae, 1998), 95: "It is the consistent image of Jesus as the son of Mary (which is a constant denial of an image of Jesus as the 'Son of God')…which constitutes the essential doctrinal point which affirms the Qur'anic proclamation of the pure Oneness of God." See also Jane Smith and Yvonne Haddad, "The Virgin Mary in Islamic Tradition and Commentary," *The Muslim World* 79, nos. 3–4 (1989): 161–87.

5. Barbara Stowasser, *Women in the Qur'an, Traditions, and Interpretation* (Oxford: Oxford University Press, 1994), 77. Stowasser notes that some Muslim (Zahiri) theologians, including Ibn Hazm (d. 1064), consider her a prophet, but neither mainstream Islam nor popular piety does, 69. For more on Mary as an Islamic prophet, see chap. 3.

6. Mona Siddiqui, *Christians, Muslims, and Jesus* (New Haven, CT: Yale University Press, 2013), 150–60, 167–68.

7. For more on New Testament Apocrypha in general, see Andrew Gregory and Christopher Tuckett, eds., *The Oxford Handbook of Early Christian Apocrypha* (Oxford: Oxford University Press, 2015), and Tony Burke, *Secret Scriptures Revealed: A New Introduction to the Christian Apocrypha* (Grand Rapids, MI: Eerdmans Publishing, 2013). For an introduction to and translation of the *Protevangelium*, see J. K. Elliott, *The Apocryphal New Testament* (Oxford: Clarendon, 1993), 48–67. See also Irene Backus, "Guillaume Postel, Theodore Bibliander et le Protévangile de Jacques," *Apocrypha* 6 (1995): 7–65; and Cornelia Horn, "Mary between the Bible and Qur'an," *Islam and Christian-Muslim Relations* 18, no. 4 (2007): 509–38.

8. Bart Ehrman and Zlatko Pleše, eds., *The Other Gospels* (Oxford: Oxford University Press, 2014), 18. For a discussion of the *Protevangelium*'s influence on early Christian iconography, see Robin M. Jensen, "The Apocryphal Mary in Early Christian Art," in *The Oxford Handbook of Early Christian Apocrypha*, ed. Gregory and Tuckett, 289–305.

9. Stephen Shoemaker, *Mary in Early Christian Faith and Devotion* (New Haven, CT: Yale University Press, 2016), 47. Ehrman, *The Other Gospels*, 19, notes that this title is found in Bodmer V, the earliest manuscript of the *Protevangelium*, which dates to the third/fourth century.

10. Shoemaker, *Mary in Early Christian Faith*, 49–50, calls it "quasi-canonical," especially in the East, where it was read during the liturgy on Marian feasts; it remained influential in the Western Church as well, despite being declared heretical by Jerome and others due to its mention of Joseph's previous marriage.

11. For more on the *Protevangelium*'s role in the development of early Marian piety, see Shoemaker, *Mary in Early Christian Faith*, and Andrew Louth, "John of Damascus on the Mother of God as a Link between Humanity and God," in *The Cult of the Mother of God in Byzantium*, ed. Leslie Brubaker and Mary Cunningham (Surrey, UK: Ashgate, 2011), 154–55.

12. The Vatican II document *Dei Verbum* (1965) stresses the equal importance of both Scripture and Tradition for Catholics. For more on the idea of Catholic Tradition (capital *T*), see Yves Congar, *Tradition and Traditions* (New York: Macmillan, 1967).

13. Cornelia Horn suggests that a "permeability of boundaries between Eastern Christianity and Islam" allowed for the exchange of ideas and images between Christians and Muslims, and argues that the reception history of the *Protevangelium* shows this text to be "a meeting ground for a cross-fertilization of the Christian and

Islamic traditions with regard to their perceptions of Mary," in "Mary between the Bible and Qur'an," 510 and 513. Horn also suggests that some of this cross-pollination could have taken place in a liturgical (lectionary and homiletic) context rather than simply through textual transmission, 519. See also Gabriel Said Reynolds, *The Qur'an and Its Biblical Subtext* (Oxford: Routledge, 2008) and Hosn Abboud, *Mary in the Qur'an: A Literary Reading* (London: Routledge, 2014), especially chap. 5, "The Infancy Story of Mary: Gender and Narrative Analysis and Intertextuality between the Qur'an and the Protevangelium."

14. Quotations from the Bible are taken from the New Revised Standard Version.

15. Translation by J. K. Elliott in *The Apocryphal New Testament* (Oxford: Clarendon, 1993), 57–67.

16. Translation by M. A. S. Abdel Haleem (Oxford: Oxford University Press, 2010).

17. Islamic tradition (Hadith) also names the mother of Mary as Hanna; see Stowasser, *Women in the Qur'an*, 68.

18. A major point of contention both for Islamic exegetes (and Christian polemicists) is interpreting what the Qur'an means when it calls Mary the daughter of ʿImran, given that in the Bible, Amram is the father of Mariam, sister of Moses, not Mary, mother of Jesus. Some have argued that the qur'anic reference to Mary as "daughter of ʿImran" or "sister of Aaron" suggests her connection to that lineage in general, not a specific person. See Suleiman Mourad, "Mary in the Qur'an: A Reexamination of Her Presentation," in *The Qur'an in Its Historical Context*, ed. Gabriel Reynolds (London: Routledge, 2008), 163–74; also Mourad, "On the Qur'anic Stories about Mary and Jesus," *Bulletin of the Royal Institute for Inter-Faith Studies* 1 (1999): 13–24; and Reynolds, *The Qur'an and Its Biblical Subtext*, 132.

19. Schleifer, *Mary the Blessed Virgin of Islam*, 24.

20. See Suleiman Mourad, "From Hellenism to Christianity and Islam: The Origin of the Palm Tree Story Concerning Mary and Jesus in the Gospel of Pseudo-Matthew and the Qur'an," *Oriens Christianus* 86 (2002): 206–16. The *Apocryphal Gospel of Matthew*, chap. 20, mentions dates, according to A. J. Wensinck and P. Johnstone, "Maryam," in *Encyclopedia of Islam*, 2nd ed. (Leiden: Brill, 1954–2005).

21. In the *Book of Mary's Repose* (*Liber Requiei*), Jews who had been blinded for trying to destroy Mary's body during her funeral procession are healed with a palm from the tree of life that Mary had been given before she died. Steven Shoemaker, *Ancient Traditions of*

the Virgin Mary's Dormition and Assumption (Oxford: Oxford University Press, 2002), 32–42.

22. John Kaltner, "The Muslim Mary," in *New Perspectives on the Nativity*, ed. Jeremy Corley (London: T & T Clark, 2009), 175.

23. Mary Thurlkill, *Chosen among Women: Mary and Fatima in Medieval Christianity and Shi'ite Islam* (Notre Dame, IN: University of Notre Dame Press, 2007).

24. Schleifer, *Mary the Blessed Virgin of Islam*, 65–66.

25. This is a point of ecumenical dialogue. Christians disagree about how far back Mary's sinlessness extends; even among Catholics there has been a lively historical debate about the immaculate conception before it was declared a dogma in 1854. For a recent ecumenical discussion of Mary, see the joint Anglican-Catholic document, "Mary: Grace and Hope in Christ" (2004).

26. Schleifer, *Mary the Blessed Virgin of Islam*, 62. See also Hosn Abboud, *Mary in the Qur'an: A Literary Reading* (London: Routledge, 2014).

27. Stowasser, *Women in the Qur'an*, 69. Stowasser also says that in Ibn Kathir, Anna's prayer to protect Mary from Satan is interpreted to mean that neither Mary nor Jesus were pricked or kicked at birth by Satan, 73.

28. Winter, "Pulchra ut Luna," 446–48.

29. Ibid., and Schleifer, *Mary the Blessed Virgin of Islam*, 66.

30. Schleifer, *Mary the Blessed Virgin of Islam*, 62.

31. Ibid., 64.

32. Louth, "John of Damascus," 154.

33. For more on patristic Mariology, see chap. 2.

34. A few later Islamic sources that give additional details about Jesus include Ibn Kathir's *Stories of the Prophets* and Ibn 'Arabi's *Bezels of Wisdom*.

CHAPTER 2

1. *Akathistos* hymn, strophes 9 and 23, and Prooemium II, trans. Leena Peltomaa in *The Image of the Virgin Mary in the Akathistos Hymn* (Boston: Brill, 2001), 3, 9, 19.

2. Nonnus of Nisibis, *Apologetic Treatise*, as quoted by Sidney Griffith in *The Beginnings of Christian Theology in Arabic* (Aldershot, UK: Ashgate, 2002), 127. Griffith notes that the Syriac word for pagan here, *hanpe*, is related to the Arabic word *hanif*, which Muslims would eventually use to refer to pre-Islamic monotheists such

as Abraham. See also Mark Swanson, "Folly to the Hunafa," in *The Encounter of Eastern Christianity with Early Islam*, ed. E. Grypeou et al. (Leiden: Brill, 2006), 237–38.

3. The literature on patristic Mariology is voluminous. Useful sources include Brian Daley, "Woman of Many Names: Mary in Orthodox and Catholic Theology," *Theological Studies* 71, no. 4 (2010): 846–69; Stephen Shoemaker, *Mary in Early Christian Faith and Devotion* (New Haven, CT: Yale University Press, 2016); and Maria Vassilaki, ed., *Images of the Mother of God: Perceptions of Theotokos in Byzantium* (Surrey, UK: Ashgate, 2005).

4. Brian Daley, *On the Dormition of Mary: Early Patristic Homilies* (Crestwood, NY: St. Vladimir's Press, 1998), 6.

5. For more on early Islam's response to Christianity, see Sidney Griffith, *Church in the Shadow of the Mosque* (Princeton, NJ: Princeton University Press, 2010), 92–93; and David Thomas, *Christian Doctrines in Islamic Theology* (Leiden: Brill, 2008).

6. Griffith, *Church in the Shadow*, 45–47. In fact, Griffith notes that the earliest extant Christian text in Arabic (ca. 755) explicitly mentions the Qur'an, 54–56. See also Kenneth Cragg, *The Arab Christian: A History in the Middle East* (Louisville, KY: Westminster John Knox Press, 1991), 71–94.

7. Another commonality early Christians recognized is monotheism; they praised Muhammad as a good man who turned Arabs away from polytheism and toward belief in one God. Griffith, *Church in the Shadow*, 38 and 104.

8. As outlined by Griffith, *The Beginnings of Christian Theology in Arabic*, 64.

9. John of Damascus, *De haeresibus*, in *John of Damascus on Islam*, trans. Daniel Sahas (Leiden: Brill, 1972). John's presentation of Islam, while certainly rooted in some knowledge of Islamic doctrine and practice (he lived his whole life in the Levant and surely knew Arabic), is far from charitable. Some scholars question whether John wrote the section on Islam at all; see Andrew Louth, *St. John Damascene* (Oxford: Oxford University Press, 2002), 76–83.

10. Bissera Pentcheva, *Icons and Power: The Mother of God in Byzantium* (University Park, PA: Pennsylvania State University Press, 2006).

11. For more on the idea of Mary as *la conquistadora* in medieval Spain and the early modern New World, see the eponymous book by Amy Remensnyder (New York: Oxford University Press, 2014).

12. Griffith, *Church in the Shadow*, 17.

13. In later Byzantium (after the tenth century), when the Ottomans began to push into the Orthodox Christian lands of Southeastern Europe, Mary was still seen as a barrier, but one that comforted them in defeat rather than protected them from invasion. On this neglected idea, see Matthew Milliner, *The Last Madonna* (Oxford: Oxford University Press, forthcoming).

14. Daley, "Woman of Many Names," 846–69, esp. 851.

15. Shoemaker, *Mary in Early Christian Faith and Devotion.*

16. Two recent attempts to remedy this lacuna include Averil Cameron, "The Early Cult of the Virgin," in *Mother of God,* ed. Maria Vassilaki (Athens: Benaki Museum Exhibition Catalogue, 2001), 3–15; and Shoemaker, *Mary in Early Christian Faith.*

17. Shoemaker, *Mary in Early Christian Faith,* 17, 23, 27.

18. Ibid., 6.

19. Shoemaker notes that because most Church fathers are silent about Marian devotion prior to the late fourth century, it is possible that "Marian piety initially emerged within a more popular and less culturally elite context," ibid., 70.

20. Andrew Louth, "John of Damascus, 154.

21. *Sub Tuum Praesidium,* as cited by Shoemaker in *Mary in Early Christian Faith,* 69.

22. Dirk Krausmüller, "Making the Most of Mary," in Brubaker and Cunningham, *Cult of the Mother of God,* 220.

23. Shoemaker, *Mary in Early Christian Faith,* 221.

24. Possibly the earliest reference to the Kathisma is from an Armenian lectionary dated 419–39, according to Rina Avner, "Theotokos at Kathisma," in Brubaker and Cunningham, *Cult of the Mother of God,* 19–20.

25. Avner, "Theotokos at Kathisma," 14–15, 19–20.

26. Shoemaker, *Mary in Early Christian Faith,* 212, 220–22.

27. Pentcheva and other scholars argue for *Akathistos*'s origins in the early fifth century; traditionally the hymn had been dated to the sixth century. For a book-length study of *Akathistos,* see Leena Peltomaa, *Images of the Virgin Mary in the Akathistos Hymn* (Leiden: Brill, 2001).

28. Leena Peltomaa, "Epithets of the Theotokos in the 'Akathistos Hymn,'" in Brubaker and Cunningham, *Cult of the Mother of God* 114–15, and Margaret Barker, "Wisdom Imagery," in Brubaker and Cunningham, *Cult of the Mother of God,* 94–95.

29. Barker, "Wisdom Imagery," 107; Peltomaa, "Epithets," 113.

CHRISTIANS, MUSLIMS, AND MARY

30. According to Pentcheva, *Icons and Power*: "In the course of the hymn the image of the Theotokos transforms from a vessel of the Incarnation to an active power able to secure victory and protection," 14.

31. Of course, exceptions exist on both sides. One of the medieval Latin names for Mary was *turris Davidica* (tower of David), while some patristic-era Byzantine icons feature Mary breastfeeding Jesus. Milliner in *The Last Madonna* suggests that recent scholarship has focused too much on Mary as a victor in fifth-century Byzantium, and neglected an important counterpoint image of Mary as a comforter of the defeated.

32. Pentcheva, *Icons and Power*: "By the tenth century the hymn [*akathistos*] was performed on the eve of Saturday of the fifth week of Lent, a day intended to commemorate the Virgin Mary's victory over the barbarians and to offer thanks to her for her unfailing protection of Constantinople," 67.

33. Ibid., 63–65.

34. George of Pisidia as quoted in ibid., 66, and Theodore Synkellos as quoted in ibid., 64.

35. Severian of Gabala as quoted in Shoemaker, *Mary in Early Christian Faith*, 177–78.

36. Ibid., 178.

37. *Akathistos* hymn (strophe 11), 11.

38. Pentcheva, *Icons and Power*, 61.

39. Ibid., 38. Early accounts of the Avar siege include a poem by George of Pisidia, a sermon by Theodore Synkellos, and an excerpt in the *Chronicon Paschale*.

40. Pentcheva, *Icons and Power*, 62–63.

41. Pentcheva, ibid., 59, notes "the cult of images appeared after and was always dependent on the more established cult of relics."

42. Ibid., 55–56.

43. The medieval text is *Anonymous Tarragonensis* (ca. 1075–98). Pentcheva, *Icons and Power*, 56–57.

44. *Cantiga* 28, translated by Kathleen Kulp-Hill in *Songs of Holy Mary of Alfonso X the Wise* (Tempe, AZ: Arizona Center for Medieval and Renaissance Studies, 2000), 39.

45. Pentcheva, *Icons and Power*, 33. August 15 is the Feast of the Assumption/Dormition, a date that also commemorates a 718 Byzantine victory over Saracens, and a 1715 Croatian victory over Ottomans in Sinj. For more on Sinj, see chap. 5.

46. *Cantiga* 28, in Kulp-Hill, *Songs of Holy Mary*, 39–40.

47. See Michele Bacci, "The Legacy of the Hodegetria: Holy Icons and Legends between East and West," in Vassilaki, *Images of the Mother of God*, 321–36.

48. Matthew Milliner has highlighted Mary's role as "Our Lady of Losers" (his term). In his book *The Last Madonna*, he notes that Mary's "'affective piety' was long thought to have arisen in Byzantium's ninth century, or in the eleventh in the West. But Maximus offers evidence" of late antique origins for the compassionate Mary, who would "become the mainstay of Byzantine Marian devotion in centuries to come, later to be visualized in the mourning Marys of Ohrid, Nerezi, Studenica and Kastoria," 26.

49. Key sources on early Arabophone Christian theology include Emmanouela Grypeou, Mark Swanson, and David Thomas, eds., *The Encounter of Eastern Christianity with Early Islam* (Leiden: Brill, 2006); Griffith, *Church in the Shadow*; R. G. Hoyland, *Seeing Islam as Others Saw It: A Survey and Evaluation of Christian, Jewish, and Zoroastrian Writings on Early Islam* (Princeton, NJ: Princeton University Press, 1997); *Christian-Muslim Relations: A Bibliographical History, Volume 1 (600–900 CE)*, ed. David Thomas and Barbara Roggema (Leiden: Brill, 2009).

50. Griffith, *Church in the Shadow*, 75–77. Of course, Muslim theology of the time was also influenced by Christian theology. See, for example, Thomas, *Christian Doctrines in Islamic Theology*, and David Cook, "New Testament Citations in the Hadith Literature," in Grypeou et al., *Encounter of Eastern Christianity with Early Islam*. Also, Irfan Shahid, "Islam and Oriens Christianus," in Grypeou et al., *Encounter of Eastern Christianity with Early Islam*, suggests that Mecca's seventh-century Ethiopian colony influenced the development of Islamic theology and specifically its Christology.

51. The *majlis* was the place Christian monks or bishops were summoned by Muslim leaders to debate religious issues. For more on Arabophone Christian polemical/apologetic genres, see Griffith, *Church in the Shadow*, 77–81.

52. Ibid., 57–60.

53. Ibid., 17.

54. Christians failed to understand that Muslims took the qur'anic references to Amram and Aaron allegorically. See Suleiman Mourad, "Mary in the Qur'an," in *The Qur'an in Its Historical Context*, ed. Gabriel Said Reynolds (Oxford: Routledge, 2008), 164–74, esp. 163–66. For more on this topic, see chap. 3 of this book on the Muslim Mary.

55. The *shahada* is the first of five pillars of Islam; it is the basic Muslim creed that proclaims, "There is no God but God and Muhammad is the messenger of God." Gerrit Reinink, "Political Power and Right Religion," in Grypeou et al., *Encounter of Eastern Christianity with Early Islam*, 154.

56. Cook, "Gospel in Hadith," in Grypeou et al., *Encounter of Eastern Christianity with Early Islam*, 190.

57. Reinink, "Political Power," 166.

58. Irfan Shahid argues that Ethiopian Christian colonies living outside Mecca in the first half of the seventh century influenced early Islam; he notes the preponderance of Ethiopian characters in early Islam, including Muhammad's wet nurse Baraka, Bilal the first muezzin, and the story of Muslim refugees at the court of the Ethiopian Negus. See Irfan Shahid, "Islam and Oriens Christianus," in Grypeou et al., *Encounter of Eastern Christianity with Early Islam*, 13.

59. "Common Christological Statement between the Catholic Church and the Assyrian Church of the East," (1994), §5. http://www.vatican.va/roman_curia/pontifical_councils/chrstuni/documents/rc_pc_chrstuni_doc_11111994_assyrian-church_en.html.

60. For more on Eastern Christians, see Ronald Roberson, *Eastern Churches: A Brief Survey*, 7th edition (Rome: Edizioni Orientalia Christiana, 2008), and Cragg, *The Arab Christian*, 15–22.

61. Except Georgians, Armenians, and Ethiopians—all of whom remained Christian-majority nations. However, Georgia, Armenia, and Ethiopia are all Christian nations that have been "islands" surrounded by Islamic civilization.

62. An unedited Syriac text from the late 7th century is believed to be an early example of an experimental Christian polemic against Islam formulated from older, anti-Jewish arguments. See Muriel Debié, "Muslim-Christian Controversy in an Unedited Syriac Text: Revelations and Testimonies about Our Lord's Dispensation," in Grypeou et al., *Encounter of Eastern Christianity with Early Islam*, 233.

63. Jacob of Edessa, *Letter on the Genealogy of the Virgin*, trans. Robert Hoyland in "Jacob of Edessa on Islam," in *After Bardaisan*, ed. G. Reinink and A. Klugkist (Leuven: Peeters, 1999), 156. Text (Syriac) and translation (French) of Jacob's *Letter on the Genealogy* is in François Nau, "Lettre de Jacques D'Edesse sur la généalogie de la Sainte Vierge," *Revue de L'Orient Chrétien* 6 (1901): 512–31.

64. R. G. Hoyland, "Jacob of Edessa on Islam," in Reinink and Klugkist, *After Bardaisan*, 149–60.

65. Andrew's biography in Mary Cunningham, *Wider Than Heaven: Eighth Century Homilies on the Mother of God* (Crestwood, NY: St. Vladimir's Press, 2008), 41–44.

66. Jacob, *Letter*, 525 and 526. Translations from Nau's French are my own.

67. Ibid., 524.

68. Ibid.

69. Ibid.

70. Ibid., as quoted by Hoyland, "Jacob of Edessa on Islam," 156.

71. Jacob, *Letter*, 526.

72. Syriac original and English translation by Alphonse Mingana in "The Apology of Timothy the Patriarch before the Caliph Mahdi," in *Woodbrooke Studies: Christian Documents in Syriac, Arabic, and Garshuni*, vol. 2 (Cambridge: Heffer, 1928), 15–162. The translation can be found at http://www.tertullian.org/fathers/timothy_i_apology_01_text.htm. For commentary on this text, see Martin Heimgartner, "Letter 59 (Disputation with the Caliph al-Mahdi)," in Thomas and Roggema, *Christian-Muslim Relations*, 522–26, and Charles Tieszen, "Can You Find Anything Praiseworthy in My Religion?" in *The Character of Christian-Muslim Encounter*, ed. Douglas Pratt et al. (Leiden: Brill, 2015), especially 132–40.

73. "The Apology of Timothy," 17.

74. Ibid.

75. Ibid., 18.

76. Ibid.

77. Ibid.

78. Al-Kindi, *Risalat*, trans. Anton Tien and N. A. Newman in *Early Christian-Muslim Dialogue: A Collection of Documents from the First Three Islamic Centuries*, ed. N. A. Newman (Hatfield, PA: Interdisciplinary Biblical Research Institute, 1993), 381–545. See also the new English translation and critical edition by Sandra Toenies Keating and Krisztina Szilagyi (Leiden: Brill, forthcoming). The *Risalat* eventually became part of the so-called Toledan Collection, Peter the Venerable's influential corpus that included the first Latin Qur'an and other Islamic texts. See Marie d'Alverny, "Deux traductions latines du Coran au Môyen Age," *Archives d'histoire doctrinale et litteraire du môyen age* 16 (1948): 69–131; James Kritzeck, *Peter the Venerable and Islam* (Princeton, NJ: Princeton University Presss, 1964); and José Martínez Gázquez, "Translations of the Qur'an and Other Islamic Texts before Dante (Twelfth and Thirteenth Centuries)," *Dante Studies* 125 (2007): 79–92.

79. Griffith, *Church in the Shadow*, 85–88.

80. Al-Kindi, *Risalat*, 500.

81. Ibid., 501. For more on the *Risalat*, see A. Abel, "L'apologie d'Al-Kindi et sa place dans la polémique islamo-chrétien," in *Atti del convegno internazionale sul tema: L'oriente christiano nella storia della civiltà* (Rome, 1964), 501–23; P. van Konigsveld, "The Apology of al-Kindi," in *Religious Polemics in Context*, ed. T. L. Hettema and A. van der Kooij (Leiden: Brill, 2005), 69–92; and Laura Bottini, "The Apology of al-Kindi," in Thomas and Roggema, *Christian-Muslim Relations*, 584–94.

82. See David Thomas, *Early Muslim Polemic against Christianity* (Cambridge: Cambridge University Press, 2002), 199n45: "The distinction between the two forms Yasu‘ and ʿIsa suggests that al Warraq [a ninth-century Muslim polemicist] may be reproducing a brief Christian statement he knows in which the name has intentionally been preserved in its non-Qur'anic Arabic form in order to distinguish the figure of Christian belief from the ʿIsa of the Qur'an. The convert Ali al-Tabari customarily uses the form Yasu‘ when referring to Christian teachings about Jesus…but ʿIsa when referring to Jesus as one of the line of prophets."

83. Bartholomew of Edessa, *Refutation of the Hagarene* (PG 104:1397), as quoted by Jaroslav Pelikan, *Mary through the Centuries* (New Haven, CT: Yale University Press, 1996), 77. Pelikan placed Bartholomew in the ninth century, but scholars now date him to the twelfth.

84. Jane Baum, "Apocalyptic Panagia," in Brubaker and Cunningham, *Cult of the Mother of God*, 202.

CHAPTER 3

1. Qurtubi is commenting on Sura 3:40–42. As quoted in Mahmoud Ayoub, *The Qur'an and Its Interpreters*, vol. 2 (New York: State University of New York, 1992), 124.

2. Two major examples include the ecumenical Christian Statement of Seelisberg (1947) and the Catholic conciliar document *Nostra Aetate* (1965), §4.

3. Ibn Ishaq, *The Life of Muhammad*, trans. A. Guillaume (Oxford: Oxford University Press, 1955), 152.

4. Aliah Schleifer, *Mary the Blessed Virgin of Islam* (Louisville, KY: Fons Vitae, 1998), 73–74.

5. For more on this topic in Islamic theology, see Mohammad Hassan Khalil, ed., *Between Heaven and Hell: Islam, Salvation, and*

Notes

the Fate of Others (Oxford: Oxford University Press, 2013); Sherman Jackson, *On the Boundaries of Theological Tolerance in Islam* (Oxford: Oxford University Press, 2002); Joseph Lumbard, "The Quranic View of Sacred History and Other Religions," in *The Study Qur'an*, trans. and ed. Seyyed Hossein Nasr, Caner K. Dagli, Maria Massi Dakake, Joseph Lumbard, and Mohammed Rustom (New York: HarperCollins, 2015); Seyyed Hossein Nasr, "The Creation of the World and of Human Beings," "Religion and Religions," "Islam and the Encounter of Religions," and "Islam's Attitude towards Other Religions in History," in *The Religious Other: Towards a Muslim Theology of Other Religions in a Post-prophetic Age*, ed. Muhammad Suheyl Umar (Lahore: Iqbal Academy Pakistan, 2008) , 47–58, 59–81, 83–120, 121–34; Fazlur Rahman, "The People of the Book and the Diversity of 'Religions,'" in *Christianity through Non-Christian Eyes*, ed. Paul J. Griffiths (Maryknoll, NY: Orbis, 1990); Abdulaziz Sachedina, "The Qur'an and Other Religions," in *The Cambridge Companion to the Qur'an*, ed. Jane Dammen McAuliffe (Cambridge: Cambridge University, 2006); Mun'im Sirry, "'Compete with One Another in Good Works': Exegesis of Qur'an Verse 5.48 and Contemporary Muslim Discourses on Religious Pluralism," *Islam and Christian-Muslim Relations* 20, no. 4 (2009): 424–38; M. Hakan Yavuz, *Toward an Islamic Enlightenment: The Gülen Movement* (Oxford: Oxford University Press, 2013), 173–97.

    6. Brian Daley, "Woman of Many Names: Mary in Orthodox and Catholic Theology," *Theological Studies* 71 (2010): 851.

    7. Schleifer, *Mary the Blessed Virgin of Islam*, 56.

    8. The NRSV footnote to Luke 1:28 comments, "Other ancient authorities add *Blessed are you among women.*"

    9. Jane Smith and Yvonne Haddad, "The Virgin Mary in Islamic Tradition and Commentary," *The Muslim World* 79, nos. 3–4 (1989): 172–73.

    10. Ibid., 173–74.

    11. ʿAbd al-Jabbar, *Critique of Christian Origins: A Parallel English-Arabic Text*, trans. and ed. Gabriel Said Reynolds and Samir Khalil Samir (Provo, UT: Brigham Young University Press, 2010), 81.

    12. Barbara Stowasser, *Women in the Qur'an, Traditions, and Interpretation* (Oxford: Oxford University Press, 1994), 77.

    13. Ibn Hazm, *Risala fi al-Mufadala bayna al-Sahaba* (Treatise of differentiation between the prophet's companions) as quoted by Hosn Abboud in "Idhan Maryam Nabiyya' (Hence Maryam is a Prophetess)," in *Mariam, the Magdalen, and the Mother*, ed. Deirdre Joy Good (Bloomington: Indiana University Press, 2005), 184.

183

14. Ibn Hazm, *Al Fasl fi al-Miala wa l-Ahwa wa l-Nihal* (The decisive word on sects, heterodoxies, and denominations) as quoted by Abboud in "Idhan Maryam," 184.

15. Stowasser, *Women in the Qur'an*, 77.

16. The Qur'an describes her as receiving *wahy*, in Sura 28:7.

17. Stowasser, *Women in the Qur'an*, 77.

18. Joseph Lumbard, "The Qur'anic View of Sacred History and Other Religions," in Nasr et al., *Study Qur'an*, 763; Schleifer, *Mary the Blessed Virgin of Islam*, 78–79, 81.

19. Stowasser, *Women in the Qur'an*, 82–84.

20. Ibid., 82–84, 90.

21. Perpetua in *The Passion of Perpetua and Felicity*, trans. W. H. Shewring (London, 1931), §10. There are many other examples of early Christians defining female virtue in terms of masculinity—these appear in sources as diverse as Gregory of Nyssa's *Life of Macrina* (Greek) and the sayings of the Desert Mothers (Coptic). These associations make sense in Latin, where the word *virtus* can be translated as "virtue," "strength," and "masculinity."

22. Jalal ad din Rumi, *Fihi ma fihi*, chap. 5, as quoted by Annemarie Schimmel in "Jesus and Mary as Poetical Images in Rumi's Verse," in *The Routledge Reader in Christian-Muslim Relations*, ed. Mona Siddiqui (London: Routledge, 2013), 289.

23. Abboud, "Idhan Maryam," 185–86.

24. Ibid.

25. Smith and Haddad, "The Virgin Mary in Islamic Tradition," 178.

26. Al-Razi, *Al-Tafsir al-Kabir*, as quoted by Abboud in "Idhan Maryam," 187.

27. Schleifer, *Mary the Blessed Virgin of Islam*, 78–80, 88–89.

28. Ibid., 81.

29. Ibid., 93.

30. Stowasser, *Women in the Qur'an*, 81.

31. Ibid.

32. In the first decade of the twenty-first century, Maryam consistently made the top ten list of the most popular baby names for girls in Arab countries.

33. Ibn Taymiyya, *Majmu'at al-fatawa*, vol. 27 (Mansura, Egypt: Dar al-wafa', 2005).

34. Christopher S. Taylor, *In the Vicinity of the Righteous: Ziyara and the Veneration of Muslim Saints in Late Medieval Egypt* (Leiden: Brill, 1999).

35. Women are more likely than men to engage in such popular religious practices because they have traditionally been excluded from other more orthodox Islamic rituals such as Friday prayer, according to Willy Jansen and Meike Kühl, "Shared Symbols: Muslims, Marian Pilgrimages and Gender," *European Journal of Women's Studies* 15, no. 3 (2008): 295–311.

36. See Ondrej Beranek and Pavel Tupek, "From Visiting Graves to Their Destruction: The Question of Ziyara through the Eyes of Salafis," *Brandeis University Crown Center for Middle East Studies* (July 2009): 3, 8. For the general exclusion of women from mosque prayer in the Arabian peninsula, see Eleanor Abdella Doumato, *Getting God's Ear: Women, Islam, and Healing in Saudi Arabia and the Gulf* (New York: Columbia University Press, 2000), 94–112. Doumato cites one exception: Oman, where women sometimes have had their own separate mosques, 102.

37. Josef W. Meri, *The Cult of Saints among Muslims and Jews in Medieval Syria* (Oxford: Oxford University Press, 2002), 188.

38. Rabia's tomb is noted by Nasir al-Din, "Guide for Muslim Pilgrims" (*Al-Mustaqsa fi Fada'il al-Masjid al-Aqsa*) in Amikam Elad, *Medieval Jerusalem and Islamic Worship* (Leiden: Brill, 1995), 170. See also Elad's commentary, 145.

39. Two recent exceptions: Virgin Mary Mosque in Australia (2004) and Sayyida Maryam Mosque in Syria (2014). But these are mosques, not shrines visited by pilgrims.

40. Elad, *Medieval Jerusalem*, 138–39.

41. Ibid.

42. Ibid., 141.

43. Muslim women who visited the Marian shrines in Germany, Portugal, and Turkey were interviewed by Jansen and Kühl, "Shared Symbols." Thanks to Lucinda Mosher for bringing to my attention the Bulgarian Orthodox Church in Dearborn as a recent destination for Muslim pilgrims in the United States.

44. Jansen and Kühl, "Shared Symbols," 302.

45. Doumato, *Getting God's Ear*, 111–12.

46. Jansen and Kühl, "Shared Symbols," 302.

47. Schleifer, *Mary the Blessed Virgin of Islam*, 61.

48. Nasir al-Din, "Guide for Muslim Pilgrims," 170–71. A sixteenth-century Italian pilgrimage guide by Barbone Morosini also mentions the House of Mary as a shared Christian-Muslim site, with festivities taking place on Assumption Day, 1514. See Barbone Morosini, "Pellegrinaggio in Terra Santa," *Collectanea* 33, nos. 31–33 (2000): 251–336. Thanks to Iris Shagrir for this reference.

49. Personal correspondence from Dr. William Toma, an Assyrian Christian scholar from Iraq now living in Chicago.

50. As quoted by Anne Garrels, *Naked in Baghdad: The Iraq War and the Aftermath* (New York: Picador/Farrar, Straus, and Giroux, 2003), 55.

51. Linda Walbridge, *Christians in Pakistan: The Passion of Bishop John Joseph* (New York: Routledge, 2003), 190–91.

52. Thank you to Fr. Bonaventure Mendes and Fr. Emmanuel Asi of Pakistan for providing this information.

53. As quoted in Gauvin Bailey, *The Jesuits and the Grand Mogul: Renaissance Art at the Imperial Court of India, 1580–1630* (Washington, DC: Smithsonian Institute, 1998), 46–47.

54. Ibid., 45–46.

55. Ibid.

56. See Punam Madhok, "Christian-Islamic Relations in the Court Art of Mughal India," *International Journal of the Arts in Society* 4, no. 6 (2010): 67–78, and Milo Beach, *The Grand Mughul: Imperial Painting in India* (Williamstown, MA: The Clark Institute, 1978).

57. Bailey, *Jesuits and the Grant Mogul*, 98. The portrait of Jahangir holding an icon of Mary is at the Musée de Guimet in Paris, according to Bailey.

58. Ibid., 19.

59. Ibid.

60. Ibid., 38. For more on the Islamic use of Christian images in India, see Gregory Minissale, *Images of Thought: Visuality in Islamic India, 1550–1750* (Cambridge: Cambridge Scholars, 2009), 216–21.

61. Oleg Grabar, *Mostly Miniatures* (Princeton, NJ: Princeton University Press, 2000), 91.

62. One example: in a 1570 illustration of Yusuf (Joseph) and Zulayka, Yusuf's face is uncovered, but he has a fire halo. Sheila Canby, *Persian Painting* (London: British Museum Press, 1993), 86.

63. Ibid., 28–30, 88.

64. David Thomas, *Christian Doctrines in Islamic Theology* (Leiden: Brill, 2008), 7.

65. Another interpretation of these verses is that they do not represent actual orthodox Christian beliefs, but rather, are examples of excessive idolatry among some heterodox Christians of the time. See David Thomas, "Christian Religion (Premodern Muslim Positions)," in *Encyclopaedia of Islam 3*, ed. Kate Fleet, Gudrun Krämer, Denis Matringe, John Nawas, Everett Rowson (Leiden: Brill, 2017), http://dx.doi.org/10.1163/1573-3912_ei3_COM_25503.

66. Smith and Haddad, "The Virgin Mary in Islam," 185, note that the qur'anic description of Christians divinizing Mary may describe the Kollyridians, a heretical Christian sect of the fourth century that included female priests and eucharistic bread offered to Mary.

67. Sidney Griffith, *Church in the Shadow of the Mosque* (Princeton, NJ: Princeton University Press, 2010), 30.

68. Ibid., 29–30.

69. ʿAbd al-Jabbar, *Critique of Christian Origins*, 2.

70. Al-Warraq, *The Refutation of the Uniting*, §187–88, as quoted by David Thomas, *Early Muslim Polemic against Christianity* (Cambridge: Cambridge University Press, 2002), 127–29.

71. ʿAbd al-Jabbar, *Critique of Christian Origins*, §2.481, at 81.

72. Ibid., §2:505–507, at 83.

73. Ibid., §2:514, at 84. Reynolds and Samir note in the introduction, lxi, n113, that the prayer cited by ʿAbd al-Jabbar is similar to Jacobite prayers preserved in Coptic manuscripts of the time.

74. Ibid., §3:730, 732, 735, at 162.

75. Ibid., §3:757, at 164.

76. Ibid., §3:768, at 165.

77. Smith and Haddad, "The Virgin Mary in Islam," 187.

CHAPTER 4

1. William of Tripoli, *Notitia de Machometo*, §15, in *Wilhelm von Tripolis: Notitia de Machometo et De statu Sarracenorum*, ed. and trans. (German) Peter Engels (Würzburg: Echter, 1992), 256–58.

2. For more on Riccoldo da Montecroce, see Rita George-Tvrtković, *A Christian Pilgrim in Medieval Iraq: Riccoldo da Montecroce's Encounter with Islam* (Turnhout: Brepols, 2012).

3. For more on William, see the introduction in Engels, *Wilhelm von Tripolis*, 52–74, and also Thomas O'Meara, "The Theology and Times of William of Tripoli: A Different View of Islam," *Theological Studies* 69 (2008): 80–98.

4. William, *Notitia*, §12.

5. Nicholas of Cusa, *Cribratio alkorani*, in *Nicolai de Cusa Opera Omnia*, vol. 8, ed. Ludwig Hagemann (Hamburg: Felix Meiner Verlag, 1986), §I.1 (lies), §I.8 (truth), 40.

6. Even though the Christian theology of Islam is a recent theological subdiscipline (developed in the last sixty years), medieval texts do contain nascent theologies of Islam that are sometimes implicit

and fragmentary, and at other times more explicit and systematic. See the introduction for a definition of the Christian theology of religions, and chap. 8 for recent developments in the Christian theology of Islam.

7. The classic discussion of the mainstream medieval theology of Islam is still Norman Daniel, *Islam and the West* (Edinburgh: Edinburgh University Press, 1960). The new classic is John Tolan, *Saracens* (New York: Columbia University Press, 2002).

8. Riccoldo, *Epistolae ad Ecclesiam Triumphantem*, trans. George-Tvrtković in *A Christian Pilgrim in Medieval Iraq*, 149. Riccoldo repeats the Mary-Miriam mix-up in other writings, including *Liber Peregrinationis*, trans. George-Tvrtković in *A Christian Pilgrim in Medieval Iraq*, 219; and *Contra Legem Sarracenorum*, ed. Jean-Marie Mérigoux in "L'ouvrage d'un frère prêcheur en Orient à la fin du XIIIe s. suivi de l'édition du Contra legem Sarracenorum," *Memorie Domenicane*, 17 (1986): §9 and §11.

9. Riccoldo, *Epistolae*, 161.

10. On Riccoldo's questions about the divine status of the Qur'an and the legitimacy of Islam, see *Epistolae*, esp. 141–42, 157, 161. He answers the question in *Contra Legem*, §§4, 6–10. For an extended discussion of these questions, see George-Tvrtković, *A Christian Pilgrim in Medieval Iraq*, chap. 5.

11. On the medieval *dialogus* genre (which relates to both Christian-Jewish and Christian-Muslim polemics), see Amos Funkenstein, "Basic Types of Christian Anti-Jewish Polemics in the Later Middle Ages," *Viator* 2 (1971): 373–82. For more on the idea of constructed images of Jews and Muslims in medieval Christian polemics, see Jeremy Cohen, *Living Letters of the Law: Ideas of the Jew in Medieval Christianity* (Berkeley: University of California Press, 1999), and Ryan Szpiech, "Rhetorical Muslims: Islam as Witness in Western Christian Anti-Jewish Polemic," *Al-Qantara* 34, no. 1 (2013): 153–85.

12. William, *Notitia*, §11, 238.

13. Ibid., §10, 230.

14. Ibid., §10, 232. This is my translation of William's Latin quote of the Qur'an; scholars do not know if William translated the passage himself, or if he was consulting another Latin version of the Qur'an.

15. Sura 57:27b claims that monasticism is not from God, but a Christian invention, and calls most Christians "lawbreakers."

16. William, *Notitia*, §15, 256–58.

17. Ibid., 258.

18. Scholars such as Peter Engels and John Tolan believe that *De statu* was written by someone in William's school of thought ("Pseudo-William"). See the introduction and critical Latin text of *De statu Saracenorum* in Engels, *Wilhelm von Tripolis*, 73–4. For a dissenting view, see O'Meara, "The Theology and Times of William Tripoli," 93, who thinks that William wrote both *Notitia* and *De statu*.

19. Pseudo-William, *De statu*, §48, 360.

20. William's phrasing here (that Muslims are "neighbors to the Christian faith") alludes to Hebrews 11:6, a text often cited in Scholastic questions on the salvation of non-Christians in order to lay down the necessity of faith and its two minimum requirements: belief in God's existence and providence. Aquinas requires explicit faith in the Trinity and Christ for salvation before the incarnation for *maiores*, but only implicit faith for *minores*. It seems that William of Tripoli anticipated more modern sixteenth or seventeenth century ways of conceiving the salvation of non-Christians, at least in the passage quoted here. Thanks to Trent Pomplun for suggesting this connection.

21. For more on Nicholas's views of Islam, see *Nicholas of Cusa and Islam: Polemic and Dialogue in the Late Middle Ages*, ed. Ian Levy, Rita George-Tvrtković, and Donald Duclow (Leiden: Brill, 2014), especially Walter Andreas Euler, "A Critical Survey of Cusanus's Writings on Islam," 20–29.

22. Jasper Hopkins, "The Role of *Pia Interpretatio* in Nicholas of Cusa's Hermeneutical Approach to the Koran," in *A Miscellany on Nicholas of Cusa*, ed. Jasper Hopkins (Minneapolis: Banning Press, 1994).

23. Pim Valkenberg, "Learned Ignorance and Faithful Interpretation of the Qur'an in Nicholas of Cusa," in *Learned Ignorance: Intellectual Humility among Jews, Christians, and Muslims*, ed. James Heft, Reuven Firestone, and Omid Safti (Oxford: Oxford University Press, 2011), 46.

24. Valkenberg, "Learned Ignorance," 42.

25. Aquinas, *Summa contra Gentiles*, §I.6. Translated by Joseph Kenny (New York: Hanover House, 1955–57).

26. According to Martínez Gázquez in his article, "A New Set of Glosses to the Latin Qur'ān Made by Nicholas of Cusa (MS Vat. Lat. 4071)" *Medieval Encounters* 21 (2015): 295–309, Nicholas consulted a Latin Qur'an (Kues MS 108) to write *De pace fidei* in 1453, but then later studied (and heavily glossed) a second Latin Qur'an that was, and still is, housed in the Vatican Library (MS Vat. Lat. 4071). Martínez Gázquez suggests that it was the Vatican MS, not Kues 108,

that Nicholas consulted while he was in Rome writing the *Cribratio alkorani*. A transcription of Cusa's marginal notes in the Vatican MS (including several about Mary) is currently being prepared for publication by Martínez Gázquez.

27. Nicholas, *Cribratio alkorani*, §I.8, 39–40. Emphasis mine.

28. In his introduction to *Wilhelm von Tripolis*, 120, Engels notes that one of three extant copies of *Notitia* (MS London British Museum Add. 19952, folios 85–111) contains the following autograph: "Iste liber est domini Nicolai de Cusa." According to Martínez Gázquez in a personal correspondence, MS 19952 contains a few marginal glosses by Nicholas. Furthermore, Nicholas does *not* include William of Tripoli in his long list of sources for information about Islam in the prologue to *Cribratio alkorani*.

29. For a comparison of the exegetical approaches of Riccoldo and Ramon, see Thomas Burman, "Two Dominicans, a Lost Manuscript, and Medieval Christian Thought on Islam," in *Commentary, Conflict, and Community in the Premodern Mediterranean*, ed. Ryan Szpiech (New York: Fordham University Press, 2015), 71–86.

30. Pim Valkenberg, "*Una Religio in Rituum Varietate*: Religious Pluralism, the Qur'an, and Nicholas of Cusa" in Levy et al., *Nicholas of Cusa and Islam*, 30–48.

31. Nicholas, *Cribratio alkorani*, second prologue, 17.

32. Ibid., §III.17, 176–77.

33. The letter can be found in Aeneas Silvius Piccolomini (Pius II), *Epistola ad Mahomatem II*, ed. and trans. (English) Albert Baca (New York: Peter Lang, 1990).

34. In fact, *Cribratio alkorani* is dedicated to Pius II. For more on Pius II's letter and its relation to Nicholas's *Cribratio alkorani,* see Andrea Moudarres, "Crusade and Conversion: Islam as Schism in Pius II and Nicholas of Cusa," *MLN* 128, no. 1 (2013), 40–52, as well as James Biechler, "Christian Humanism Confronts Islam: Sifting the Qur'an with Nicholas of Cusa," *Journal of Ecumenical Studies* 13 (1976): 14, who suggests that Nicholas's *Cribratio alkorani* influenced Pius's letter. For more on the personal relationship between Nicholas and Pius, see Christopher Bellitto, Thomas Izbicki, and Gerald Christiansen, eds., *Introducing Nicholas of Cusa: Guide to a Renaissance Man* (New York: Paulist, 2004), 44–47.

35. Nicholas, *Cribratio alkorani*, §III.17, 176.

36. Ibid., §III.17, 174–75.

37. See John Tolan, "Saracen Philosophers Secretly Deride Islam," *Medieval Encounters* 11 (2002): 184–208.

38. David Bertaina, "Christians in Medieval Shīʿī Historiography," *Medieval Encounters* 19 (2013): 379–407, esp. 385–89, 394, 406.

39. Nicholas, *De pace*, in *Nicolai de Cusa Opera Omnia*, vol. 7, ed. Raymond Klibansky and Hildebrand Bascour (Hamburg: Felix Meiner Verlag, 1959), §XVII, 57.

40. Ibid., §XVI, 55–56. Circumcision was one of the topics discussed between Latin and Coptic Christians during unity talks at the Council of Ferrara-Florence (1438).

41. "Religio una in rituum varietate," Nicholas, *De pace*, §I, 7. For a discussion of qur'anic influences on Nicholas's use of this phrase, see Valkenberg, *"Una Religio in Rituum Varietate*: Religious Pluralism, the Qur'an, and Nicholas of Cusa" in Levy et al., *Nicholas of Cusa and Islam*, 30–48. As to "in rituum varietate," Cary Nederman, *Worlds of Difference: European Discourses on Tolerance, c. 1100–1550* (University Park, PA: Pennsylvania State Press, 2000), suggests that Nicholas's distinctive contribution to the early modern discourse on pluralism "was to connect his critique of intolerance to differences in nationality," 89–90.

42. Pseudo-William, *De statu*, §55, 370.

43. Ibid., §53, 366.

44. "And if only they would conclude that the word of God is from God through divine and eternal generation, and that the Holy Spirit of God proceeds from God and through the Word generated eternally, they would know that the Father and Son and Holy Spirit are three things in themselves in their essence or person, and which is one deity," ibid., §53, 366.

45. William, *Notitia*, §12, 246–48.

46. Ibid., §15, 256–58.

47. For more on the citing of personal experience as a theological authority by medieval Latin Christians, see Ryan Szpiech, *Conversion and Narrative: Reading and Religious Authority in Medieval Polemic* (Philadelphia: University of Pennsylvania Press, 2012), 7–8, and George-Tvrtković, *A Christian Pilgrim in Medieval Iraq*, chap. 6.

48. The Dominicans' "refute error, expound the truth" strategy can be found in *Summa contra Gentiles* §1.1, where Aquinas describes the goal of wise persons in general (not missionaries in particular): "to meditate and publish the divine truth…and to refute the error contrary to truth," while Master of the Order Humbert of Romans specifically asked missionaries to have treatises against the errors of heretics, Jews, Muslims, and others. For more on the medieval Dominican missionary strategy, see Benjamin Kedar, *Crusade and*

Mission (Princeton, NJ: Princeton University Press, 1984) and Tolan, *Saracens*, "The Dominican Missionary Strategy," 233–55.

CHAPTER 5

1. Pope Pius V, *Salvatoris Domini*, March 5, 1572, as quoted by Cyril Dore in "The Popes and the Rosary," *Dominicana* 10, no. 2 (September 1925): 15–21.

2. For an extended discussion of Lepanto, see Kenneth Sutton, *The Papacy and the Levant, 1204–1571* (Philadelphia: American Philosophical Society, 1984), 1045–1104. For details on how Lepanto was celebrated in Rome soon after the battle, see Anthony Majanlahti, *The Families Who Made Rome* (London: Chatto & Windus, 2005). Also, Thomas Dandelet, *Spanish Rome 1500–1700* (New Haven, CT: Yale University Press, 2001), describes a public Easter procession in Rome commemorating the twenty-fifth anniversary of Lepanto in 1596 that might have influenced later artistic depictions of Lepanto. See also Paul Anderson, "Marcantonio Colonna and the Victory at Lepanto: The Framing of a Public Space at Santa Maria in Aracoeli," in *Perspectives on Public Space in Rome*, ed. Gregory Smith and Jan Gadeyne (London: Routledge, 2013), 131–55, for a discussion of that church's gilt Lepanto ceiling.

3. Sutton, *The Papacy and the Levant*, 1100.

4. *Salvatoris Domini*, March 5, 1572.

5. Gregory XIII renamed the feast on April 1, 1573 (*Monet Apostolus*); it was made a universal feast of the church by Clement XI in 1715. See also Annick Delfosse, *La Protectrice du Pais-Bas: Strategies Politiques et Figures de la Vierge dans les Pays Bas Espagnols* (Turnhout: Brepols, 2009).

6. Just one example of a modern-day website suggesting that praying to Our Lady of Victory will defeat terrorists is this one sponsored by uCatholic.com, an organization "dedicated to providing traditional Catholic information in the modern world": https://ucatholic .leadpages.co/pray-the-rosary-to-defeat-isis/.

7. It has perdured as part of a "memory culture," according to Jasper van der Steen, *Memory Wars in the Low Countries, 1566–1700* (Leiden: Brill, 2015), 88.

8. Amy Remensnyder describes the explicit use of Mary as patron saint of the Reconquista (along with St. James) in Spain up to 1492 but as early as 1212 in *La Conquistadora* (Oxford: Oxford University Press, 2014). See 15–118 for a discussion of the Spanish

use of Mary against the Moors during the Reconquista. Also, Italian, Spanish, and Latin poems were written soon after the Battle of Lepanto (1571) for English translations, see *The Battle of Lepanto*, ed. and trans. Elizabeth R. Wright, Sarah Spence, and Andrew Lemons (Cambridge, MA: Harvard University Press, 2014).

9. Nigel Spivey, *Enduring Creation: Art, Pain and Fortitude* (Berkeley: University of California Press), 97.

10. Van der Steen, *Memory Wars*, 88.

11. *Alcorani seu legis Mahometi et Evangelistarum concordiae liber* (1543). Number 6 on his list mentions Mary.

12. Martin Luther, "Preface to the Treatise on the Religion and Customs of the Turks" (1530), trans. Sarah Henrich and James L. Boyce in "Martin Luther—Translations of Two Prefaces on Islam," *Word & World* 16, no. 2 (1996): 259–61.

13. Louis Châtellier, *The Europe of the Devout*, trans. Jean Birrell (Cambridge: University of Cambridge, 1989), 9. See also Bridget Heal, *The Cult of the Virgin Mary in Early Modern Germany* (Cambridge: Cambridge University Press, 2007).

14. For more on this period, see John O'Malley, *Trent: What Happened at the Council* (Cambridge, MA: Harvard University Press, 2013).

15. Anthony Bryer and Michael Ursinus, ed., *Manzikert to Lepanto: The Byzantine World and the Turks, 1071–1571* (Amsterdam: Hakkert Publishers, 1991). Also see Nancy Bisaha, *Creating East and West: Renaissance Humanists and the Ottoman Turks* (Philadelphia: University of Pennsylvania Press, 2004), and Christine Isom-Verhaaren, *Allies with the Infidel: The Ottoman and French Alliance in the Sixteenth Century* (London: I. B. Tauris and Co., 2011).

16. Bisaha, *Creating East and West*, 5.

17 Ibid., 1.

18. Heal, *Cult of the Virgin*, 3.

19. Ibid., 305. See also Beth Kreitzer, *Reforming Mary* (Oxford: Oxford University Press, 2004).

20. According to Anne Winston-Allen, *Stories of the Rose: The Making of the Rosary in the Middle Ages* (University Park, PA: Penn State University Press, 1997), 70, Alain was the first to mention Dominic's vision of the Rosary; before him, no connection existed between Dominic and the Rosary.

21. Ibid., 66.

22. Christine Getz, *Music and the Early Modern Imagination: Mary, Music, and Meditation; Sacred Conversations in Post-Tridentine Milan* (Bloomington: Indiana University Press, 2013), 83.

23. Heal, *Cult of the Virgin*, 253.

24. Châtellier, *Europe of the Devout*, 3.

25. Nathan Mitchell, *The Mystery of the Rosary: Marian Devotion and the Reinvention of Catholicism* (New York: New York University Press, 2009), 32.

26. Ibid., 20–21.

27. Heal, *Cult of the Virgin*, 254.

28. Ibid.

29. Donna Spivey Ellington, *From Sacred Body to Angelic Soul: Understanding Mary in Late Medieval and Early Modern Europe* (Washington, DC: Catholic University of America Press, 2001), 219. The French preacher Christophe Cheffontaines (d. 1595) promoted wearing rosaries in this way.

30. As quoted in Lawrence Cunningham, "The Virgin Mary," in *From Trent to Vatican II: Historical and Theological Investigations*, ed. Raymond F. Bulman and Frederick J. Parrella (Oxford: Oxford University Press, 2006), 180.

31. Michael Mullett, *The Catholic Reformation* (New York: Routledge, 1999), 117.

32. Kreitzer, *Reforming Mary*, 32. See Luke 1:28.

33. Ibid., 34 and 62, discusses the preaching of Lutheran ministers Christoph Vischer, Johannes Heune, and Simon Pauli. According to Kreitzer, 170, even as early as 1529, Luther himself was criticizing the Catholic idea that the Turks could be defeated with Mary's help.

34. Ibid., 33–34.

35. Derek Krueger, "Mary at the Threshold: Mother of God as Guardian," in *The Cult of the Mother of God in Byzantium*, ed. Leslie Brubaker and Mary Cunningham (Surrey, UK: Ashgate, 2011), 32.

36. Leena Peltomaa, "Epithets of Theotokos in the Akathistos," in Brubaker and Cunningham, *The Cult of the Mother of God*, 109.

37. Matthew Milliner, *The Last Madonna* (Oxford: Oxford University Press, forthcoming), 26: "'Affective piety'…would in turn become the mainstay of Byzantine Marian devotion in centuries to come, later to be visualized in the mourning Marys of Ohrid, Nerezi, Studenica and Kastoria."

38. Linda B. Hall, *Mary, Mother and Warrior* (Austin: University of Texas Press, 2004), 23–36.

39. The phrase between the rosary and sword reads *clupeus Christianorum*. A *clupeus* (or *clipeus*) is a round Roman battle shield.

40. Heal, *Cult of the Virgin*, 259. Thanks to Dr. Heal for unearthing this image at the Historisches Stadtmuseum Köln.

41. For a book-length discussion of the transfer of Our Lady of Victory from Spain to America, see Remensnyder, *La Conquistadora*. For more on the role of Mariahilf in Reformation Germany, see Heal, *Cult of the Virgin*.

42. Châtellier, *Europe of the Devout*, 7.

43. Mitchell, *Mystery of the Rosary*, 47, observes that the ornate, baroque Marian paintings at the chapel of the Rosary at St. Dominic's Church in Bologna stand in striking contrast to Dominic's austere tomb, which recounts the events of his life but includes no mention of the Rosary.

44. Some of the many paintings include Paolo Veronese's *Allegory of Lepanto* (1572); Caravaggio's *Madonna of the Rosary* (1607), featuring a cameo of Holy League general Mark Anthony Colonna; and Lazzaro Baldi's *Pope Pius V's Vision of the Victory at Lepanto* (1673).

45. Heal, *Cult of the Virgin*, 158.

46. Ibid., 201.

47. One new image was Jan Peeter's *Preparations for the Battle of Lepanto* (1671) at St Paul's Church, Antwerp. Van der Steen, *Memory Wars*, 87–89.

48. Mitchell, *Mystery of the Rosary*, 22.

49. Ellington, *From Sacred Body to Angelic Soul*, 129.

50. The list of twenty-eight doctrines and practices shared by Protestants and Muslims can be found in Postel, *Alcorani seu legis Mahometi et evangelistarum concordiae Liber* (Paris: Gromorsus, 1543), 19–22. Early print book is at Chicago, Newberry Library, Special collections, Case C 5238.706. The year 1543 was important for the advancement of Arabic and Islamic studies in Europe, for it also saw Bibliander's publication of Ketton's Qur'an and the entire Toledan Collection.

51. Number 6 reads, "Mariam non debere coli aut honorare." Postel, *Alcorani*, 21.

52. For more on Postel, see Yvonne Petry, *Gender, Kabbalah and the Reformation: The Mystical Theology of Guillaume Postel* (Leiden: Brill, 2004), and William Bouwsma, *Concordia Mundi* (Cambridge, MA: Harvard University Press, 1957).

53. Postel published the first print edition of the *Protevangelium* in Latin (giving it its name) in *Protevangelium sive de natalibus Jesu Christi et ipsius Matris virginis Mariae* (Basel, 1552). See Petry, *Gender, Kabbalah, and Reformation*, 109. See also Irene Backus, "Guillaume Postel, Theodore Bibliander et le Protévangile de Jacques," *Apocrypha* 6 (1995): 7–65.

54. Petry, *Gender, Kabbalah, and Reformation*, 105.

55. Postel's use of the Qur'an to defend Mary's immaculate conception can be found in *Du souverain effect de la plus excellente Corone du mond*, Paris BNF MS Fons Français 2114. Folio 61ff. According to Petry, *Gender, Kabbalah, and Reformation*, 106, manuscripts 2112–16 contain (autograph) texts by Postel, including several about Mary. The only other example of a Christian using Muslim texts to support the immaculate conception is Marquard von Lindau, OFM (d. 1392), who did not know Arabic but relied on quotes from Ramon Martí and Riccoldo da Montecroce. See Stephen Mossman, "The Western Understanding of Islamic Theology in the Later Middle Ages," *Recherches de Théologie et Philosophie Médiévales* 74, no. 1 (2007): 169–224.

56. Postel, *Alcorani*, 31.

57. Ibid.

58. Ibid., 32.

59. Ibid.

60. Guillaume Postel, *De orbis terrae Concordia libri quattuor* (Basel: Oporinus, 1544), 175–76.

61. Ibid., 204–5. Sura 19:1–40 discusses the story of John, Mary, Jesus, and how Christians err about Jesus and Mary; 19:41–98 discuss other prophets.

62. For more on Augsburg, see Heal, *Cult of the Virgin*, 2–3. For a discussion of several examples of the Protestant disdain for images, such as their wholesale destruction in Basel in 1529, see Nelson Minnich, "Debate on the Use of Sacred Images," in *The Catholic Reformation* (Aldershot, UK: Variorum, 1993), 393. See also William Dyrness, *Reformed Theology and Visual Culture: The Protestant Imagination from Calvin to Edwards* (Cambridge: Cambridge University Press, 2004).

63. The first preface is to the 1530 *Libellus de ritu et moribus Turcorum* (Pamphlet on the religion and customs of the Turks), and the second is to Bibliander's 1543 Qur'an. Translations and commentary by Henrich and Boyce, "Martin Luther—Translations of Two Prefaces." For a comprehensive study of Luther's views of Islam, see Adam S. Francisco, *Martin Luther and Islam: A Study in Sixteenth-Century Polemics and Apologetics* (Leiden: Brill, 2007).

64. Luther, "Preface to Qur'an," in Henrich and Boyce, "Martin Luther—Translations of Two Prefaces," 265. Francisco argues that Luther's approach to Islam was more theological (and apologetic) than scholars have acknowledged in the past, *Martin Luther and Islam*, 3.

65. Henrich and Boyce, "Martin Luther—Translations of Two Prefaces," 254–55.

66. Luther, *Preface to Libellus*, 259.

67. Ibid.

68. Ibid., 260–61.

69. Adam Francisco, in *Martin Luther and Islam*, 47, 71–73, argues that Luther's fight against Islam initially stressed spiritual warfare, but later turned toward actual war; Catholics tended to be more constant in describing a military struggle against Islam.

70. Ibid., 69, describes Luther as more concerned with the internal, Catholic threat than the external, Turkish threat.

71. Luther, *Preface to Libellus*, 262.

72. Kreitzer, *Reforming Mary*, and Heal, *Cult of the Virgin*, however, show that a strong devotion to Mary continued among many Lutherans for centuries after the Reformation.

73. George Sale, *The Koran: Translated into English with Explanatory Notes and Preliminary Discourse* (Philadelphia: J. W. Moore, 1853), preface, v–vi. For more on Sale's original 1734 Qur'an, the edition possessed by Thomas Jefferson, see Denise Spellberg, *Thomas Jefferson's Qur'an: Islam and the Founders* (New York: Vintage, 2013).

74. Sale, *The Koran*, Preliminary Discourse (§2), 24.

75. Ibid., (§2), 25.

76. Ibid.

77. Despite Sale's anti-Marian rhetoric, it should be remembered that Anglicans (along with Lutherans) have traditionally been more pro-Marian than other Christians. See A. M. Allchin, *The Joy of All Creation: Anglican Meditation on the Place of Mary* (Hyde Park, NY: New City Press, 1993), as well as chap. 8 for a discussion of contemporary Anglican-Catholic ecumenical dialogues about Mary.

78. I am grateful to Devorah Schoenfeld for raising this question.

79. Pope Pius IX, *Aeterni Patris* (1868), as quoted by Lester Kurtz, *The Politics of Heresy: The Modernist Crisis in Roman Catholicism* (Berkeley: University of California Press, 1986), 35.

80. According to Pope Pius X in Kurtz, *Politics of Heresy*, 7.

81. Leo's Rosary encyclicals are *Supremi Apostolatus Officio* (1883); *Superiore Anno* (1884); *Vi E Ben Noto* (1887); *Octobri Mense* (1891); *Magnae Dei Matris* (1892); *Laetitiae Sanctae* (1893); *Iucunda Semper Expectatione* (1894); *Adiutricem* (1895); *Fidentem Piumque Animum* (1896); *Augustissimae Virginis Mariae* (1897); *Diuturni Temporis* (1898).

82. Leo XIII, *Supremi Apostolatus Officio*, §2–3. David Schultenover argues that one of Leo's main strategies for consolidating papal authority was to appeal directly to the people, *A View from Rome: On the Eve of the Modernist Crisis* (New York: Fordham University Press, 1999), 22–23.

83. Leo XIII, *Supremi*, §4–5.

84. Leo XIII, *Diuturni*, §2.

85. Leo XIII, *Laetitiae*, §16.

86. As stated in his 1577 book, *De Maria Virgine incomparabili*.

87. Georg Daltrop, "Galleria dei Candelabri," in *The Vatican: Spirit and Art of Ancient Rome*, ed. Philippe de Montebello and Kathleen Howard (New York: Metropolitan Museum of Art, 1983), 188–89.

88. See "The History of the Feast of Our Lady of Victory," accessed August 25, 2017, http://www.olvrc.com/reference/general/documents/The%20History%20of%20the%20Feast%20of%20Our%20Lady%20of%20Victory.pdf.

89. Ibid.

90. For devotions and prayers to Our Lady of Sinj, see, for example, the official website of the shrine in Croatia: http://www.gospa-sinjska.hr/pdf/poboznosti_gospi_sinjskoj_2009.pdf.

91. See Anđelko Vlašić and Janja Kovač, "Elements of Ottoman Legacy in the Alka of Sinj" (unpublished conference paper, International Symposium on Balkan Studies, Podgorica, Montenegro, January 2014).

92. "Sinj: About Us," accessed August 25, 2017, http://www.dalmacija.net/sinj/sinj_1.htm.

93. "Sinjska Alka, a Knights' Tournament in Sinj," accessed August 25, 2017, http://www.unesco.org/culture/ich/en/RL/sinjska-alka-a-knights-tournament-in-sinj-00357.

94. It would be interesting to compare Croatia's Our Lady of Sinj (Our Lady of Victory) with Serbian and Macedonian icons of Mary as a kind of "Our Lady of Losers" (Ohrid, Studenica), given that Croatia was never under Ottoman control, but Serbia and Macedonia were. For the term "Our Lady of Losers," see Milliner, *The Last Madonna*.

95. "Novena to Our Lady (Assumption Feast)," website of St. Jerome Croation Catholic Church of Chicago, accessed August 25, 2017, http://www.stjeromecroatian.org/eng/assumpt.htm.

96. Ivan Markešić. "Our Lady of Mercy: A Unique Cult in Two Places," in *Cult Places on the Border*, ed. B. Đorđević, B. Dragoljub, D. Todorović, and D. Krstić (Niš, Serbia: YSSSR, 2014), 15–28.

97. Another popular Balkan Marian site—perhaps the most popular—is Međugorje in Bosnia. Possibly due to its location in Hercegovina, which saw heavy fighting between Catholics and Muslims during the Bosnian War of the 1990s, Međugorje has remained almost an exclusively Catholic site. (Muslims do visit, but usually as tourists, not religious pilgrims.) Some contemporary websites tout Međugorje's ability to convert Muslims to Christianity. For more on Međugorje, see Chris Maunder, *Our Lady of the Nations: Apparitions of Mary in the Twentieth Century* (Oxford: Oxford University Press, 2016), 153–70.

CHAPTER 6

1. *Cantigas de Santa Maria*, cantiga 46, trans. Kathleen Kulp-Hill in *Songs of Holy Mary of Alfonso X the Wise* (Tempe, AZ: Arizona Center for Medieval and Renaissance Studies, 2000), 62.
2. A critical edition of the original Galician text is in Walter Mettmann, ed., *Cantigas de Santa Maria*, v. 1–3, (Madrid: Editorial Castalia, 1986). A full-color facsimile version of the illustrations is in *Cantigas de Santa María: Edición Facsímil del Códice T.1.1 de la Biblioteca de San Lorenzo de El Escorial*, Siglo XIII, 2 vols. (Madrid: Edilán, 1979). There is a huge corpus of scholarship on the *cantigas*, much in Spanish. Three useful Anglophone resources are Joseph O'Callaghan, *Alfonso X and the Cantigas de Santa Maria* (Leiden: Brill, 1998); Kirstin Kennedy, "Seeing Is Believing: The Miniatures in the *Cantigas de Santa Maria* and Medieval Devotional Practices," *Portuguese Studies* 32, no. 1 (2015): 169–82; and Francisco Prado-Vilar, "The Gothic Anamorphic Gaze: Regarding the Worth of Others," in *Under the Influence: Questioning the Comparative in Medieval Castile*, ed. Cynthia Robinson and Leyla Rouhi (Leiden: Brill, 2005), 67–100.
3. *Cantiga* 329 presents a relatively accurate outline of Muslim Mariology, while other *cantigas* illustrate connections between Muslim Marian devotion and conversion.
4. O'Callaghan calls it a "poetic biography" in *Alfonso X and the Cantigas*, 2–3. Scholars today believe Alfonso was its editor and patron, but not the primary author, 6.
5. *Cantiga* 46, 62.
6. Ibid.
7. *Cantiga* 205, 247.
8. *Cantiga* 183, 219.
9. *Cantiga* 181, 217.
10. Folio 240r.

11. *Cantiga* 329, 400.

12. MS T.I.1, folios 221v and 222r.

13. Prado-Vilar, *Under the Influence*, 80–81.

14. Sixteenth-century Seville retained a sizable Morisco (converted or secret Muslim) population; Moriscos were sent to Seville from other parts of Andalusia, according to Mary Elizabeth Perry, *The Handless Maiden: Moriscos and the Politics of Religion in Early Modern Spain* (Princeton, NJ: Princeton University Press, 2005), 1.

15. Prado-Vilar, *Under the Influence*, 81.

16. John Tolan, "*Veneratio Sarracenorum*: Shared Devotion among Muslims and Christians, according to Burchard of Strasbourg," in *Sons of Ishmael* (Gainesville, FL: University Press of Florida, 2008), 101–12.

17. Burchard, *Itinerarium*, as quoted by Tolan in "*Veneratio Sarracenorum*," 108–9.

18. Eugenio Garosi, "The Incarnated Icon of Saydnaya: Light and Shade," *Journal of Islam and Muslim-Christian Relations* 26, no. 3 (2015): 339–58. For more on "Our Lady of Sardenay" (or Sardonay), see Bernard Hamilton, "Our Lady of Saidnaya: An Orthodox Shrine Revered by Muslims and Knights Templars at the Time of the Crusades," in *Holy Land, Holy Lands, and Christian History*, ed. R. N. Swanson (Woodbridge, UK: Boydell Press, 2000), 207–15, at 207; Denys Pringle, "Saidnaiya," in *The Churches of the Crusader Kingdom of Jerusalem*, vol. 2, ed. Denys Pringle (Cambridge: Cambridge University Press, 2009), 219–21; D. Baraz, "The Incarnated Icon of Saidnaya Goes West," *Le Museon* 108 (1995): 181–91; and Amikam Elad, *Medieval Jerusalem and Islamic Worship* (Leiden: Brill, 1995).

19. Burchard, *Itinerarium*, as quoted by Tolan in "*Veneratio Sarracenorum*," 108–9.

20. Ibid.

21. Riccoldo, *Liber peregrinationis*, in *A Christian Pilgrim in Medieval Iraq: Riccoldo da Montecroce's Encounter with Islam*, trans. Rita George-Tvrtković (Turnhout: Brepols, 2012), 184.

22. Ibid., 179, 183, 184.

23. Felix Fabri, *Wanderings in the Holy Land*, trans. Aubrey Stewart (London: Palestine Pilgrims Text Society, 1892), 100. Critical Latin edition in Jean Meyers and Nicole Chareyron, ed., *Félix Fabri. Les errances de Frère Félix, pèlerin en Terre sainte, en Arabie et en Égypte (1480–1483)*, 2 vols. (Montpellier: Publications de l'Université Paul-Valéry et du CERCAM, 2000 and 2003).

24. Fabri, *Wanderings*, 100.

25. Ibid., 129.

26. The pre–Vatican II idea that other religions can be a "preparation for the gospel" is still expressed in some magisterial documents such as *Dominus Iesus* §21 (2000). For more on this idea, see Jacques Dupuis, *Towards a Christian Theology of Religious Pluralism* (Maryknoll, NY: Orbis, 1997), 130–57.

27. Elad, *Medieval Jerusalem*, 93–95.

28. Ibid., 117.

29. Ibid., 138, notes that "as far back as 661, an early Syrian chronicle states that Mu'awiya visited this church. According to another tradition (al-Aziz d. 783), Umr al-Khattab 'prayed two rak'as at [this] church....' Another tradition by the same transmitter states, 'When Umr al-Khattab conquered Jerusalem he passed by the church of Mary peace be upon her in the valley, prayed and performed two rakas there.'"

30. Ibid., 138.

31. Ibid., 139–40.

32. Yazid, as quoted in ibid., 139–40.

33. Ibid., 140–41.

34. Ibid.

35. Nasir al-Din as quoted in ibid., 170.

36. On the mission work of these orders in the seventeenth century, see Bernard Heyberger, "Polemic Dialogues between Christians and Muslims in the Seventeenth Century," *Journal of the Economic and Social History of the Orient* 55 (2012): 495–516, and Emanuele Colombo, "Jesuits and Islam in Seventeenth-Century Europe: War, Preaching and Conversions," in *L'Islam visto da Occidente. Cultura e religione del Seicento europeo di fronte all'Islam*, ed. Bernard Heyberger et al. (Milan: Marietti, 2009), 315–40.

37. Muzaffar Alam and Sanjay Subrahmanyam, *Writing the Mughal World* (New York: Columbia University Press, 2012), 258.

38. As reported by Du Jarric in Edward Maclagan, *The Jesuits and the Great Mogul* (London: Burns, Oates & Washbourne, 1932), 54.

39. Ibid., 48, 54.

40. According to a 1608 letter by Jerome Xavier, as quoted in ibid., 69–70.

41. Guerriero, as quoted in ibid., 229–30.

42. Guerriero, as quoted in ibid., 233.

43. Gauvin Bailey calls the Jesuit Mission to India a "fantastic and extravagant failure" in "The Truth-Showing Mirror: Jesuit Catechism and the Arts in Mughal India," in *The Jesuits: Cultures, Sciences, and the Arts, 1540–1773*, vol. 1, ed. John W. O'Malley (Toronto: University of Toronto Press, 1999), 381.

44. For more on Baldassarre, see Emanuele Colombo, "Muslim Turned Jesuit: Baldassarre Loyola Mandes (1631–1667)," *Journal of Early Modern History* 17, nos. 5–6 (2013): 479–504.

45. This text is written in Persian and extant only in manuscript form. For a discussion of this text in relation to Mughal devotional art, see Bailey, "The Truth-Showing Mirror." For more on Xavier's writings, see Arnulf Camps, "Persian Works of Jerome Xavier: A Jesuit at the Mogul Court," in *Studies in Asian Missionary History, 1956–1998* (Leiden: Brill, 2000), and Maclagan, *Jesuits and the Great Mogul*, 206–9.

46. Bailey, "The Truth-Showing Mirror," 395. *Hilya* is an Islamic genre comprising verbal descriptions of the physical characteristics of Muhammad and other prophets and saints.

47. For more on Xavier, see Arnulf Camps, *Jerome Xavier SJ and the Muslims of the Mogul Empire: Controversial Works and Missionary Activity* (Fribourg, 1957), and Alam and Subrahmanyam, *Writing the Mughal World*, 249–310.

48. Xavier, *Mirat al-Quds (The Mirror of Holiness): A Life of Christ for Emperor Akbar*, trans. Wheeler Thackston, with commentary by Pedro Moura Carvalho (Leiden: Brill, 2012).

49. Carvalho, introduction to *Mirat al-Quds*, 3. One of the most complete illustrated manuscripts of this book is at the Cleveland Art Museum; this is the prime object of Carvalho's study. Another is at Victoria & Albert Museum, London.

50. Xavier, *Mirat al-Quds*, 140. Since the Bible says nothing about Mary before the annunciation, Xavier likely consulted extra-biblical sources such as the *Protevangelium of James* and the *Golden Legend* of Jacob of Voraigne.

51. Xavier, *Mirat al-Quds*, 152 (on the physical aspects of Mary's virginity). Mary's virginity (and specifically her being "intact" after giving birth) is also discussed on 149, 153, and 157.

52. Ibid., 150. This unusual image is discussed in detail by Carvalho, ibid., 84–85. Even though Xavier's text says "they cleaned," only Mary is depicted as doing housework here! Several men are milling about at the bottom of the illustration, but they are not helping her clean.

53. Ibid., 145.

54. Carvalho, commentary on *Mirat al-Quds*, 39n332 cites a 1595 letter from Xavier to Jesuit Superior General Acquaviva, noting Akbar's Marian devotion.

55. Xavier, *Mirat al-Quds*, 157. Cf. Luke 2:26.

56. Ibid., 233. Cf. John 20, Mark 16, and Matthew 28, where Mary Magdalene is the first to see the risen Christ; in Luke 24, the women are the first to see the empty tomb, and disciples on the Road to Emmaus are the first to see the risen Christ.

57. Two early Christian sources, George of Nicomedia's *Homily 9 on the Virgin's Vigil at the Tomb* (ninth c.) and Maximos the Confessor's *Life of the Virgin* (seventh c.) both claim that Mary witnessed the resurrection itself. See excerpts translated by Shoemaker in *Life of the Virgin* (New Haven, CT: Yale University Press, 2012), 119–20. There is also a medieval homiletic and iconic tradition that supports the idea that Mary saw Jesus first. See James D. Breckenridge, "'Et Prima Vidit': The Iconography of the Appearance of Christ to His Mother," *Art Bulletin* 39, no. 1 (March 1957): 9–32.

58. In his notes to the translation, Thackston mentions this point in Xavier, *Mirat al-Quds*, 142. While the Bible does not accord Friday any importance, the main public Marian services at the Blachernai in Constantinople took place on Fridays beginning in the seventh century. Bissera Pentcheva, *Icons and Power: The Mother of God in Byzantium* (University Park, PA: Pennsylvania State University Press, 2006), 12.

59. Carvalho, introduction to Xavier, *Mirat al-Quds*, 5–6.

60. Ludovico De Dieu, *Historia Christi Persice, conscripta simulque multis modis contaminata* (Leiden, 1639).

61. "Iesuitas Mariam magis quam Christum praedicasse," ibid., 5. De Dieu's translation of Xavier's book was placed on the Catholic index of forbidden books in 1660–61, Carvalho, Xavier, *Mirat al-Quds*, 27. Was this because of De Dieu's critique of Xavier and the Jesuits, or Xavier's "enculturation" of Christ's life to the Mughal context?

62. De Dieu, *Historia Christi Persice*, 581, 582; and 632, respectively.

63. Ibid., 632.

64. Zwemer, *Islam: A Challenge to Faith* (New York: Student Volunteer Movement for Foreign Missions, 1907), 195.

65. Ibid., 185. On 194, Zwemer does mention briefly the mission work of the Jesuit Xavier in Mughal India, but mistakes Jerome for his more famous great-uncle, Francis.

66. Eleanor H. Tejirian and Reeva Spector Simon, *Conflict, Conquest, and Conversion: Two Thousand Years of Christian Missions in the Middle East* (New York: Columbia University Press, 2014), xii.

67. David Walls, "Africa as the Theatre of Engagement with Islam in the Nineteenth Century," in *Christianity and the African*

Imagination: Essays in Honour of Adrian Hastings, ed. David Maxwell and Ingrid Lawrie (Leiden: Brill, 2013), 47.

68. Ibid., 43.

69. It is important to note the rising interest in Mary as an example of ideal womanhood among nineteenth-century American Protestants, for example, Congregationalists and Lutherans, even as they rejected Catholic veneration to her. See Elizabeth Hayes Alvarez, *Valiant Woman: The Virgin Mary in Nineteenth-Century American Culture* (Chapel Hill, NC: University of North Carolina, 2016).

70. See Heather Sharkey, *American Evangelicals in Egypt: Missionary Encounters in an Age of Empire* (Princeton, NJ: Princeton University Press, 2008), chap. 2.

71. Another key resource on the history of American Protestant missions in Egypt is Thomas Kidd, *American Christians and Islam: Evangelical Culture and Muslims from the Colonial Period to the Age of Terrorism* (Princeton, NJ: Princeton University Press, 2009).

72. W. A. Essery, *The Ascending Cross* (London, 1905), 34–35.

73. Just two examples among many: Mary Bird devotes three chapters to "Darkness and Light," in her *Persian Women and Their Creed* (London: CMS, 1908), while chap. 2 of Essery's *Ascending Cross* is entitled "Light, Shadow, Gross Darkness."

74. Mariolatry is described by Charles Watson, *In the Valley of the Nile* (New York: Fleming Revell Co., 1908); Henry Jessup, *The Women of the Arabs* (New York: Dodd & Meade, 1873); and W. A. Essery, *The Ascending Cross*, 34.

75. Giulian Lansing, *Egypt's Princes* (New York: Carter & Brothers, 1865), 110.

76. Ibid., 111.

77. Sharkey, *American Evangelicals in Egypt*, 39–40.

78. Walls, "Africa as the Theatre of Engagement," 52–53.

79. Gabriel Said Reynolds, "Evangelizing Islam," *First Things* (January 2011).

80. For more on the White Fathers, see Aylward Shorter, *The Cross and Flag in Africa: The White Fathers during the Colonial Scramble* (Maryknoll, NY: Orbis, 2006). There is little recent scholarship in English about the White Fathers. A good French source is Joseph Cuoq, *Lavigerie, Les Pères Blancs et les Musulmans Maghrebins* (Rome: Missionaries of Africa), 1986.

81. Lavigerie as quoted in *Missionaries of Africa: Selected Texts* (London: Samuel Walker, 1990), 53.

82. Adrian Hastings, *The Church in Africa, 1450–1950* (Oxford: Clarendon, 1994), 25.

83. Lavigerie in an 1878 letter to the first caravan of White Fathers traveling to equatorial Africa, as quoted in *Missionaries of Africa*, 40.

84. Dionigi Albera, "Religious Antagonism and Shared Sanctuaries in Algeria," in *Choreographies of Shared Sacred Sites*, ed. Elazar Barkan and Karen Barkey (New York: Columbia University Press, 2015), 108.

85. Lavigerie, as quoted in *Missionaries of Africa*, 63.

86. Pope Leo XIII, *Adiutricem* (1895), 4.

87. Viera Pawlikova-Vilhanova, "The Role of Early Missionaries of Africa or White Fathers in the Study and Development of African Languages," *Asian and African Studies* 20, no. 2 (2011): 267–88.

88. Albera, "Religious Antagonism," 101–2.

89. Pavy in ibid., 102.

90. Ibid., 107–8.

91. Ibid., 108.

92. Sharkey, *American Evangelicals in Egypt*, notes that a century of Presbyterian mission work in Egypt produced only two hundred converts, most of whom had formerly been Coptic Christians. See also Ussama Makdisi, *Artillery of Heaven: American Missionaries and the Failed Conversion of the Middle East* (Ithaca, NY: Cornell University Press, 2007), and Robin Vose, *Dominicans, Muslims and Jews in the Medieval Crown of Aragon* (Cambridge: Cambridge University Press, 2009), who challenges the idea that the main concern of medieval Dominicans was mission at all, suggesting instead that the priority of Iberian Dominicans was to foster Christian faith, not convert Muslims.

93. Sharkey, *American Evangelicals in Egypt*, 19, 63.

94. Shorter, *The Cross and Flag in Africa*, 41. The White Fathers fared much better among non-Muslims in equatorial Africa.

95. Pallavicino as quoted by Colombo in "Jesuits and Islam," 332. However, some new studies suggest that seventeenth-century Jesuit missionaries in Spain were somewhat successful in converting Muslims to Christianity. See ibid., 334–35.

96. Sharkey, *American Evangelicals in Egypt*, 15, notes that "people involved in missionary encounters changed significantly—and changed each other—without necessarily converting" in the technical sense.

97. Albera, "Religious Antagonism," 116.

98. Ibid., 119.

CHAPTER 7

1. *Acta Synodalia* III.3, General Congregation XC (Vatican City, 1972), 54.

2. In November 2006, Pope Benedict XVI celebrated mass at Meryem Ana Evi, ending his homily with the following prayer: "Mary, Mother of the Church, accompany us always on our way! Holy Mary, Mother of God, pray for us! *Aziz Meryem Mesih'in Annesi bizim için Dua et.* Amen." His full speech can be found on the Vatican website: https://w2.vatican.va/content/benedict-xvi/en/homilies/2006/documents/hf_ben-xvi_hom_20061129_ephesus.html.

3. Bishop Yves Plumey, OMI, of Cameroon listed all these during his speech. *Acta Synodalia* III.3, 16.

4. The three bishops were Sfair, Descuffi, and Plumey.

5. Heather Abraham, "The Shrine of Our Lady of Ephesus: A Study of the Personas of Mary as Lived Religion" (Master's thesis, University of Georgia, 2008), 38–39.

6. Fulton Sheen, *The World's First Love: Mary, Mother of God* (New York: McGraw-Hill, 1952).

7. Examples of Traditionalist Catholic websites putting forth the idea of Mary as a tool for mission: "Our Lady Will Convert Muslims" (http://www.ewtn.com/v/experts/showmessage.asp?number = 331944&Pg = &Pgnu = &recnu =); "A Fatima Novena for the Conversion of Muslims" (http://www.onepeterfive.com/a-fatima-novena -for-the-conversion-of-muslims/); "Traditional Catholic Rosary and Muslims" (http://www.traditionalcatholicpriest.com/2015/02/08/ feast-holy-rosary-muslims/).

8. While *Nostra Aetate* emphasizes dialogue, it does not completely ignore mission; §2 repeatedly mentions the duty to proclaim Christ and the necessity of Christian witness. Furthermore, other conciliar documents do discuss mission.

9. *Dialogue and Proclamation* (1991), Council for Interreligious Dialogue and Congregation for the Evangelization of Peoples, §77.

10. Pope John XXIII dubbed the decade a "Marian era" in 1959. See Paula M. Kane, "Marian Devotion since 1940: Continuity or Casualty?" in *Habits of Devotion: Catholic Religious Practice in Twentieth-Century America*, ed. James O'Toole (New York: Cornell University Press, 2004), 89–119.

11. Pius XII, *Munificentissimus Deus*, 1950, §2.

12. Ibid., §8–9. The *sensus fidelium* is defined by the 2014 document *"Sensus Fidei* in the Life of the Church," (2014) by the International Theological Commission (ITC) as follows: "The faithful have an instinct for the truth of the Gospel, which enables them to recognise and endorse authentic Christian doctrine and practice, and to reject what is false. That supernatural instinct, intrinsically linked to the gift of faith received in the communion of the Church, is called the *sensus fidei*," §2.

13. Frank Coppa, *The Life and Pontificate of Pope Pius XII: Between History and Controversy* (Washington, DC: Catholic University Press, 2013), 11.

14. The Marian year was proclaimed by Pius XII in *Fulgens Corona*.

15. *Ad caeli reginam*. For more on the mariological documents of Pius XII, see Matthew Rocco Mauriello, "Venerable Pope Pius XII and the 1954 Marian Year" (Master's thesis, University of Dayton, 2010).

16. Pius XII, *Fulgens corona*, §33–34, 39, 41–43, respectively.

17. Nathan Mitchell, *The Mystery of the Rosary: Marian Devotion and the Reinvention of Catholicism* (New York: New York University Press, 2009), 239.

18. See Jonathon Herzog, *The Hammer and the Cross: America's Holy War against Communism* (Palo Alto, CA: Stanford University Press, 2008).

19. April 24, 1954, *L'Osservatore Romano*.

20. Sheen, *The World's First Love*, 208.

21. Thomas Reeves, *America's Bishop: The Life and Times of Fulton Sheen* (San Francisco: Encounter Books, 2001), 264–65.

22. Sheen, *World's First Love*, 193–94.

23. Kathleen Riley, *Fulton Sheen: An American Catholic Response to the Twentieth Century* (Staten Island, NY: Alba House, 2004), 248–49. Fulton Sheen, "The Sword, the Hammer, the Sickle, and the Cross," *Worldmission* 2 (Winter 1951): 3, 6.

24. Riley, *Fulton Sheen*, 248–49.

25. Book-length biographies of Massignon include Mary Louise Gude, *Crucible of Compassion* (Notre Dame, IN: University of Notre Dame, 1997) and Christian Destremau and Jean Moncelon, *Massignon* (Paris: Plon, 1994).

26. This was common among French intellectuals of the time; see Anthony O'Mahony, "Louis Massignon: A Catholic Encounter with God and the Middle East," in *God's Mirror: Renewal and Engagement in French Catholic Intellectual Culture in the Mid Twentieth Century*, ed.

Katherine Davies and Toby Garfitt (New York: Fordham University Press, 2015).

27. For example, the founding documents state this goal: "que l'Islam comprenne la réalité et efficacé de la crucifixion...Ce but qui est la manifestation du Christ en Islam," Badaliya as cited by Amira El-Zein in "L'autre dans la spiritualité massignonienne," in *Louis Massignon: Au Coeur de Notre Temps*, ed. Jacques Keryell (Paris: Éditions Karhala, 1999), 41. Scholars disagree whether this means conversion or not. Jean-Jacques Pérennès, OP, in *Passion Kaboul: Le père Serge de Beaurecueil* (Paris: Cerf, 2014), chap. 2, says conversion was not intended. However, Christian Destremau and Jean Moncelon disagree in *Massignon*, 246. Also, some Muslims in the 1950s accused Massignon of attempting to convert them, according to El-Zein, "L'autre dans la spiritualité," 41. For correspondence related to the founding of Badaliya, see Dorothy Buck, *Louis Massignon: A Pioneer of Interfaith Dialogue; The Badaliya Prayer Movement, 1947–1962* (London: Blue Dome Press, 2016).

28. For a discussion of Badaliya's development into a truly interfaith group, see Anthony O'Mahony, "Louis Massignon, the Seven Sleepers of Ephesus and the Christian Muslim Pilgrimage at Vieux-Marche," in *Explorations in a Christian Theology of Pilgrimage*, ed. Craig Bartholomew and Fred Hughes (Aldershot, UK: Ashgate, 2003). The group's evolution continues; in 2003, Badaliya was resurrected as an international, interfaith prayer group based in Boston. See Buck, *The Badaliya Prayer Movement*, "Badaliya Today."

29. This is clear in the table of contents of *Opera Minora*, the three-volume compendium of Massignon's scholarship: *Opera Minora*, vols. 1–3, ed. Y. Moubarac (Beirut: Dar al-Maaref, 1963). Earlier writings (1920s and 1930s) focus on Islamic theology, Arabic philology, and historical studies. Later writings (1950s and 1960s) center on interreligious themes, such as the Christian-Muslim connections present in the shrine of Our Lady of Fatima in Portugal. Eventually, Massignon expands to include dialogue with Indian and Japanese religions. One could argue that his approach to interreligious dialogue is distinct from post–Vatican II approaches; for example, he focused more on mystical sympathy with Islam than on theology. See Christian Krokus, *The Theology of Louis Massignon: Islam, Christ, and the Church* (Washington, DC: Catholic University of America Press, 2017).

30. Jacques Waardenberg lists three groups influenced by Massignon, including "Catholic Orientalists," 171, in *Muslims as Actors: Islamic Meanings and Muslim Interpretation* (Berlin: Walter de

Gruyter, 2007). Several scholars report that Montini was a member of Massignon's Badaliya; see Christian Krokus, "Louis Massignon's Influence on the Teaching of Vatican II on Muslims and Islam," *Islam and Christian-Muslim Relations* 23, no. 3 (2012): 329–45, and Andrew Unsworth, "Louis Massignon, the Holy See, and the Ecclesial Transition from *Immortale Dei* to *Nostra Aetate*: A Brief History of the Development of Catholic Church Teaching on Muslims and the Religion of Islam," *Aram Society for Syro-Mesopotamian Studies* 20 (2008).

31. Georges Anawati, "Excursus on Islam," in *Commentary on the Documents of Vatican II*, ed. Herbert Vorgrimler, 3 vols. (New York: Herder & Herder, 1967–69), 3:151–60. Anawati, 152, names Massignon as the primary reason for the sea change in Catholic attitudes toward Islam. See also Robert Caspar in "La vision de l'Islam chez Louis Massignon et son influence sur l'église," in *L'Herne Massignon*, ed. J. Six (Paris, 1970), 126–47.

32. Krokus, "Louis Massignon's Influence," 334–36.

33. Gavin D'Costa, *Vatican II: Catholic Doctrines on Jews and Muslims* (Oxford: Oxford University Press, 2014), acknowledges Massignon's importance, but includes him in a broader complex of influences, 187. See also Julian Baldick, "Massignon: Man of Opposites," *Religious Studies* 23, no. 1 (1987): 29–39.

34. See, for example, Krokus, "Louis Massignon's Influence," and Neal Robinson, "Massignon, Vatican II, and Islam as an Abrahamic Religion," *Islam and Christian-Muslim Relations* 2, no. 2 (1991): 182–205.

35. Unsworth, "Louis Massignon," 310.

36. Ibid., 303.

37. Ibid., 304–5.

38. Even the second claim (one God) has been contested in the years following 9/11; yet as we have seen, this was not an issue for patristic and medieval theologians, most of whom acknowledged Islam as monotheistic. For more on the contested reception of Vatican II, see "Interpreting the Interpreters" in D'Costa, *Catholic Doctrines on Jews and Muslims*, where he characterizes the two groups who have received *Nostra Aetate* as "weepers" and "cheerers," and criticizes both for misrepresenting what the Council actually taught.

39. One book that supports the idea of Abrahamic faiths is F. E. Peters, *The Children of Abraham* (Princeton, NJ: Princeton University Press, 1982); another book that challenges and further nuances the idea is Jon D. Levenson, *Inheriting Abraham: The Legacy of the*

Patriarch in Judaism, Christianity, and Islam (Princeton, NJ: Princeton University Press, 2012).

40. Massignon, "Les trois prières de Abraham," *Opera Minora*, 3:811–12. English translation in *Testimonies and Reflections: Essays of Louis Massignon*, ed. and trans. Herbert Mason (Notre Dame, IN: University of Notre Dame Press, 1989), 3–20.

41. One could argue that this is neither unique to Massignon, nor a new *theologoumenon*, since as we have already seen, earlier theologians like Jacob of Edessa, William of Tripoli, and Nicholas of Cusa discuss Mary as a commonality between Christians and Muslims. But Massignon's scholarship stressed the devotional aspects of Mary over the theological.

42. While orthodox Islam technically does not have "saints" (the preferred term is *wali*, or "friend of God"), and frowns upon the veneration of any human being, it is nevertheless the case that a significant percentage of ordinary Muslims throughout the world (not only Sufis) engage in heterodox practices such as visiting the graves of Muslim holy people (*ziyara*) or the shrines of Christian saints.

43. See the speeches of Sfair and Descuffi, and an excellent discussion of their influence on drafts of *Nostra Aetate* 3, in D'Costa, *Catholic Doctrines on Jews and Muslims*, 197–200.

44. D'Costa notes that Massignon's focus on devotion was shared by Pope Paul VI, Daniélou, and de Lubac, "all of whom emphasized adoration and prayer as traits to be highly valued in Islam," *Catholic Doctrines on Jews and Muslims*, 186.

45. Three of these articles are cited in the notes below.

46. Massignon, "La Mubahala de Medine et L'Hyperdulie de Fatima," *Opera Minora*, 1:550–72.

47. "Fatima se trouve constituée *l'otage humain de l'affirmation de l'Inaccessibilité divine*—face à Maryam, *hôtesse surhumaine de l'immanence divine*. Tandis que le 'kun' (fiat) chez Maryam c'est l'Annonciation par un ange d'une Naissance dans le temps (selon les chrétiens: Incarnation)—le 'kun' chez Fatima c'est le Rappel, par le Ruh-al-Amr (Esprit de Dieu dans la Nuit de Destin) d'un destin dans la prééternité, la marque créatrice, Fitra, prédestinant les Elus à la Pitié paternelle du Rahman Rahim," Massignon, "Mubahala," 567. Emphasis is Massignon's.

48. Francis X. Clooney, *Comparative Theology: Deep Learning across Religious Borders* (Oxford: Blackwell, 2010), 10. Clooney founded comparative theology in the 1980s; his project has an interesting precedent in the 1948 book cowritten by Massignon's students Georges Anawati and Louis Gardet, *Introduction à la Théologie Musulmane:*

Essai de Theologie Comparée (Paris: Vrin, 1948), to which Massignon wrote an introduction.

49. Massignon, "La notion de Voeu et la dévotion musulmane à Fatima," *Opera Minora*, 1:573–91. These heterodox (usually Shi'i) practices would be frowned upon by most Sunni Muslims.

50. For more on the history of Islamic devotion and pilgrimages, see Christopher S. Taylor, *In the Vicinity of the Righteous: Ziyara and the Veneration of Muslim Saints in Late Medieval Egypt* (Leiden: Brill, 1999).

51. Massignon, "L'Oratoire de Marie à l'Aqça [Al Aqsa], vu sous le voile de deuil de Fatima," *Opera Minora*, 1:591–618.

52. Ibid., 591. Massignon does not cite the origin of the Sheen quote.

53. Ibid., 603–9.

54. Ibid., 605.

55. Ibid., 606.

56. Ibid., 608.

57. Edward Said's classic book, *Orientalism* (New York: Pantheon, 1979), includes an entire chapter on Massignon.

58. For a hagiographical account of Marie de Mandat-Grancey, see Carl G. Schulte, *The Life of Sr. Marie de Mandat-Grancey and Mary's House in Ephesus* (Charlotte, NC: TAN Books, 2011).

59. Eugène Poulin, *La Maison de la Sainte Vierge: La véritable histoire de sa découverte* (Istanbul, 1999 [1905]), 162.

60. Abraham, "Our Lady of Ephesus," 31. Boyer D'Agen, "Maison de Marie à Éphèse," *La Nouvelle Revue* 16 (1902): 41–44, also mentions the Kirkindje.

61. Manoël Pénicaud, "La Maison de la Vierge à Éphèse: De la fondation à la patrimonialisation d'un sanctuaire « international »," *European Journal of Turkish Studies* 19 (2014): 6–7.

62. Ibid., 9.

63. Massignon provides little patristic evidence for his claim; he mentions only Epiphanius in "L'oratoire," 595.

64. Just one example is "Le Culte Liturgique et Populaire des VII Dormants Martyrs d'Ephese," *Opera Minora*, 3:119–80.

65. Miltner was the Austrian archaeologist who conducted the excavation in 1926; see Ernest Honigmann, "Stephen of Ephesus and the Legend of the Seven Sleepers," *Patristic Studies, Studi e testi* 173 (1953): 125–68. For more on Ephesus in general, see Clive Foss, *Ephesus after Antiquity: A Late Antique, Byzantine, and Turkish City* (Cambridge: Cambridge University Press, 1979).

66. Indeed, Massignon explicitly connects Mary, the Seven Sleepers, and Ephesus: "Sans qu'il se rende compte que ce mystère de la Dormition distincte de la Mort est posé à Ephèse, pour S. Jean, et les VII Dormants, ce qui incite en faveur de la Dormition de Marie à Ephese," "L'oratoire," 607.

67. Pénicaud, "La Maison," 9.

68. A letter of Pope Pius XII to Descuffi on July 22, 1957, praises him for building Meryem Ana Evi.

69. According to Descuffi, who reported that the House of Mary had one hundred thousand Muslim pilgrims and one hundred thousand Christian pilgrims per year for the past decade during his September 29, 1964, intervention, *Acta Synodalia* III.3, 54.

70. Pénicaud, "La Maison," 9.

71. In his letter to Descuffi, the pope says the House of Mary is open "à toute personne, même nonchrétienne, ayant une dévotion spéciale à la Vierge Marie," as cited in Pénicaud, "La Maison," 9. Massignon also refers to these same words of the pope in a September 2, 1962, letter to Plumey.

72. Pénicaud, "La Maison," 16.

73. Ibid.

74. Füsun Türkmen and Emre Öktem, "Foreign Policy as a Determinant in the Fate of Turkey's Non-Muslim Minorities: A Dialectical Analysis," *Turkish Studies* 14 (2013): 463–82.

75. Proceedings from General Congregation 90, September 28–29, 1964, can be found in *Acta Synodalia* III.3, 9–55.

76. The Latin text of this first draft is in *Acta Synodalia* III.8, 637–42. The short section on Muslims reads, "Sic amplectamur imprimis etiam Musulmanos qui unicum Deum personalem atque remuneratorum adorant et sensu religioso atque permultis humanae culturae communicationibus propius ad nos accesserunt," 639.

77. Bishop Yves Joseph Marie Plumey, OMI, of Garoua, Cameroon, *Acta Synodalia* III.3, 15–17; Maronite Archbishop Pietro Sfair (Titular Bishop of Nisibis) of Syria, 41–43; and Archbishop Joseph Descuffi, CM, of Smyrna (Izmir), Turkey, 53–55.

78. Plumey, *Acta Synodalia* III.3, 15–16.

79. Ibid., III.3, 16.

80. Plumey, private letter to Massignon, August 10, 1962. I am grateful to Fr. Maciej Michalski, archivist at the Oblate General Archives in Rome, who sent me copies of the unpublished Plumey-Massignon correspondence of 1962, filed under *Media & Edition (Different Issus—Correspondence: 1949–1965) B - 43S2.*

81. In his September 2, 1962, reply to Plumey, Massignon quotes Pope Pius XII's letter to Descuffi, which says that the House of Mary is open to anyone with a devotion to Mary, even non-Christians.

82. For more on the connections between Descuffi, Massignon, and the House of the Virgin in Ephesus, see Krokus, "Louis Massignon's Influence," 337, and Pénicaud, "La Maison," 8–10.

83. The first and second Latin drafts are published side by side in *Acta Synodalia* III.8, 637–42.

84. The influence of Dominicans and White Fathers was explicitly affirmed by Cardinal Bea at the Council in October 1964, notes D'Costa, *Catholic Doctrines on Jews and Muslims*, 193.

85. For more by and about the *periti* involved in writing *Nostra Aetate* 3, see especially Anawati, "Excursus on Islam;" D'Costa, *Catholic Doctrines on Jews and Muslims*; and the forthcoming book, *The Genesis and Development of Nostra Aetate*, by Thomas Stransky, CSP, and John Borelli.

86. For a discussion of the theological considerations that influenced the draft, see D'Costa, *Catholic Doctrines on Jews and Muslims*, esp. 186–206, and John Flannery, "Christ in Islam and Muhammad, a Christian Evaluation: Theological Reflections on Tradition and Dialogue," in *The Catholic Church in the Contemporary Middle East*, ed. Anthony O'Mahony and John Flannery (London: Melisende, 2010), 331–52.

87. "Matremque eius virginalem honorant Mariam et aliquando eam devote etiam invocant." *Acta Synodalia* IV.4, 692.

88. Unsworth suggests that Anawati and Caspar "drew directly upon Descuffi's intervention while drafting *Nostra Aetate* 3," in "Louis Massignon," 315.

89. ITC, "*Sensus Fidei* in the Life of the Church," identifies the following: patristic period (§24, Mary's perpetual virginity and §26, Mary's divine motherhood), medieval period (§27, immaculate conception), modern period (§38–39, immaculate conception), twentieth c. (§41–52, assumption).

90. D'Costa, *Catholic Doctrines on Jews and Muslims*, 200, suggests that "many Fathers would have been moved by their accounts, especially given their own devotion and veneration to Mary and also the protracted controversy about Mary that had taken place earlier at the Council."

91. *Nostra Aetate* 3.

92. Interestingly, the decline in the Rosary among Catholics after the Council coincides with a postconciliar rise in Catholic understanding of other religions, including Islam.

CHAPTER 8

1. Miguel Ángel Ayuso Guixot, "La Vierge Marie et la Dialogue Islamo-Chrétien," *Pro Dialogo Bulletin* 146/147 (2014): 203. Translation from the French is my own.

2. Lebanon's Christian minority represents 38 percent of the total population, which is the highest percentage of Christians in any Middle Eastern country, according to the *Religious Composition by Country Report* by the Pew Charitable Trust, 2015.

3. For an interview with Nokkari, see "Lebanon: How the Annunciation Came to Be a Joint Christian-Muslim Holiday," by Marialaura Conte in *Oasis: Christians and Muslims in the Global World*, March 29, 2010, http://www.oasiscenter.eu/articles/interreligious -dialogue/2010/03/29/lebanon-how-the-annunciation-came-to-be-a -joint-muslim-christian-national-holiday.

4. The "Our Lady" vs. "Your Lady" distinction was made by Rabbi Michael Signer, a Jewish medievalist of blessed memory and my professor at the University of Notre Dame (also Our Lady).

5. Mustafa Akyol, "Why It's Not Wrong to Wish Muslims a Merry Christmas," *The New York Times*, December 23, 2016.

6. Eric Ross, "Christmas in Cambérène, or How Muhammad Begets Jesus in Senegal," in *Muslims and Others in Sacred Space*, ed. Margaret Cormack (Oxford: Oxford University Press, 2013), 85.

7. The other document that contributes to the conciliar theology of Islam is *Lumen Gentium* 16, which affirms Islamic monotheism and states that Muslims are "included in God's plan for salvation."

8. Michael Fitzgerald, "Dialogue and Proclamation: A Reading in the Perspective of Christian-Muslim Relations," in *In Many and Diverse Ways: In Honor of Jacques Dupuis*, ed. Daniel Kendall and Gerard O'Collins (Maryknoll, NY: Orbis, 2003), 184.

9. Pontifical Council for Interreligious Dialogue, *Recognize the Spiritual Bonds Which Unite Us* (Rome: Vatican City, 1994), 7–11. For a good discussion of the postconciliar Catholic theology of Islam, see Christian Troll, "Changing Catholic Views of Islam," in *Islam and Christianity: Mutual Perceptions since the Mid-20th Century*, ed. Jacques Waardenburg (Leuven: Peeters, 1998), 19–77.

10. For a list of these speeches, see Christian Troll, "Catholic Teachings on Interreligious Dialogue, with Special Reference to Christian-Muslim Relations," in *Muslim-Christian Perceptions of Dialogue Today*, ed. Jacques Waardenburg (Leuven: Peeters, 2000), 241.

11. Pope John Paul II, as quoted in *Recognize the Spiritual Bonds*, 15.

12. Some of these theologians include Georges Anawati, "Polémique, apologie, et dialogue islamo-chrétien, positions classiques médiévals et positions contemporaines," *Euntes Docete* 22 (1969): 375–452; Robert Caspar, *Pour un regard chrétien sur l'Islam* (Centurion, 1990); Jacques Jomier, *Pour connaître Islam* (Paris: Les éditions du Cerf, 1988); Thomas Michel, "Pope John Paul II's Teaching on Islam in His Addresses to Muslims," *Bulletin* n. 62, vol. 21, no. 2 (1986): 182–91; Troll, "Changing Catholic Views."

13. Caspar, *Pour un regard*, 179–97.

14. David Kerr, "He Walked in the Path of the Prophets: Towards Christian Theological Recognition of the Prophethood of Muhammad," in *Muslims in Dialogue: The Evolution of a Dialogue*, ed. Leonard Swidler (Lewiston, NY: Mellen Press, 1992); Kenneth Cragg, *Muhammad and the Qur'an: A Question of Response* (Maryknoll, NY: Orbis, 1984), 140–41.

15. Cragg, *The Christ and the Faiths* (London: SPCK, 1986), 328 and 337.

16. World Council of Churches (WCC), "Planning Meeting for Next Steps in Christian-Muslim Dialogue" (1976), in *Christians Meeting Muslims: WCC Papers on Ten Years of Christian-Muslim Dialogue*, ed. John Taylor (Geneva: World Council of Churches, 1980), 150.

17. Caspar, *Pour un Regard*, 196–97.

18. "Group Report on Christian-Muslim Relations" in Taylor, *Christians Meeting Muslims*, 61.

19. Yvonne Yazbeck Haddad and Wadi Zaidan Haddad, eds., *Christian-Muslim Encounters* (Gainesville: University Press of Florida, 1995), and Waardenburg, *Islam and Christianity*, both include notable scholars in Muslim-Christian relations such as Willem Bijlefeld, Maymoud Ayoub, Seyyed Hossain Nasr, Christian Troll, David Kerr, Annemarie Schimmel, Jane Smith, among many others.

20. *Prayer: Christian and Muslim Perspectives* (Building Bridges Seminar), ed. David Marshall and Lucinda Mosher (Washington, DC: Georgetown University Press, 2011) does not mention Mary. There is no entry for Mary in the index of Clinton Bennett, *Understanding Christian-Muslim Relations* (New York: Continuum, 2008). John Renard, *Islam and Christianity: Theological Themes in Comparative Perspective* (Berkeley: University of California Press, 2011), briefly compares Mary and Muhammad, and notes that Islam reveres Mary along with Khadija and other founding Muslimas.

21. C. Jonn Block, *The Qur'an in Christian-Muslim Dialogue: Historical and Modern Interpretations* (London: Routledge, 2014), includes these sections on Mary: pp. 48, 93, 214.

22. Clare Amos, "Vatican and World Council of Churches Initiatives," in *Contemporary Muslim-Christian Encounters*, ed. Paul Hedges (New York: Bloomsbury Academic, 2015), 193. Comparative theologians such as James Fredericks and Francis Clooney have called for a "moratorium" on the theology of religions project.

23. Zeki Saritoprak, *Islam's Jesus* (Gainesville: University Press of Florida, 2014); Tarif Khalidi, *The Muslim Jesus* (Cambridge, MA: Harvard University Press, 2001); Mona Siddiqui, *Christians, Muslims, and Jesus* (New Haven, CT: Yale University Press, 2013). A recent exception is the brand-new *Marie au regard de l'Islam*, ed. Mustapha Cherif (Paris: Albouraq, 2017), which was published as this book was going to press.

24. For more on Zeitoun, see Maura Hearden, "Lessons from Zeitoun: A Marian Proposal for Christian-Muslim Dialogue," *The Journal of Ecumenical Studies* 47, no. 3 (Summer 2012) and Angie Heo, "The Virgin between Christianity and Islam: Sainthood, Media, and Modernity in Egypt," *Journal of the American Academy of Religion* (2013): 1–22.

25. "Mosque Dedicated to Virgin Mary Opens in Tartous," *Lebanon Daily Star*, June 8, 2015, http://www.dailystar.com.lb/News/Middle-East/2015/Jun-08/301021-mosque-dedicated-to-virgin-mary-opens-in-tartous.ashx.

26. Nathan Mitchell in *The Mystery of the Rosary: Marian Devotion and the Reinvention of Catholicism* (New York: New York University Press, 2009), 213, quotes a Pew Trust Survey from 2008 ("US Religious Landscape Survey") that says about one-fifth of American Catholics still pray the Rosary once a week. This statistic does not include gender or generational breakdowns.

27. A brief sampling of feminist discussions of Mary: Rosemary Radford Ruether, *Mary the Feminine Face of God* (Philadelphia: Westminster, 1977); Marina Warner, *Alone in All Her Sex* (New York: Vintage Books, 1983); Elizabeth Johnson, *Truly Our Sister* (New York: Continuum, 2006); Amy-Jill Levine, ed., *A Feminist Companion to Mariology* (London: T & T Clark International, 2005); Sarah Jane Boss, *Mary the Complete Resource* (Oxford: Oxford University Press, 2007); Miri Rubin, *Mother of God: A History of the Virgin Mary* (New Haven, CT: Yale University Press, 2009).

28. *Marianismo* is a term coined by Rosa M. Gil and Carmen Inoa Vázquez in *The María Paradox* (New York: Putnam's Sons, 1996), 7.

29. Johnson cites the observation of Mary Hines in *Truly Our Sister*, 9. Anecdotally, I too have seen this enrollment pattern in my own classes.

30. Johnson, *Truly Our Sister*, chap. 11 (the last) is entitled "Friend of God and Prophet."

31. Matthew Milliner, *The Last Madonna* (Oxford: Oxford University Press, forthcoming), makes this point, and highlights the importance of Our Lady of Compassion in Byzantium, using the neologism "Our Lady of Losers."

32. See Anna Niedzwiedz, *Image and Figure: Our Lady of Czestochowa in Polish Culture and Popular Religion* (Krakow: Jagellonian University Press, 2015), and Jalane D. Schmidt, *Cachita's Streets: The Virgin of Charity, Race, and Revolution in Cuba* (Durham, NC: Duke University Press, 2015).

33. Sölle as quoted in Johnson, *Truly Our Sister*, 15.

34. See, for example, Ivone Gebara and Maria Clara Bingemer, *Mary, Mother of God, Mother of the Poor* (Maryknoll, NY: Orbis, 1989).

35. Retta Blaney, "One-Woman Play Uses Biblical Mary's Life to Tell Story of Black Mothers, Sons," *National Catholic Reporter*, February 16, 2017.

36. For more on Mary as mother of mourning, see Christopher Clohessy, "Weeping Mothers: Tears and Power in Fatima and Mary," *Islamochristiana* 36 (2010): 101–15. For Islamic perspectives on gender and related issues, see Ednan Aslan, Marcia Hermensen, and Elif Medeni, eds., *Muslima Theology: The Voices of Muslim Women Theologians* (Frankfurt: Peter Lang, 2013).

37. See Heal, *The Cult of the Virgin Mary*, and Beth Kreitzer, *Reforming Mary*.

38. Miguel de la Torre, personal correspondence. For a contrasting view, see Nora Lozano-Díaz, "Ignored Virgin or Unaware Woman: A Mexican-American Protestant Reflection on the Virgin of Guadalupe," in *Blessed One: Protestant Perspectives on Mary*, ed. Beverly Roberts Gaventa and Cynthia Rigby (Louisville, KY: Westminster John Knox Press, 2002), 85–96.

39. Gaventa and Rigby, *Blessed One*.

40. Bonnie Miller-McLemore, "Pondering All These Things: Mary and Motherhood," in Gaventa and Rigby, *Blessed One*, 97.

41. Anglican-Roman Catholic International Commission (ARCIC), *Mary: Grace and Hope in Christ*, §3. For background on this

document, see Adelbert Denaux and Nicholas Sagovsky, eds., *Studying Mary: The ARCIC Working Papers* (London: T & T Clark, 2007).

42. See Tim Perry, *Mary for Evangelicals* (Downers Grove, IL: IVP Academic, 2006), and David Gustafson and Dwight Longenecker, *Mary: A Catholic-Evangelical Debate* (Grand Rapids, MI: Brazos, 2003).

43. Editorial by Timothy George, Morgan Lee, and Mark Galli, *Christianity Today*, December 22, 2016.

44. Alan Cowell and Joel Greenberg, "Mideast Turmoil: Aftermath; In Church of the Nativity, the Refuse of a Siege," *The New York Times*, May 11, 2002. Thanks to Melanie Webb for bringing this article and the examples of Holy Land pilgrimage sites visited by Protestants to my attention.

45. Willy Jansen, "Marian Images and Religious Identities in the Middle East," in *Moved by Mary: The Power of Pilgrimage in the Modern World*, ed. Anna-Karina Hermkens, Willy Jansen, and Catrien Notermans (Surrey, UK: Ashgate, 2009), 39.

46. For a discussion of the connections between conversion and coercion in the medieval period, see Marcia L. Colish, *Faith, Fiction, and Force in Medieval Baptism Debates* (Washington, DC: Catholic University of America Press, 2014).

47. Translating the Arabic word *jihad* as "holy war" is inaccurate. A better definition based on the word's Arabic root letters would be "striving or struggle in the way of God." This struggle could include the use of spiritual, political, economic, rhetorical, or physical means.

48. One of the talking points in the 2016 presidential election revolved around the terminology for terrorism: Trump used "radical Islamic terrorism" but Clinton (and Obama) preferred "violent jihadist terrorism" because the latter two did not want to suggest that the United States is at war with Islam.

49. Colombo, "Jesuits and Islam," 340.

50. Leo XIII, *Supremi Apostolatus* (1883), §3.

51. Leo XIII, *Adiutricem* (1895), §4.

52. Zwemer, *Islam: A Challenge to Faith,* 255–56.

53. For a recent survey of American Catholic attitudes about Islam, see the Bridge Initiative Report, "Danger and Dialogue: American Catholic Public Opinion and Portrayals of Islam," Georgetown University, 2016.

54. Gazing at images of Mary and Jesus was considered auspicious, and this *Falnama* image is relevant to this book because it combines Islamic and Christian religious themes and artistic conventions.

See Farhad, Massumeh and Serpil Bagci, *Falnama: The Book of Omens* (Washington, DC: Sackler Gallery/Smithsonian Institution, 2009), 319n22.

55. Scott Alexander, *The Race to Goodness: An End to Triumphalism in Christian-Muslim Relations* (Oxford: Oxford University Press, forthcoming).

56. Thanks to Kim Wagner for bringing this meme to my attention.

57. The "Danger and Dialogue" report indicates that most American Catholics polled do not know basic facts about Islam—for example, 86 percent think that Muslims worship Muhammad, while 88 percent do not know Muslims honor Mary, 37–38.

58. Commonalities include not only doctrines and symbols, but also shared values, such as belief in interfaith cooperation itself as a desideratum. For example, Eboo Patel, an American Muslim who has pioneered the youth interfaith movement, suggests that young people must "be aggressive about spreading the vision of interfaith cooperation," *Acts of Faith* (Boston: Beacon Press, 2007), 187.

EPILOGUE

1. Excellent articles about Islam and Mary by Muslim scholars exist, e.g., Timothy Winter, "Pulchra ut Luna: Some Reflections on the Marian Theme in Muslim-Catholic Dialogue," *Journal of Ecumenical Studies* 36 (1999): 439–69, and Jane Smith and Yvonne Haddad, "The Virgin Mary in Islamic Tradition and Commentary," *The Muslim World* 79, nos. 3–4 (1989): 161–87, but they were written in 1999 and 1989, respectively. The index of a more recent (2013) volume on the Islamic theology of religions, Mohammad Hassan Khalil, ed., *Between Heaven and Hell: Islam, Salvation, and the Fate of Others* (Oxford: Oxford University Press, 2013), lists just two page references for Mary (in contrast, Jesus has seventeen). A full-length volume about the Muslim Mary from an Islamic scholarly perspective, comparable to recent books written about the Muslim Jesus, would be most welcome.

2. Pontifical Council of Interreligious Dialogue and Congregation for the Evangelization of Peoples, *Dialogue and Proclamation* (1991), §42.

3. Ibid., §85.

4. Thanks to Andreatte Brachman for sharing the Bridgeview women dialogue group's reflections.

5. Mona Siddiqui, *Christians, Muslims, and Jesus* (New Haven, CT: Yale University Press, 2013), 170.

6. Anne Hege Grung, "Gender and Christian-Muslim Dialogue," in *Contemporary Muslim-Christian Encounters*, ed. Paul Hedges (New York: Bloomsbury Academic, 2015), 67–81, at 76.

7. Ibid., 76–77. For more on this topic, see also Grung's *Dialogue with and without a Veil*, with Lena Larsen (Oslo: Pax, 2000).

BIBLIOGRAPHY

PRIMARY SOURCES

ʿAbd al-Jabbar. *Critique of Christian Origins: A Parallel English-Arabic Text*. Translated and edited by Gabriel Said Reynolds and Samir Khalil Samir. Provo, UT: Brigham Young University Press, 2010.

Acta Synodalia III.3. General Congregation XC. Vatican City, 1972.

Akathistos Hymn. In *The Image of the Virgin Mary in the Akathistos Hymn*, translated by Leena Peltomaa, 2–19. Leiden: Brill, 2001.

Alfonso X. *Cantigas de Santa Maria*. In *Songs of Holy Mary of Alfonso X the Wise*, translated by Kathleen Kulp-Hill. Tempe AZ: Arizona Center for Medieval and Renaissance Studies, 2000.

Al-Kindi. *Apology of Al-Kindi*. In *Early Christian-Muslim Dialogue: A Collection of Documents from the First Three Islamic Centuries*, translated (English) by Anton Tien and N. A. Newman, edited by N. A. Newman, 381–545. Hatfield, PA: Interdisciplinary Biblical Research Institute, 1993. Translated (French) by Georges Tartar, *Dialogue islamo-chrétien sous le Calife al-Maʾmun (813–834): Les épîtres d'al-Hashimi et d'al-Kindi*. Paris: Nouvelles Éditions Latines, 1985.

Al-Warraq. *The Refutation of the Uniting*, §187–88. Quoted by David Thomas in *Early Muslim Polemic against Christianity*, 127–29. Cambridge: Cambridge University Press, 2002.

Anawati, Georges and Louis Gardet. *Introduction à la Théologie Musulmane: Essai de Theologie Comparée*. Paris: Vrin, 1948.

Anglican-Roman Catholic International Commission (ARCIC). *Mary: Grace and Hope in Christ*. 2004.

Arinze, Francis Cardinal. "Message at Ramadan." Pontifical Council for Interreligious Dialogue, 1988.

Ayuso Guixot, Miguel Ángel. "La Vierge Marie et la Dialogue Islamo-Chrétien." *Pro Dialogo Bulletin* 146–147 (2014): 201–4.

Bartholomew of Edessa. *Refutation of the Hagarene* (PG 104:1397). Quoted by Jaroslav Pelikan, *Mary through the Centuries*, 77. New Haven, CT: Yale University Press, 1996.

Bible. New Revised Standard Version, Anglicized Edition, Division of Christian Education of the National Council of the Churches of Christ in the United States of America, 1995.

Bird, Mary. *Persian Women and Their Creed*. London: CMS, 1908.

Caspar, Robert. *Pour un regard chrétien sur l'Islam*. Paris: Centurion, 1990.

Common Christological Statement. The Catholic Church and the Assyrian Church of the East, 1994.

Cragg, Kenneth. *The Christ and the Faiths*. London: SPCK, 1986.

———. *Muhammad and the Qur'an: A Question of Response*. Maryknoll, NY: Orbis, 1984.

D'Agen, Boyer. "Maison de Marie à Éphèse." *La Nouvelle Revue* 16 (1902).

De Dieu, Ludovico. *Historia Christi Persice, conscripta simulque multis modis contaminata*. Leiden, 1639.

Dialogue and Proclamation. Pontifical Council for Interreligious Dialogue and Congregation for the Evangelization of Peoples, 1991.

Essery, W. A. *The Ascending Cross*. London, 1905.

Felix Fabri. *Wanderings in the Holy Land*. Translated by Aubrey Stewart. London: Palestine Pilgrims Text Society, 1892. Critical Latin edition in Jean Meyers and Nicole Chareyron, ed., *Félix Fabri. Les errances de Frère Félix, pèlerin en Terre sainte, en Arabie et en Égypte (1480–1483)*, 2 vols. Montpellier: Publications de l'Université Paul-Valéry et du CERCAM, 2000 and 2003.

Ibn Hazm. *Al Fasl fi al-Miala wa l-Ahwa wa l-Nihal* (The decisive word on sects, heterodoxies and denominations). Quoted by Hosn Abboud, "Idhan Maryam Nabiyya' (Hence Maryam is a prophetess)." In *Mariam, the Magdalen, and the Mother*, edited by Deirdre Joy Good, 183–96. Bloomington: Indiana University Press, 2005.

———. *Risala fi al-Mufadala bayna al-Sahaba* (Treatise of differentiation between the prophet's companions). Quoted by Hosn Abboud, "Idhan Maryam Nabiyya' (Hence Maryam is a prophetess)." In *Mariam, the Magdalen, and the Mother*, edited by Deirdre Joy Good, 183–96. Bloomington: Indiana University Press, 2005.

Ibn Ishaq. *The Life of Muhammad*. Translated by A. Guillaume. Oxford: Oxford University Press, 1955.

Ibn Taymiyya. *Majmu'at al-fatawa*. Vol. 27. Mansura, Egypt: Dar al-wafa', 2005.

International Theological Commission (ITC). *Sensus Fidei in the Life of the Church*. 2014.

Jacob of Edessa. *Letter on the Genealogy of the Virgin*. Text (Syriac) and translation (French) by François Nau in "Lettre de Jacques D'Edesse sur la généalogie de la Sainte Vierge." *Revue de L'Orient Chrétien* 6 (1901): 512–31. Excerpts (English) translated by Robert Hoyland in "Jacob of Edessa on Islam." In *After Bardaisan*, edited by G. Reinink and A. Klugkist. Leuven: Peeters, 1999.

Jessup, Henry. *The Women of the Arabs*. New York: Dodd & Meade, 1873.

John of Damascus. *De haeresibus*. Translated by Daniel Sahas in *John of Damascus on Islam*. Leiden: Brill, 1972.

Jomier, Jacques. *Pour connaître Islam*. Paris: Les éditions du Cerf, 1988.

Keeler, William Cardinal. "How Mary Holds Muslims and Christians in Conversation." *Origins: CNS Documentary Service* 25, no. 36 (February 29, 1996).

Kerr, David. "He Walked in the Path of the Prophets: Towards Christian Theological Recognition of the Prophethood of Muhammad." In *Muslims in Dialogue: The Evolution of a Dialogue*, ed. Leonard Swidler. Lewiston, NY: Edwin Mellen Press, 1992.

Lansing, Gulian. *Egypt's Princes*. New York: Carter & Brothers, 1865.

Lavigerie, Charles. *Missionaries of Africa: Selected Texts*. London: Samuel Walker, 1990.

Luther, Martin. "Preface to the Qur'an." (1553). In "Martin Luther—Translations of Two Prefaces on Islam," translated by Sarah Henrich and James L. Boyce. *Word & World* 16, no. 2 (1996): 262–66.

———. "Preface to the Treatise on the Religion and Customs of the Turks" (1530). In "Martin Luther—Translations of Two Prefaces on Islam," translated by Sarah Henrich and James L. Boyce. *Word & World* 16, no. 2 (1996): 258–62.

Massignon, Louis. "Badaliya Statutes (1947)." In *Louis Massignon: A Pioneer of Interfaith Dialogue. The Badaliya Prayer Movement, 1947–1962*, translated by Dorothy Buck. London: Blue Dome Press, 2016.

———. "Le culte liturgique et populaire des VII dormants martyrs d'Ephese." In *Opera Minora*, edited by Y. Moubarac, 3:119–80. Beirut: Dar al-Maaref, 1963.

———. "La Mubahala de Medine et l'hyperdulie de Fatima." In *Opera Minora*, edited by Y. Moubarac, 1:550–72. Beirut: Dar al-Maaref, 1963.

———. "La notion de voeu et la dévotion musulmane à Fatima." In *Opera Minora*, edited by Y. Moubarac, 1:573–91. Beirut: Dar al-Maaref, 1963.

———. *Opera Minora*. Edited by Y. Moubarac. 3 vols. Beirut: Dar al-Maaref, 1963.

———. "L'oratoire de Marie à l'Aqça [Al Aqsa], vu sous le voile de deuil de Fatima." In *Opera Minora*, edited by Y. Moubarac, 1:591–618. Beirut: Dar al-Maaref, 1963.

———. "Les trois prières de Abraham." In *Opera Minora*, edited by Y. Moubarac, 3:811–12. English translation in *Testimonies and Reflections: Essays of Louis Massignon*, edited and translated by Herbert Mason, 3–20. Notre Dame, IN: University of Notre Dame Press, 1989.

Nasir al-Din. *Guide for Muslim Pilgrims (Al-Mustaqsa fi Fada'il al-Masjid al-Aqsa)*. In Amikam Elad, *Medieval Jerusalem and Islamic Worship*. Leiden: Brill, 1995.

Nicholas of Cusa. *Cribratio alkorani*. In *Nicolai de Cusa Opera Omnia*, edited by Ludwig Hagemann, vol. 8. Hamburg: Felix Meiner Verlag, 1986.

———. *De pace fidei*. In *Nicolai de Cusa Opera Omnia*, edited by Raymond Klibansky and Hildebrand Bascour, vol. 7. Hamburg: Felix Meiner Verlag, 1959.

Nonnus of Nisibis. *Apologetic Treatise*. In Sidney Griffith, *Beginnings of Christian Theology in Arabic*, 127. Surrey: Ashgate, 2002.

Nostra Aetate (*On the Church's Relation to Non-Christian Religions*). Vatican II Council, 1965.

Perpetua. *The Passion of Perpetua and Felicity*. Translated by W. H. Shewring. London, 1931.

Pius II, Pope. *Epistola ad Mahomatem II*. Edited and translated (English) by Albert Baca. New York: Peter Lang, 1990.

Pius V, Pope. *Salvatoris Domini*. March 5, 1572. Translated by Cyril Dore in "The Popes and the Rosary." *Dominicana* 10, no. 2 (September, 1925): 15–21.

Plumey, Yves, OMI. Letter to Louis Massignon, August 10, 1962. OMI Archives *Media & Edition (Different Issues—Correspondence: 1949–1965) B-43S2*.

Pontifical Council for Interreligious Dialogue. *Recognize the Spiritual Bonds Which Unite Us*. Vatican City, 1994.

Postel, Guillaume. *Alcorani seu legis Mahumeti et evangelistarum concordiae Liber*. Paris: Gromorsus, 1543.

———. *De orbis terrae Concordia libri quattuor*. Basel: Oporinus, 1544.

———. *Du souverain effect de la plus excellente Corone du mond*. Paris BNF MS Fons Français 2114. Folio 61ff.

Poulin, Eugène. *La Maison de la Sainte Vierge: La véritable histoire de sa découverte*. Istanbul, 1999 (1905).

Protevangelium of James. In *The Apocryphal New Testament*, translated by J. K. Elliott, 57–67. Oxford: Clarendon, 1993.

Protevangelium sive de natalibus Jesu Christi et ipsius Matris virginis Mariae. Translated by Guillaume Postel (Latin). Basel, 1552.

Pseudo-William of Tripoli. *De statu sarracenorum*. In *Wilhelm von Tripolis: Notitia de Machometo et De statu Sarracenorum*, edited and translated by (German) Peter Engels, 266–371. Würzburg: Echter, 1992.

Qur'an. Translated by M. A. S. Abdel Haleem. Oxford: Oxford University Press, 2016.

Riccoldo da Montecroce. *Contra Legem Sarracenorum*. In "L'ouvrage d'un frère prêcheur en Orient à la fin du XIIIe s. suivi de l'édition du Contra legem Sarracenorum," edited by Jean-Marie Mérigoux, in *Memorie Domenicane* 17 (1986): 60–142.

———. *Epistolae ad Ecclesiam Triumphantem*. In *A Christian Pilgrim in Medieval Iraq: Riccoldo da Montecroce's Encounter with Islam*, translated by Rita George-Tvrtković. Turnhout: Brepols, 2012.

———. *Liber peregrinationis*. In *A Christian Pilgrim in Medieval Iraq: Riccoldo da Montecroce's Encounter with Islam*, translated by Rita George-Tvrtković. Turnhout: Brepols, 2012.

Rumi, Jalal ad din. *Fihi ma fihi*, chap. 5. Quoted by Annemarie Schimmel in "Jesus and Mary as Poetical Images in Rumi's Verse." In *The Routledge Reader in Christian-Muslim Relations*, edited by Mona Siddiqui. London: Routledge, 2013.

Sale, George. *The Koran, translated into English with Explanatory Notes and Preliminary Discourse*. London: 1734; revised edition Philadelphia: J.W. Moore, 1853.

Sheen, Fulton. "The Sword, the Hammer, the Sickle, and the Cross." *Worldmission* 2 (Winter, 1951): 3, 6.

———. *The World's First Love: Mary, Mother of God*. New York: McGraw-Hill, 1952.

Timothy. *The Apology of Timothy*. In "The Apology of Timothy the Patriarch before the Caliph Mahdi," text and translated by

(English) Alphonse Mingana, 15–162. In *Woodbrooke Studies: Christian Documents in Syriac, Arabic, and Garshuni*. Vol. 2. Cambridge: Heffer, 1928.

Watson, Charles. *In the Valley of the Nile*. New York: Fleming Revell Co., 1908.

William of Tripoli. *Notitia de Machometi*. In *Wilhelm von Tripolis: Notitia de Machometo et De statu Sarracenorum*, edited and translated by (German) Peter Engels, 194–261. Würzburg: Echter, 1992.

World Council of Churches. "Group Report on Christian-Muslim Relations." In *Christians Meeting Muslims: WCC Papers on Ten Years of Christian-Muslim Dialogue*. Geneva: World Council of Churches, 1977.

———. "Planning Meeting for Next Steps in Christian-Muslim Dialogue (1976)." In *Christians Meeting Muslims: WCC Papers on Ten Years of Christian-Muslim Dialogue*, edited by John Taylor. Geneva: World Council of Churches, 1980.

Xavier, Jerome. *Mirat al-Quds (The Mirror of Holiness): A Life of Christ for Emperor Akbar*. Translated by Wheeler Thackston with commentary by Pedro Moura Carvalho. Leiden: Brill, 2012.

Zwemer, Samuel. *Islam: A Challenge to Faith*. New York: Student Volunteer Movement for Foreign Missions, 1907.

SECONDARY SOURCES

Abboud, Hosn. "Idhan Maryam Nabiyya' (Hence Maryam is a Prophetess)." In *Mariam, the Magdalen, and the Mother*, edited by Deirdre Joy Good, 183–96. Bloomington: Indiana University Press, 2005.

———. *Mary in the Qur'an: A Literary Reading*. London: Routledge, 2014.

Abel, A. "L'apologie d'Al-Kindi et sa place dans la polémique islamo-chrétien." *Atti del convegno internazionale sul tema: L'oriente christiano nella storia della civiltà*. Rome, 1964.

Abraham, Heather. "The Shrine of Our Lady of Ephesus: A Study of the Personas of Mary as Lived Religion." Master's thesis, University of Georgia, 2008.

Akyol, Mustafa. "Why It's Not Wrong to Wish Muslims a Merry Christmas." *The New York Times*. December 23, 2016.

Alam, Muzaffar, and Sanjay Subrahmanyam. *Writing the Mughal World*. New York: Columbia University Press, 2012.

Bibliography

Albera, Dionigi. "Religious Antagonism and Shared Sanctuaries in Algeria." In *Choreographies of Shared Sacred Sites*, edited by Elazar Barkan and Karen Barkey, 97–129. New York: Columbia University Press, 2015.

Allchin, A. M. *The Joy of All Creation: Anglican Meditation on the Place of Mary*. Hyde Park, NY: New City Press, 1993.

Alvarez, Elizabeth Hayes. *Valiant Woman: The Virgin Mary in Nineteenth-Century American Culture*. Chapel Hill, NC: University of North Carolina, 2016.

Amos, Clare. "Vatican and World Council of Churches Initiatives." In *Contemporary Muslim-Christian Encounters*, edited by Paul Hedges, 185–200. New York: Bloomsbury Academic, 2015.

Anawati, Georges. "Excursus on Islam." In *Commentary on the Documents of Vatican II*, edited by Herbert Vorgrimler, 3:151–60. New York: Herder & Herder, 1967–69.

———. "Polémique, apologie, et dialogue islamo-chrétien, positions classiques médiévals et positions contemporaines." *Euntes Docete* 22 (1969): 375–452.

Anderson, Paul. "Marcantonio Colonna and the Victory at Lepanto: The Framing of a Public Space at Santa Maria in Aracoeli." In *Perspectives on Public Space in Rome*, edited by Gregory Smith and Jan Gadeyne, 131–55. London: Routledge, 2013.

Arnaldez, Roger. *Jesus fils de Marie prophete de l'Islam*. Paris: Desclee, 1980.

Aslan, Ednan, Marcia Hermensen, and Elif Medeni, eds. *Muslima Theology: The Voices of Muslim Women Theologians*. Frankfurt: Peter Lang, 2013.

Avner, Rina. "Theotokos at Kathisma." In *The Cult of the Mother of God*, edited by Leslie Brubaker and Mary Cunningham, 9–30. Surrey: Ashgate, 2011.

Bacci, Michele. "The Legacy of the Hodegetria: Holy Icons and Legends between East and West." In *Images of the Mother of God*, edited by Maria Vassilaki, 321–36. Surrey, UK: Ashgate, 2005.

Backus, Irene. "Guillaume Postel, Theodore Bibliander et le Protévangile de Jacques." *Apocrypha* 6 (1995): 7–65.

Bailey, Gauvin. *The Jesuits and the Grand Mogul: Renaissance Art and the Imperial Court of India, 1580–1630*. Washington: Smithsonian Institute, 1998.

———. "The Truth-Showing Mirror: Jesuit Catechism and the Arts in Mughal India." In *The Jesuits: Cultures, Sciences, and the Arts, 1540–1773*, edited by John W. O'Malley, 1:380–401. Toronto: University of Toronto Press, 1999.

Baldick, Julian. "Massignon: Man of Opposites." *Religious Studies* 23, no. 1 (1987): 29–39.

Baraz, D. "The Incarnated Icon of Saidnaya Goes West." *Le Museon* 108 (1995): 181–91.

Barker, Margaret. "Wisdom Imagery." In *The Cult of the Mother of God*, edited by Leslie Brubaker and Mary Cunningham, 91–108. Surrey, UK: Ashgate, 2011.

Baum, Jane. "Apocalyptic Panagia." In *The Cult of the Mother of God*, edited by Leslie Brubaker and Mary Cunningham, 199–218. Surrey, UK: Ashgate, 2011.

Beach, Milo. *The Grand Mughul: Imperial Painting in India*. Williamstown, MA: The Clark Institute, 1978.

Bellitto, Christopher, Thomas Izbicki, and Gerald Christiansen, eds. *Introducing Nicholas of Cusa: Guide to a Renaissance Man*. New York: Paulist Press, 2004.

Bennett, Clinton. *Understanding Christian-Muslim Relations*. New York: Continuum, 2008.

Beranek, Ondrej, and Pavel Tupek. "From Visiting Graves to Their Destruction: The Question of Ziyara through the Eyes of Salafis." *Brandeis University Crown Center for Middle East Studies* (July 2009).

Bertaina, David. "Christians in Medieval Shi'i Historiography." *Medieval Encounters* 19 (2013): 379–407.

Biechler, James. "Christian Humanism Confronts Islam: Sifting the Qur'an with Nicholas of Cusa." *Journal of Ecumenical Studies* 13 (1976).

Bisaha, Nancy. *Creating East and West: Renaissance Humanists and the Ottoman Turks*. Philadelphia: University of Pennsylvania Press, 2004.

Blaney, Retta. "One-Woman Play Uses Biblical Mary's Life to Tell Story of Black Mothers, Sons." *National Catholic Reporter*. February 16, 2017.

Block, C. Jonn. *The Qur'an in Christian-Muslim Dialogue: Historical and Modern interpretations*. London: Routledge, 2014.

Boss, Sarah Jane. *Mary the Complete Resource*. Oxford: Oxford University Press 2007.

Bottini, Laura. "The Apology of al-Kindi." In *Christian-Muslim Relations: A Bibliographic History*, edited by D. Thomas et al., 1:584–594. Leiden: Brill, 2009.

Bouwsma, William. *Concordia Mundi: The Career and Thought of Guillaume Postel*. Cambridge, MA: Harvard University Press, 1957.

Breckenridge, James D. "Et Prima Vidit: The Iconography of the Appearance of Christ to His Mother." *Art Bulletin* 39, no. 1 (1957): 9–32.

Bridge Initiative. *Danger and Dialogue: American Catholic Public Opinion and Portrayals of Islam*. Georgetown University Report, 2016.

Bryer, Anthony, and Michael Ursinus, eds. *Manzikert to Lepanto: The Byzantine World and the Turks, 1071–1571*. Amsterdam: Hakkert Publishers, 1991.

Buck, Dorothy. *Dialogues with Saints and Mystics: In the Spirit of Louis Massignon*. London: Khaniqahi Nimatullahi Publications, 2002.

———. *Louis Massignon: A Pioneer of Interfaith Dialogue. The Badaliya Prayer Movement, 1947–1962*. London: Blue Dome Press, 2016.

Bulman, Raymond F., and Frederick J. Parrella, eds. *From Trent to Vatican II: Historical and Theological Investigations*. Oxford: Oxford University Press, 2006.

Burke, Tony. *Secret Scriptures Revealed: A New Introduction to the Christian Apocrypha*. Grand Rapids, MI: Eerdmans Publishing, 2013.

Burman, Thomas. *Reading the Qur'an in Latin Christendom, 1140–1560*. Philadelphia: University of Pennsylvania Press, 2007.

———. "Two Dominicans, A Lost Manuscript, and Medieval Christian Thought on Islam." In *Commentary, Conflict, and Community in the Premodern Mediterranean*, edited by Ryan Szpiech, 71–86. New York: Fordham University Press, 2015.

Cameron, Averil. "The Early Cult of the Virgin." In *Mother of God*, edited by Maria Vassilaki. Athens: Benaki Museum Exhibition Catalogue, 2001.

Camps, Arnulf. *Jerome Xavier, S.J. and the Muslims of the Mogul Empire: Controversial Works and Missionary Activity*. Fribourg, 1957.

———. "Persian Works of Jerome Xavier: A Jesuit at the Mogul Court." In *Studies in Asian Missionary History, 1956–1998*. Leiden: Brill, 2000.

Canby, Sheila. *Persian Painting*. London: British Museum Press, 1993.

Caspar, Robert. "La vision de l'Islam chez Louis Massignon et son influence sur l'église." In *Cahier Massignon*, edited by Jean-François Six, 126–47. Paris: L'Herne, 1970.

Châtellier, Louis. *The Europe of the Devout*. Translated by Jean Birrell. Cambridge: University of Cambridge Press, 1989.

Cherif, Mustapha, ed. *Marie au regard de l'Islam*. Paris: Albouraq, 2017.

Clohessy, Christopher. "Weeping Mothers: Tears and Power in Fatima and Mary." *Islamochristiana* 36 (2010): 101–15.

Clooney, Francis X. *Comparative Theology: Deep Learning across Religious Borders*. Oxford: Blackwell, 2010.

Cohen, Jeremy. *Living Letters of the Law: Ideas of the Jew in Medieval Christianity*. Berkeley, CA: University of California Press, 1999.

Colish, Marcia L. *Faith, Fiction, and Force in Medieval Baptism Debates*. Washington, DC: Catholic University of America Press, 2014.

Colombo, Emanuele. "Jesuits and Islam in Seventeenth-Century Europe: War, Preaching and Conversions." In *L'Islam visto da Occidente. Cultura e religione del Seicento europeo di fronte all'Islam*, edited by Bernard Heyberger et al., 315–40. Milan: Marietti, 2009.

———. "Muslim Turned Jesuit: Baldassarre Loyola Mandes (1631–1667)." *Journal of Early Modern History* 17, nos. 5–6 (2013): 479–504.

Congar, Yves. *Tradition and Traditions*. New York: Macmillan, 1967.

Conte, Marialaura. "Lebanon: How the Annunciation Came to Be a Joint Christian-Muslim Holiday." *Oasis: Christians and Muslims in the Global World*. March 29, 2010.

Cook, David. "New Testament Citations in the Hadith Literature." In *The Encounter of Eastern Christianity with Early Islam*, edited by Emmanouela Grypeou, Mark Swanson, and David Thomas, 185–223. Leiden: Brill, 2006.

Coppa, Frank. *The Life and Pontificate of Pope Pius XII: Between History and Controversy*. Washington, DC: Catholic University Press, 2013.

Cowell, Alan, and Joel Greenberg. "Mideast Turmoil: In Church of the Nativity, the Refuse of a Siege." *The New York Times*, May 11, 2002.

Cragg, Kenneth. *The Arab Christian: A History in the Middle East*. Louisville, KY: Westminster John Knox Press, 1991.

Cunningham, Lawrence. "The Virgin Mary." In *From Trent to Vatican II: Historical and Theological Investigations*, edited by Raymond F. Bulman and Frederick J. Parrella, 179–92. Oxford: Oxford University Press, 2006.

Cunningham, Mary. *Wider Than Heaven: Eighth-Century Homilies on the Mother of God*. Crestwood, NY: St. Vladimir's Press, 2008.

Cuoq, Joseph. *Lavigerie, Les Pères Blancs et les Musulmans Maghrebins*. Rome: Missionaries of Africa, 1986.

Daley, Brian. *On the Dormition of Mary: Early Patristic Homilies*. Crestwood, NY: St. Vladimir's Press, 1998.

———. "Woman of Many Names: Mary in Orthodox and Catholic Theology." *Theological Studies* 71, no. 4 (2010): 846–69.

Daltrop, Georg. "Galleria dei Candelabri." In *The Vatican: Spirit and Art of Ancient Rome*, edited by Philippe de Montebello and Kathleen Howard. New York: Metropolitan Museum of Art, 1983.

D'Alverny, Marie. "Deux traductions latines du Coran au Môyen Age." *Archives d'histoire doctrinale et litteraire du môyen age* 16 (1948): 69–131.

Dandelet, Thomas. *Spanish Rome 1500–1700*. New Haven, CT: Yale University Press, 2001.

Daniel, Norman. *Islam and the West*. Edinburgh: Edinburgh University Press, 1960.

D'Costa, Gavin. *Vatican II: Catholic Doctrines on Jews and Muslims*. Oxford: Oxford University Press, 2014.

Debié, Muriel. "Muslim-Christian Controversy in an Unedited Syriac Text: Revelations and Testimonies about Our Lord's Dispensation." In *The Encounter of Eastern Christianity with Early Islam*, edited by Emmanouela Grypeou, Mark Swanson, and David Thomas, 225–35. Leiden: Brill, 2006.

Delfosse, Annick. *La Protectrice du Pais-Bas: Strategies Politiques et Figures de la Vierge dans les Pays Bas Espagnols*. Turnhout: Brepols, 2009.

Denaux, Adelbert, and Nicholas Sagovsky, eds. *Studying Mary: The ARCIC Working Papers*. London: T & T Clark, 2007.

Destremau, Christian, and Jean Moncelon. *Massignon*. Paris: Plon, 1994.

Duomato, Eleanor Abdella. *Getting God's Ear: Women, Islam, and Healing in Saudi Arabia and the Gulf*. New York: Columbia University Press, 2000.

Dupuis, Jacques. *Towards a Christian Theology of Religious Pluralism*. Maryknoll, NY: Orbis, 1997.

Dyrness, William. *Reformed Theology and Visual Culture: The Protestant Imagination from Calvin to Edwards*. Cambridge: Cambridge University Press, 2004.

Ehrman, Bart, and Zlatko Pleše, eds. *The Other Gospels*. Oxford: Oxford University Press, 2014.

Elad, Amikam. *Medieval Jerusalem and Islamic Worship*. Leiden: Brill, 1995.

Ellington, Donna Spivey. *From Sacred Body to Angelic Soul: Understanding Mary in Late Medieval and Early Modern Europe*. Washington, DC: Catholic University of America Press, 2001.

Elliott, J. K. Introduction to the *Protevangelium of James*. In *The Apocryphal New Testament*, 48–67. Oxford: Clarendon Press, 1993.

El-Zein, Amira. "L'autre dans la spiritualité massignonienne." In *Louis Massignon: Au Coeur de Notre Temps*, edited by Jacques Keryell. Paris: Éditions Karhala, 1999.

Euler, Walter Andreas. "A Critical Survey of Cusanus's Writings on Islam." In *Nicholas of Cusa and Islam: Polemic and Dialogue in the Late Middle Ages*, edited by Ian Levy, Rita George-Tvrtković, and Donald Duclow, 20–29. Leiden: Brill, 2014.

Farhad, Massumeh, and Serpil Bagci. *Falnama: The Book of Omens*. Washington, DC: Sackler Gallery/Smithsonian Institution, 2009.

Fitzgerald, Michael. "Dialogue and Proclamation: A Reading in the Perspective of Christian-Muslim Relations." In *In Many and Diverse Ways: In Honor of Jacques Dupuis*, edited by Daniel Kendall and Gerard O'Collins. Maryknoll, NY: Orbis, 2003.

Flannery, John. "Christ in Islam and Muhammad, a Christian Evaluation: Theological Reflections on Tradition and Dialogue." In *The Catholic Church in the Contemporary Middle East*, edited by Anthony O'Mahony and John Flannery, 331–52. London: Melisende, 2010.

Foss, Clive. *Ephesus after Antiquity: A Late Antique, Byzantine, and Turkish City*. Cambridge: Cambridge University Press, 1979.

Francisco, Adam S. *Martin Luther and Islam: A Study in Sixteenth-Century Polemics and Apologetics*. Leiden: Brill, 2007.

Funkenstein, Amos. "Basic Types of Christian Anti-Jewish Polemics in the Later Middle Ages." *Viator* 2 (1971): 373–82.

Garosi, Eugenio. "The Incarnated Icon of Saydnaya: Light and Shade." *Journal of Islam and Muslim-Christian Relations* 26, no. 3 (2015): 339–58.

Garrels, Anne. *Naked in Baghdad: The Iraq War and the Aftermath*. New York: Picador/Farrar, Straus, and Giroux, 2003.

Gaventa, Beverly Roberts, and Cynthia Rigby, eds. *Blessed One: Protestant Perspectives on Mary*. Louisville, KY: Westminster John Knox Press, 2002.

Gebara, Ivone, and Maria Clara Bingemer. *Mary, Mother of God, Mother of the Poor*. Maryknoll, NY: Orbis, 1989.

George, Timothy, Morgan Lee, and Mark Galli. "What Evangelicals Can Love about Mary: What Protestants Can Affirm in the 'Hail Mary,' What Luther Thought about the Mother of God, and

Why Christmas Shouldn't Be the Only Time Protestants Give Her Some Love." *Christianity Today.* December 22, 2016.

George-Tvrtković, Rita. "Bridge or Barrier? Mary and Islam in William of Tripoli and Nicholas of Cusa." *Medieval Encounters* 22, no. 4 (2016): 307–25.

———. *A Christian Pilgrim in Medieval Iraq: Riccoldo da Montecroce's Encounter with Islam.* Turnhout: Brepols, 2012.

———. "Meryem Ana Evi, Marian Devotion, and the Making of *Nostra aetate* 3." *Catholic Historical Review* 103, no. 4 (Autumn 2017): 755–81.

Getz, Christine. *Music and the Early Modern Imagination: Mary, Music, and Meditation: Sacred Conversations in Post-Tridentine Milan.* Bloomington: Indiana University Press, 2013.

Gil, Rosa M., and Carmen Inoa Vázquez, eds. *The María Paradox.* New York: Putnam's Sons, 1996.

Grabar, Oleg. *Mostly Miniatures.* Princeton, NJ: Princeton University Press, 2000.

Gregory, Andrew, and Christopher Tuckett, eds. *The Oxford Handbook of Early Christian Apocrypha.* Oxford: Oxford University Press, 2015.

Griffith, Sidney. *The Beginnings of Christian Theology in Arabic.* Aldershot, UK: Ashgate, 2002.

———. *The Church in the Shadow of the Mosque.* Princeton, NJ: Princeton University Press, 2010.

Grung, Anne Hege. "Gender and Christian-Muslim Dialogue." In *Contemporary Muslim-Christian Encounters*, edited by Paul Hedges, 67–81. New York: Bloomsbury Academic, 2015.

Grung, Anne Hege, and Lena Larsen. *Dialogue with and without a Veil.* Oslo, Norway: Pax, 2000.

Grypeou, Emmanouela, Mark Swanson, and David Thomas, eds. *The Encounter of Eastern Christianity with Early Islam.* Leiden: Brill, 2006.

Gude, Mary Louise. *Louis Massignon: The Crucible of Compassion.* Notre Dame, IN: University of Notre Dame Press, 1997.

Gustafson, David, and Dwight Longenecker. *Mary: A Catholic-Evangelical Debate.* Grand Rapids, MI: Brazos, 2003.

Haddad, Yvonne Yazbeck, and Wadi Zaidan Haddad, eds. *Christian-Muslim Encounters.* Gainesville: University Press of Florida, 1995.

Hall, Linda B. *Mary, Mother and Warrior.* Austin: University of Texas Press, 2004.

Hamilton, Bernard. "Our Lady of Saidnaiya: An Orthodox Shrine Revered by Muslims and Knights Templars at the Time of the Crusades." In *Holy Land, Holy Lands, and Christian History*, edited by R. N. Swanson. Woodbridge, England: Boydell Press, 2000.

Hastings, Adrian. *The Church in Africa, 1450–1950*. Oxford: Clarendon, 1994.

Heal, Bridge. *The Cult of the Virgin Mary in Early Modern Germany*. Cambridge: Cambridge University Press, 2007.

Hearden, Maura. "Lessons from Zeitoun: A Marian Proposal for Christian-Muslim Dialogue." *Journal of Ecumenical Studies* 47, no. 3 (2012).

Heimgartner, Martin. "Letter 59 (Disputation with the Caliph al-Mahdi)." In *Christian-Muslim Relations: A Bibliographical History, Volume 1 (600–900)*, edited by David Thomas and Barbara Roggema, 522–26. Leiden: Brill, 2009.

Heo, Angie. "The Virgin between Christianity and Islam: Sainthood, Media, and Modernity in Egypt." *Journal of the American Academy of Religion* 81, no. 4 (2013): 1117–38.

Hermkens, Anna-Karina, Willy Jansen, and Catrien Notermans, eds. *Moved by Mary: The Power of Pilgrimage in the Modern World*. Surrey, UK: Ashgate, 2009.

Herzog, Jonathon. *The Hammer and the Cross: America's Holy War against Communism*. Palo Alto, CA: Stanford University Press, 2008.

Heyberger, Bernard. "Polemic Dialogues between Christians and Muslims in the Seventeenth Century." *Journal of the Economic and Social History of the Orient* 55 (2012): 495–516.

Honigmann, Ernest. "Stephen of Ephesus and the Legend of the Seven Sleepers." *Patristic Studies, Studi e testi* 173 (1953): 125–68.

Hopkins, Jasper. "The Role of *Pia Interpretatio* in Nicholas of Cusa's Hermeneutical Approach to the Koran." In *A Miscellany on Nicholas of Cusa*, edited by Jasper Hopkins, 39–55. Minneapolis: Banning Press, 1994.

Horn, Cornelia. "Mary between the Bible and Qur'an." *Islam and Christian-Muslim Relations* 18, no. 4 (2007): 509–38.

Hoyland, Robert. "Jacob of Edessa on Islam." In *After Bardaisan*, edited by G. Reinink and A. Klugkist, 149–60. Leuven: Peeters, 1999.

―――――. *Seeing Islam as Others Saw It: A Survey and Evaluation of Christian, Jewish, and Zoroastrian Writings on Early Islam*. Princeton, NJ: Princeton University Press, 1997.

Isom-Verhaaren, Christine. *Allies with the Infidel: The Ottoman and French Alliance in the Sixteenth Century*. London: I. B. Tauris and Co., 2011.

Jackson, Sherman. *On the Boundaries of Theological Tolerance in Islam*. Oxford: Oxford University Press, 2002.

Jansen, Willy. "Marian Images and Religious Identities in the Middle East." In *Moved by Mary: The Power of Pilgrimage in the Modern World*, edited by Anna-Karina Hermkens, Willy Jansen, and Catrien Notermans, 33–48. Surrey, UK: Ashgate, 2009.

Jansen, Willy, and Meike Kühl. "Shared Symbols: Muslims, Marian Pilgrimages and Gender." *European Journal of Women's Studies* 15, no. 3 (2008): 295–311.

Jensen, Robin M. "The Apocryphal Mary in Early Christian Art." In *The Oxford Handbook of Early Christian Apocrypha*, edited by Andrew Gregory and Christopher Tuckett. Oxford: Oxford University Press, 2015.

Johnson, Elizabeth. *Truly Our Sister: A Theology of Mary in the Communion of Saints*. New York: Continuum, 2006.

Kaltner, John. "The Muslim Mary." In *New Perspectives on the Nativity*, edited by Jeremy Corley, 165–79. London: T & T Clark, 2009.

Kane, Paula M. "Marian Devotion since 1940: Continuity or Casualty?" In *Habits of Devotion: Catholic Religious Practice in Twentieth-Century America*, edited by James O'Toole, 89–119. New York: Cornell University Press, 2004.

Kearns, Cleo McNelly. *The Virgin Mary, Monotheism, and Sacrifice*. Cambridge: Cambridge University Press, 2008.

Kedar, Benjamin. *Crusade and Mission*. Princeton, NJ: Princeton University Press, 1984.

Kennedy, Kirstin. "Seeing Is Believing: The Miniatures in the *Cantigas de Santa Maria* and Medieval Devotional Practices. *Portuguese Studies* 32, no. 1 (2015): 169–82.

Khalidi, Tarif. *The Muslim Jesus*. Cambridge, MA: Harvard University Press, 2001.

Khalil, Mohammad Hassan, ed. *Between Heaven and Hell: Islam, Salvation, and the Fate of Others*. Oxford: Oxford University Press, 2013.

Khalil, Samir. "Quelques expressions de la piete mariale contemporaine chez le musulmans d'Egypte (et d'Irak)." In *Maria nell'Ebraismo e nell 'Islam Oggi*, edited by Elio Peretto, 141–66. Rome: Marianum; and Bologna: Dehoniane, 1987.

Kidd, Thomas. *American Christians and Islam: Evangelical Culture and Muslims from the Colonial Period to the Age of Terrorism.* Princeton, NJ: Princeton University Press, 2009.

Krausmüller, Dirk. "Making the Most of Mary." In *The Cult of the Mother of God*, edited by Leslie Brubaker and Mary Cunningham, 219–46. Surrey, UK: Ashgate, 2011.

Kreitzer, Beth. *Reforming Mary.* Oxford: Oxford University Press, 2004.

Kritzeck, James A. *Peter the Venerable and Islam.* Princeton, NJ: Princeton University Press, 1964.

Krokus, Christian. "Louis Massignon's Influence on the Teaching of Vatican II on Muslims and Islam." *Islam and Christian-Muslim Relations* 23, no. 3 (2012): 329–45.

———. *The Theology of Louis Massignon: Islam, Christ, and the Church.* Washington, DC: Catholic University of America Press, 2017.

Krueger, Derek. "Mary at the Threshold: Mother of God as Guardian." In *The Cult of the Mother of God in Byzantium*, edited by Leslie Brubaker and Mary Cunningham, 31–38. Surrey, UK: Ashgate, 2011.

Kurtz, Lester. *The Politics of Heresy: The Modernist Crisis in Roman Catholicism.* Berkeley: University of California Press, 1986.

Levenson, Jon D. *Inheriting Abraham: The Legacy of the Patriarch in Judaism, Christianity, and Islam.* Princeton, NJ: Princeton University Press, 2012.

Levine, Amy-Jill, ed. *A Feminist Companion to Mariology.* London: T & T Clark International, 2005.

Levy, Ian Christopher, Rita George-Tvrtković, and Donald Duclow. *Nicholas of Cusa and Islam: Polemic and Dialogue in the Late Middle Ages.* Leiden: Brill, 2014.

Louth, Andrew. "John of Damascus on the Mother of God as a Link between Humanity and God." In *The Cult of the Mother of God in Byzantium*, edited by Leslie Brubaker and Mary Cunningham, 153–62. Surrey, UK: Ashgate, 2011.

Lozano-Díaz, Nora. "Ignored Virgin or Unaware Woman: A Mexican-American Protestant Reflection on the Virgin of Guadalupe." In *Blessed One: Protestant Perspectives on Mary*, edited by Beverly Roberts Gaventa and Cynthia Rigby, 85–96. Louisville, KY: Westminster John Knox Press, 2002.

Lumbard, Joseph. "The Quranic View of Sacred History and Other Religions." In *The Study Qur'an*, translated and edited by Seyyed Hossein Nasr, Caner K. Dagli, Maria Massi Dakake, Joseph Lumbard, and Mohammed Rustom. New York: HarperCollins, 2015.

Maclagan, Edward. *The Jesuits and the Great Mogul*. London: Burns, Oates & Washbourne, 1932.

Madhok, Punam. "Christian-Islamic Relations in the Court Art of Mughal India." *International Journal of the Arts in Society* 4, no. 6 (2010): 67–78.

Majanlahti, Antony. *The Families Who Made Rome*. London: Chatto & Windus, 2005.

Makdisi, Ussama. *Artillery of Heaven: American Missionaries and the Failed Conversion of the Middle East*. Ithaca, NY: Cornell University Press, 2007.

Markešić, Ivan. "Our Lady of Mercy: A Unique Cult in Two Places." In *Cult Places on the Border*, edited by B. Đorđević, B. Dragoljub, D. Todorović, and D. Krstić, 16–28. Niš, Serbia: YSSSR, 2014.

Marshall, David, and Lucinda Mosher, eds. *Prayer: Christian and Muslim Perspectives*. Building Bridges Seminar. Washington, DC: Georgetown University Press, 2011.

Martínez Gázquez, José. "A New Set of Glosses to the Latin Qur'ān Made by Nicholas of Cusa (MS Vat. Lat. 4071)." *Medieval Encounters* 21 (2015): 295–309.

———. "Translations of the Qur'an and Other Islamic Texts before Dante (Twelfth and Thirteenth Centuries)." *Dante Studies* 125 (2007): 79–92.

Maunder, Chris. *Our Lady of the Nations: Apparitions of Mary in the Twentieth Century*. Oxford: Oxford University Press, 2016.

Mauriello, Matthew Rocco. "Venerable Pope Pius XII and the 1954 Marian Year." Master's thesis, University of Dayton, 2010.

Meri, Josef W. *The Cult of Saints among Muslims and Jews in Medieval Syria*. Oxford: Oxford University Press, 2002.

Michel, Thomas. "Pope John Paul II's Teaching on Islam in His Addresses to Muslims." *Bulletin* n. 62, vol. 21, no. 2 (1986): 182–91.

Miller-McLemore, Bonnie. "Pondering All These Things: Mary and Motherhood." In *Blessed One: Protestant Perspectives on Mary*, edited by Beverly Roberts Gaventa and Cynthia Rigby, 97–116. Louisville, KY: Westminster John Knox Press, 2002.

Minissale, Gregory. *Images of Thought: Visuality in Islamic India, 1550–1750*. Cambridge: Cambridge Scholars, 2009.

Minnich, Nelson. *The Catholic Reformation*. Aldershot, UK: Variorum, 1993.

Mitchell, Nathan. *The Mystery of the Rosary: Marian Devotion and the Reinvention of Catholicism*. New York: New York University Press, 2009.

Mossman, Stephen. "The Western Understanding of Islamic Theology in the Later Middle Ages." *Recherches de Théologie et Philosophie Médiévales* 74, no. 1 (2007): 169–224.

Moudarres, Andrea. "Crusade and Conversion: Islam as Schism in Pius II and Nicholas of Cusa," *MLN* 128, no. 1 (2013): 40–52.

Mourad, Suleiman. "From Hellenism to Christianity and Islam: The Origin of the Palm Tree Story Concerning Mary and Jesus in the Gospel of Pseudo-Matthew and the Qur'an." *Oriens Christianus* 86 (2002): 206–16.

———. "Mary in the Qur'an: A Reexamination of Her Presentation." In *The Qur'an in Its Historical Context*, edited by Gabriel Said Reynolds, 163–74. London: Routledge, 2008.

———. "On the Qur'anic Stories about Mary and Jesus." *Bulletin of the Royal Institute for Inter-Faith Studies* 1 (1999): 13–24.

Mullett, Michael. *The Catholic Reformation*. New York: Routledge, 1999.

Nederman, Cary. *Worlds of Difference: European Discourses of Toleration, c. 1100–1550*. University Park, PA: Pennsylvania State Press, 2000.

Niedzwiedz, Anna. *Image and Figure: Our Lady of Czestochowa in Polish Culture and Popular Religion*. Krakow: Jagellonian University Press, 2015.

O'Callaghan, Joseph. *Alfonso X and the Cantigas de Santa Maria*. Leiden: Brill, 1998.

O'Mahony, Anthony. "Louis Massignon: A Catholic Encounter with God and the Middle East." In *God's Mirror: Renewal and Engagement in French Catholic Intellectual Culture in the Mid Twentieth Century*, edited by Katherine Davies and Toby Garfitt. Fordham University Press: New York, 2015.

———. "Louis Massignon, the Seven Sleepers of Ephesus and the Christian Muslim Pilgrimage at Vieux-Marche." In *Explorations in a Christian Theology of Pilgrimage*, edited by Craig Bartholomew and Fred Hughes. Aldershot, UK: Ashgate, 2003.

O'Malley, John. *Trent: What Happened at the Council*. Cambridge, MA: Harvard University Press. 2013.

O'Meara, Thomas. "The Theology and Times of William of Tripoli: A Different View of Islam." *Theological Studies* 69 (2008): 80–98.

Pallavicini, Shaikh 'Abd al-Wahid. "Corrispondenze Mariane nella tradizione Islamica: elementi per un dialogo." In *Maria nell'Ebraismo e nell 'Islam Oggi*, edited by Elio Peretto, 119–40. Rome: Marianum; and Bologna: Dehoniane, 1987.

Patel, Eboo. *Acts of Faith*. Boston: Beacon Press, 2007.

Pawlikova-Vilhanova, Viera. "The Role of Early Missionaries of Africa or White Fathers in the Study and Development of African Languages." *Asian and African Studies* 20, no. 2 (2011): 267–88.

Pelikan, Jaroslav. *Mary through the Centuries: Her Place in the History of Culture*. New Haven, CT: Yale University Press, 1996.

Peltomaa, Leena. "Epithets of the Theotokos in the Akathistos Hymn." In *The Cult of the Mother of God*, edited by Leslie Brubaker and Mary Cunningham, 109–16. Surrey, UK: Ashgate, 2011.

———. *The Image of the Virgin Mary in the Akathistos Hymn*. Boston: Brill, 2001.

Pénicaud, Manoël. "La Maison de la Vierge à Éphèse: De la fondation à la patrimonialisation d'un sanctuaire « international »." *European Journal of Turkish Studies* 19 (2014).

Pentcheva, Bissera V. *Icons and Power: The Mother of God in Byzantium*. University Park, PA: Pennsylvania State University Press, 2006.

Pérennès, Jean-Jacques. *Passion Kaboul: Le père Serge de Beaurecueil*. Paris: Cerf, 2014.

Perry, Mary Elizabeth. *The Handless Maiden: Moriscos and the Politics of Religion in Early Modern Spain*. Princeton, NJ: Princeton University Press, 2005.

Perry, Tim. *Mary for Evangelicals*. Downers Grove, IL: IVP Academic, 2006.

Peters, F. E. *The Children of Abraham*. Princeton, NJ: Princeton University Press, 1982.

Petry, Yvonne. *Gender, Kabbalah and the Reformation: The Mystical Theology of Guillaume Postel*. Leiden: Brill, 2004.

Prado-Vilar, Francisco. "The Gothic Anamorphic Gaze: Regarding the Worth of Others." In *Under the Influence: Questioning the Comparative in Medieval Castile*, edited by Cynthia Robinson and Leyla Rouhi, 67–100. Leiden: Brill, 2005.

Pringle, Denys. "Saidnaiya." In *The Churches of the Crusader Kingdom of Jerusalem*, edited by Denys Pringle, 2:219–21. Cambridge: Cambridge University Press, 2009.

Rahman, Fazlur. "The People of the Book and the Diversity of 'Religions.'" In *Christianity through Non-Christian Eyes*, edited by Paul J. Griffiths, 102–10. Maryknoll, NY: Orbis, 1990.

Reeves, Thomas C. *America's Bishop: The Life and Times of Fulton Sheen*. San Francisco: Encounter Books, 2001.

Reinink, Gerrit. "Political Power and Right Religion." In *The Encounter of Eastern Christianity with Early Islam*, edited by Emmanouela Grypeou, Mark Swanson, and David Thomas, 153–70. Leiden: Brill, 2006.

Remensnyder, Amy. *La Conquistadora*. New York: Oxford University Press, 2014.

Renard, John. *Islam and Christianity: Theological Themes in Comparative Perspective*. Berkeley: University of California Press, 2011.

Reynolds, Gabriel Said. "Evangelizing Islam." *First Things* (January 2011).

———. *The Qur'an and Its Biblical Subtext*. London: Routledge, 2008.

Riley, Kathleen. *Fulton Sheen: An American Catholic Response to the Twentieth Century*. Staten Island, NY: Alba House, 2004.

Roberson, Ronald. *Eastern Churches, A Brief Survey*. 7th edition. Rome: Edizioni Orientalia Christiana, 2008.

Robinson, Neal. "Massignon, Vatican II, and Islam as an Abrahamic Religion." *Islam and Christian-Muslim Relations* 2, no. 2 (1991): 182–205.

Ross, Eric. "Christmas in Cambérène, or How Muhammad Begets Jesus in Senegal." In *Muslims and Others in Sacred Space*, edited by Margaret Cormack. Oxford: Oxford University Press, 2013.

Rubin, Miri. *Emotion and Devotion: The Meaning of Mary in Medieval Religious Cultures*. Budapest: SEU Press, 2009.

———. *Mother of God: A History of the Virgin Mary*. New Haven, CT: Yale University Press, 2009.

Ruether, Rosemary Radford. *Mary the Feminine Face of God*. Philadelphia: Westminster, 1977.

Sachedina, Abdulaziz. "The Qur'an and Other Religions." In *The Cambridge Companion to the Qur'an*, edited by Jane Dammen McAuliffe, 291–309. Cambridge: Cambridge University, 2006.

Said, Edward. *Orientalism*. New York: Pantheon, 1979.

Saritoprak, Zeki. *Islam's Jesus*. Gainesville: University Press of Florida, 2014.

Schleifer, Aliah. *Mary the Blessed Virgin of Islam*. Louisville, KY: Fons Vitae, 1998.

Schmidt, Jalene D. *Cachita's Streets: The Virgin of Charity, Race, and Revolution in Cuba*. Durham, NC: Duke University Press, 2015.

Schulte, Carl G. *The Life of Sr. Marie de Mandat-Grancey and Mary's House in Ephesus*. Charlotte, NC: TAN Books, 2011.

Schultenover, David. *A View from Rome: On the Eve of the Modernist Crisis*. New York: Fordham University Press, 1999.

Shahid, Irfan. "Islam and Oriens Christianus." In *The Encounter of Eastern Christianity with Early Islam*, edited by Emmanouela Grypeou, Mark Swanson, and David Thomas, 9–31. Leiden: Brill, 2006.

Sharkey, Heather. *American Evangelicals in Egypt: Missionary Encounters in an Age of Empire*. Princeton, NJ: Princeton University Press, 2008.

Shoemaker, Stephen. *Ancient Traditions of the Virgin Mary's Dormition and Assumption*. Oxford: Oxford University Press, 2002.

———. *Mary in Early Christian Faith and Devotion*. New Haven, CT: Yale University Press, 2016.

Shorter, Aylward. *The Cross and Flag in Africa: The White Fathers during the Colonial Scramble*. Maryknoll, NY: Orbis, 2006.

Siddiqui, Mona. *Christians, Muslims, and Jesus*. New Haven, CT: Yale University Press, 2013.

Sirry, Mun im. "'Compete with One Another in Good Works': Exegesis of Qur an Verse 5.48 and Contemporary Muslim Discourses on Religious Pluralism." *Islam and Christian-Muslim Relations* 20, no. 4 (2009): 424–38.

Smith, Jane I., and Yvonne H. Haddad. "The Virgin Mary in Islamic Tradition and Commentary." *The Muslim World* 79, nos. 3–4 (1989): 161–87.

Spellberg, Denise. *Thomas Jefferson's Qur'an: Islam and the Founders*. New York: Vintage, 2013.

Spivey, Nigel. *Enduring Creation: Art, Pain and Fortitude* Berkeley: University of California Press, 2001.

Stowasser, Barbara. *Women in the Qur'an, Traditions, and Interpretation*. Oxford: Oxford University Press, 1994.

Sutton, Kenneth. *The Papacy and the Levant, 1204–1571*. Philadelphia: American Philosophical Society, 1984.

Swanson, Mark. "Folly to the Hunafa." In *The Encounter of Eastern Christianity with Early Islam*, edited by E. Grypeou et al., 237–56. Leiden: Brill, 2006.

Swanson, R. N. *The Church and Mary*. Woodbridge, UK: Boydell, 2004.

Szpiech, Ryan. *Conversion and Narrative: Reading and Religious Authority in Medieval Polemic*. Philadelphia: University of Pennsylvania Press, 2012.

———. "Rhetorical Muslims: Islam as Witness in Western Christian Anti-Jewish Polemic." *Al-Qantara* 34, no. 1 (2013): 153–85.

Tavard, George. *The Thousand Faces of the Virgin Mary*. Collegeville, MN: Liturgical Press, 1996.

Taylor, Christopher S. *In the Vicinity of the Righteous: Ziyara and the Veneration of Muslim Saints in Late Medieval Egypt*. Leiden: Brill, 1999.

Tejirian, Eleanor, and Reeva Spector Simon. *Conflict, Conquest, and Conversion: Two Thousand Years of Christian Missions in the Middle East*. New York: Columbia University Press, 2014.

Thomas, David. *Christian Doctrines in Islamic Theology*. Leiden: Brill, 2008.

———. "Christian Religion (Premodern Muslim Positions)." In *Encyclopaedia of Islam 3*, edited by Kate Fleet, Gudrun Krämer, Denis Matringe, John Nawas, Everett Rowson. Leiden: Brill, 2007–.

Thomas, David, et al., eds. *Christian-Muslim Relations: A Bibliographical History*. 11 volumes. Leiden: Brill, 2009–.

Thurlkill, Mary. *Chosen among Women: Mary and Fatima in Medieval Christianity and Shi'ite Islam*. Notre Dame, IN: University of Notre Dame Press, 2007.

Tieszen, Charles. "Can You Find Anything Praiseworthy in My Religion?" In *The Character of Christian-Muslim Encounter*, edited by Douglas Pratt et al. Leiden: Brill, 2015.

Tolan, John. "Saracen Philosophers Secretly Deride Islam." *Medieval Encounters* 8, no. 2 (2002): 184–208.

———. *Saracens*. New York: Columbia University Press, 2002.

———. "*Veneratio Sarracenorum*: Shared Devotion among Muslims and Christians, according to Burchard of Strasbourg." In *Sons of Ishmael*, edited by John Tolan, 101–12. Gainesville: University Press of Florida, 2008.

Troll, Christian. "Catholic Teachings on Interreligious Dialogue, with Special Reference to Christian-Muslim Relations." In *Muslim-Christian Perceptions of Dialogue Today*, edited by Jacques Waardenburg. Leuven: Peeters, 2000.

———. "Changing Catholic Views of Islam." In *Islam and Christianity: Mutual Perceptions since the Mid-20th Century*, edited by Jacques Waardenburg, 19–77. Leuven: Peeters, 1998.

Türkmen, Füsun, and Emre Öktem. "Foreign Policy as a Determinant in the Fate of Turkey's Non-Muslim Minorities: A Dialectical Analysis." *Turkish Studies* 14 (2013): 463–82.

Umar, Muhammad Suheyl, ed. *The Religious Other: Towards a Muslim Theology of Other Religions in a Post-prophetic Age.* Lahore: Iqbal Academy Pakistan, 2008.

Unsworth, Andrew. "Louis Massignon, The Holy See, and the Ecclesial Transition from *Immortale Dei* to *Nostra Aetate*: A Brief History of the Development of Catholic Church Teaching on Muslims and the Religion of Islam." *Aram Society for Syro-Mesopotamian Studies* 20 (2008).

Valkenberg, Pim. "Learned Ignorance and Faithful Interpretation of the Qur'an in Nicholas of Cusa." In *Learned Ignorance: Intellectual Humility among Jews, Christians, and Muslims*, edited by James Heft, Reuven Firestone, and Omid Safti, 34–52. Oxford: Oxford University Press, 2011.

———. "*Una Religio in Rituum Varietate*: Religious Pluralism, the Qur'an, and Nicholas of Cusa." In *Nicholas of Cusa and Islam: Polemic and Dialogue in the Late Middle Ages*, edited by Ian Levy, Rita George-Tvrtković, and Donald Duclow, 30–48. Leiden: Brill, 2014.

Van der Steen, Jasper. *Memory Wars in the Low Countries, 1566–1700.* Leiden: Brill, 2015.

Van Konigsveld, P. "The Apology of al-Kindi." In *Religious Polemics in Context*, edited by T. L. Hettema and A. van der Kooij, 69–92. Leiden: Brill, 2005.

Vassilaki, Maria, ed. *Images of the Mother of God: Perceptions of Theotokos in Byzantium.* Surrey, UK: Ashgate, 2005.

Vlašić, Anđelkom, and Janja Kovač. "Elements of Ottoman Legacy in the Alka of Sinj." Unpublished conference paper, International Symposium on Balkan Studies, Podgorica, Montenegro, January 2014.

Vose, Robin. *Dominicans, Muslims and Jews in the Medieval Crown of Aragon.* Cambridge: Cambridge University Press, 2009.

Waardenburg, Jacques. *Muslims as Actors: Islamic Meanings and Muslim Interpretation.* Berlin: Walter de Gruyter, 2007.

Walbridge, Linda. *Christians in Pakistan: The Passion of Bishop John Joseph.* New York: Routledge, 2003.

Walls, David. "Africa as the Theatre of Engagement with Islam in the Nineteenth Century." In *Christianity and the African Imagination: Essays in Honour of Adrian Hastings*, edited by David Maxwell and Ingrid Lawrie. Leiden: Brill, 2013.

Warner, Marina. *Alone in All Her Sex*. New York: Vintage Books, 1983.

Wensinck, A. J., and P. Johnstone, P. "Maryam." In *Encyclopedia of Islam.*, edited by P. Bearman et al., 2nd edition. Leiden: Brill, 1960–2007.

Winston-Allen, Anne. *Stories of the Rose: The Making of the Rosary in the Middle Ages*. University Park, PA: Penn State University Press, 1997.

Winter, Timothy. "Pulchra ut Luna: Some Reflections on the Marian Theme in Muslim-Catholic Dialogue." *Journal of Ecumenical Studies* 36 (1999): 439–69.

Wright, Elizabeth R., Sarah Spence, and Andrew Lemons, eds. and trans. *The Battle of Lepanto*. Cambridge, MA: Harvard University Press, 2014.

Yavuz, M. Hakan. *Toward an Islamic Enlightenment: The Gülen Movement*. Oxford University Press, 2013.

INDEX